THE HAMPSHIRE VILLAGE BOOK

The places, the people and their stories

**Hampshire County Federation
of Women's Institutes**

COUNTRYSIDE BOOKS
NEWBURY BERKSHIRE

First published 2018
© Hampshire County Federation of Women's Institutes

All rights reserved. No part of this publication may be reproduced, stored in a retrieval system, or transmitted by any means, electronic, mechanical, photocopying, recording or otherwise, without the prior written permission of the copyright holder and publishers.

COUNTRYSIDE BOOKS
3 Catherine Road
Newbury, Berkshire

To view our complete range of books please visit us at
www.countrysidebooks.co.uk

ISBN 978 1 84674 375 7

Front cover photo of East Statton by Gregory Davies/Alamy
Back cover picture of Oakley by Linda Burrowes, WI

Produced by The Letterworks Ltd., Reading
Designed and Typeset by KT Designs, St Helens
Printed by Holywell Press, Oxford

All materials used in the manufacture of this book carry FSC certification

Foreword

2018 marks 100 years of the WI having a presence in Hampshire and records show that during that time there has been, or still is, a WI in possibly every village in Hampshire. It is therefore time that the new version of *The Hampshire Village Book* should be published in this our Centenary year. Many WIs were both happy and proud to contribute to the book, updating life in their Hampshire village and reminding readers of the many hidden gems to be found in our County.

Maureen Levenson
Chair HCFWI

Acknowledgements

The production of this book has only been made possible by the enthusiastic research of the contributors and the untiring efforts of Sue Atrill, who co-ordinated the project brilliantly.

Dear Readers

I expect, like me, you are impatient to delve into this book on Hampshire which has been compiled from contributions from WIs across the County.

I would like to say a huge thank you to all who contributed – writers, artists and photographers. You have all played an important part in making this book a picture of life in Hampshire in the 21st century and as we read we will find out just how much life has changed, or not, since the last edition was published in 2002.

Thank you everyone.

Gina

Gina Ireland
Chair Elect HCFWI

County of HAMPSHIRE

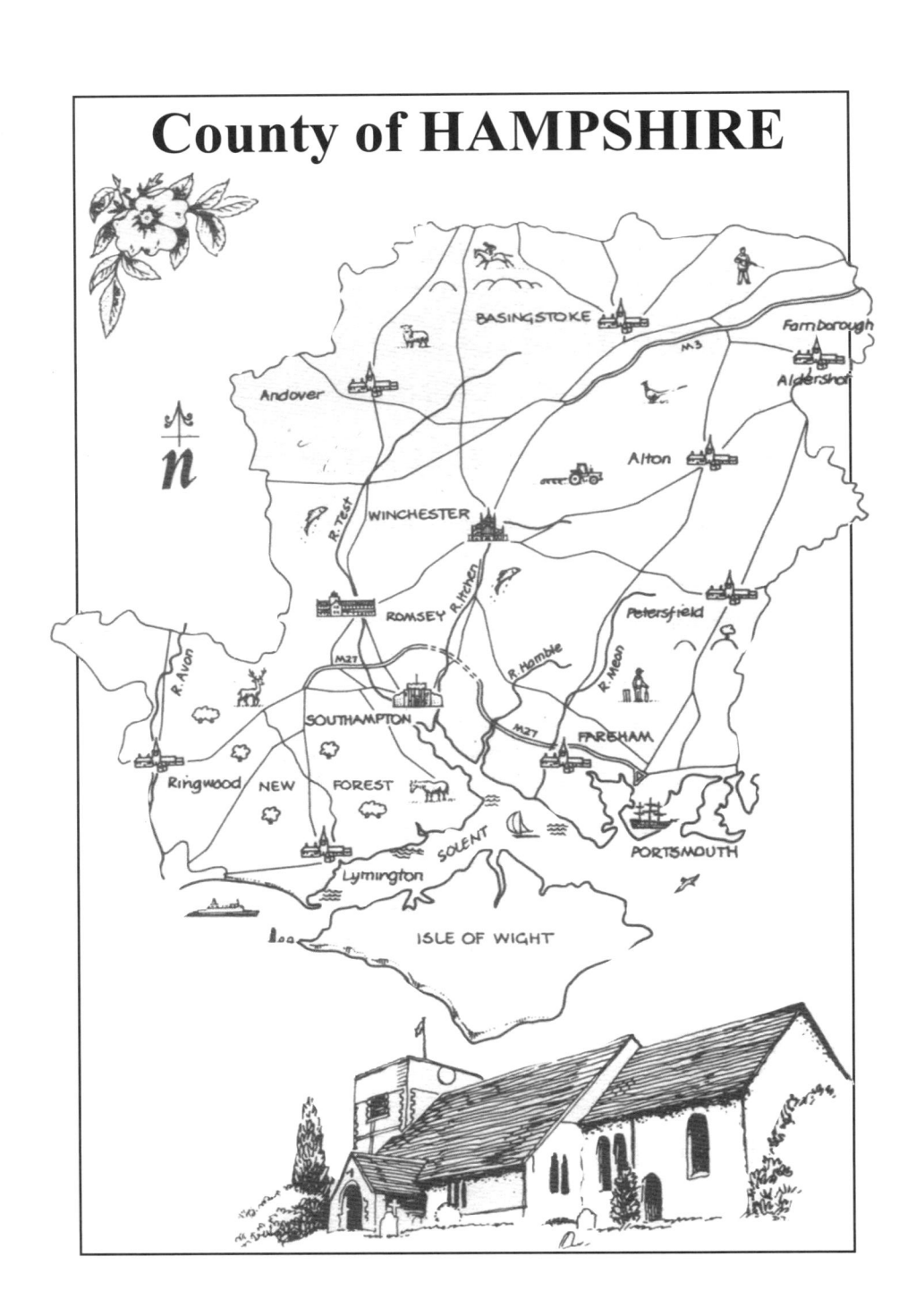

🍁 Abbotts Ann

Abbotts Ann is a village in north Hampshire, about two miles south of Andover, just off the A343 Andover-Salisbury road. The centre of the village is predominantly cottages, many of them thatched, that were originally the village labourers' rented cottages, most of them owned at one time by the Red Rice Estate. They provide good 'picture postcard' material for photographers.

St Mary's church is accessible via Church Path which runs from the village shop to Church Road. Parking is available at the Church Road end of Church Path. The church was built in 1716, on the site of a much older building; the first record of a church in Abbotts Ann is in a charter of AD 901 granted by Edward the Elder, son of King Alfred of Wessex.

St Mary's displays a number of Virgins' Crowns. They are traditionally made of newly cut hazelwood, decorated with black and white paper rosettes, and hanging from the frame are five parchment 'gauntlets'. In order to qualify for a Virgin's Crown the deceased must have been born and baptised, and lived and died in the parish. They must also have been of 'unblemished character' and unmarried. Following the funeral the crown is suspended from the gallery in the church for three weeks and if not challenged it is then hung just below ceiling level and will stay there until it finally disintegrates and falls. The present selection of crowns date from the building of the current church, in 1716. The last crown was awarded to Miss Lily Myra Annetts who died aged 73 in 1973 and is buried in the churchyard. The tradition still exists but since 1973 there have been no requests and in a modern transient society there would be very few who could meet the conditions.

Amongst Abbotts Ann's notable residents was Thomas 'Diamond' Pitt, who was Governor of Fort St George in Madras in 1699, becoming President of Madras. His eldest son was the politician William Pitt, also known as 'Pitt the Elder'. In India Thomas Pitt purchased a 410 carat uncut diamond for £20,400. Back in London the diamond was professionally cut resulting in a main diamond of 141 carats and several smaller diamonds, some of which were sold to Peter the Great of Russia. The main diamond was eventually sold to Philippe II, Duke of Orléans and became known as Le Regent. Today, it is part of the French Crown Jewels and is housed in the French Royal Treasury at the Louvre. Thomas Pitt owned a number of properties in southern England, including property in Abbotts Ann and with the money raised from the sale of the diamond he funded the demolition of the original Abbotts Ann church and the building of the present church and neighbouring Old Rectory.

Robert Tasker came to Abbotts Ann in 1806 as an apprentice blacksmith under Thomas Maslen. He was a committed nonconformist and soon came up against the rector, Thomas Burroughs who disapproved of nonconformism. Robert Tasker eventually took over the Abbotts Ann blacksmith business and prospered making farm equipment. He purchased property in the village and next to it built a chapel, now called Chapel Cottage located opposite the village shop. The business expanded rapidly and he set up the Waterloo Ironworks in Anna Valley. This provided employment for very many local people. Robert strongly believed in education for the masses and built the village school in 1830.

In 1831 Rev Samuel Best became Rector of Abbotts Ann and unlike his predecessor, collaborated with Robert Tasker. He too was committed to education and Robert handed the responsibility of the school over to him. The school was unusual for its day as children of all denominations and backgrounds were welcome. Children were charged a shilling a week but only if they could afford it, the majority being charged 2d a week!

Rev Samuel Best was also an enthusiastic antiquarian and in 1854 uncovered a Roman villa, thought to date from AD 300, in a field at the top of Dunkirt Lane. The site was the subject of a further archaeological dig in 2005 by Professor Barry Cunliffe and a large mosaic from the villa now resides in the British Museum. The site has been covered over again and returned to arable farming.

The population in the 2011 census was circa 2,500 with the majority of working age. Like many villages Abbotts Ann has expanded in recent years and a number of its residents do not work locally but make use of the nearby rail service into Salisbury, Basingstoke and London. The village is lucky enough to still have a village shop and post office, mostly staffed by volunteers. The shop also serves hot drinks and cakes. The school still thrives in a new building on the outskirts of the village and has an excellent reputation; the old school in the village centre has been transformed into a residential property. A nursery school also operates from the War Memorial Hall. There are many village organisations including an amateur dramatics group, sports association, handbells group and a thriving Women's Institute.

Alverstoke & Stokes Bay

From the Parish Centre, where St Mary's church clock chimes, and crossing the road, we start our walk. Past the lychgate, the graveyard, the imposing Victorian Gothic church itself and the large old rectory, with its mix of medieval stone and Georgian brickwork, home to generations of St Mary's rectors, but now divided into flats. Then Stokesmead, a small remnant of the old rectory land, and quite recently designated as open space. Past a derelict corner, due for renovation by the Gosport Shed – and into Crescent Road with its impressive Regency crescent and hotel on one side, and award-winning garden, beautifully maintained by volunteers, on the other.

Past the Institute of Naval Medicine, once the residence of a leading Gosport brewer, and turning left into the narrow coast road we soon enter Stokes Bay Golf Course. The course (which claims to have originated the term 'bogey' for a one-over-par hole) is bounded by Fort Monckton, still in use by Special Forces, and Fort Gilkicker, neglected for decades but now under exploration for development into luxury apartments overlooking the Solent.

Rounding the Fort, we follow the coastline to reach the Gosport and Fareham Inshore Rescue Service, exchanging cheery greetings with numerous dog walkers on the way. The GAFIRS' tractor clearing the slipway of stones reminds us how this whole beach area is transformed each New Year's morning by thousands of supporters cheering on those brave enough to plunge into the waters for a charity swim. At this point, too, we start the 'Golden Mile' together with lycra-clad runners probably in training for June's race along this iconic and aptly named promenade.

Past the Sailing Club there is a blue plaque commemorating its role as Control Centre for the D-Day landings in 1944. Opposite Pebbles café/restaurant is a pétanque pitch maintained by Friends of Stokes Bay and a small stone monument to Canadian D-Day Forces. Walk past the popular children's splash park, kite flyers, footballers and picnickers, and – across the road – tennis courts, crazy golf and a dog-agility course.

Out in the Bay, where ships assembled prior to D-Day and Naval reviews were held, sailing boats, wind surfers and kayakers now dot the waters. Occasional Naval vessels, container ships and cruise liners still plough the Solent; ferries and hovercrafts head for the Isle of Wight (even when it is totally obscured by sea mist!) and, by the water's edge, children are inevitably throwing stones.

Past remnants of the caissons for the Mulberry Harbours constructed between 1943 and 1944 on the beach, the wooden stumps of old breakwaters and the crumbling sea wall. Looking over to the island, we glimpse Queen Victoria's favoured Osborne House while, along the other side of the road, the old moat – in its heyday the scene of swan boats and swimmers but now a grassy hollow – can still be detected. We end the 'Golden Mile' at the Bayside Cabin café and The Diving Museum housed in Number 2 Battery of the old Stokes Bay Lines, then leave the coast road between two mobile home parks with their privileged location so close to the Solent.

Turning into Stanley Park to the south of Bay House School, once the home of the Sloane-Stanley family, we admire the variety of mature trees, the pet cemetery and the Monterey Cypress recently carved to depict local wildlife atop which is the emblematic Gosport longboat.

Past the Alverbank hotel, a place of sojourn for politicians and even royalty in Victorian times (now sporting another blue plaque – to Major Smith-Barry) we stop in the Osborne Walled Garden to admire the husbandry of the Alverstoke WI before leaving the park to walk along Western Way to Alverstoke village centre.

Now we pass the vintage dress shop with its stylish and colour-coordinated displays, the aptly-named Village Home pub and the gift shop, with its cleverly-themed windows. On the other side, the corner convenience store, the ever-busy hairdresser, the hardware shop selling everything from dahlias to dog-treats. The upgrading of our sub post office to a main post office reflects the resurgence of the village and its ability to buck the trend. Pilates and quilting classes, beauty salons, a Chinese restaurant, fish 'n' chips and even a bee-keeper are all testimony to a vibrant village life.

We take time, as always, for tea and scones in the cosy tea-shop, but today we have business to discuss – preparations for the Michaelmas Fayre held every last Saturday in September to raise money for charity and the community.

And so, refreshed and replete, we return to the Parish Centre, the hub of village life, while opposite, the Old Lodge hotel sports bunting and a bouncy castle ready for an afternoon wedding. Early guests, anxious not to miss the arrival of the bride in a horse-drawn carriage, attempt to decipher the inscriptions on the old tombstones, enter St Mary's church to look out through stained-glass windows or listen to the traditional pealing of bells installed in memory of those who fought and fell in the 1914-18 war.

This village may be only two miles from Gosport and a stone's throw from Portsmouth, but it retains its independent identity and special place in its residents' hearts. As Alwarestock, it pre-dated the Domesday Book but, as Alverstoke, it lives on in the 21st century – a thriving community where locals and visitors alike love more than ever to meet and chat after a walk along Stokes Bay.

AMPFIELD

Ampfield derives its name from the spring that still rises within the church's grounds. 'An-felde' was the village's earliest name, 'an' being a Celtic word for a spring.

On the site of Gosport Farm stood a pilgrims' inn called 'God's Port', drawing its business from the old Saxon road running between Romsey and Winchester, and its water from the ancient spring at Washers Well. The route of the main road has changed, however, and now the busy A31 carries its traffic well away from the site of the old inn.

The Rev W. Awdry, author of the *Thomas the Tank Engine* books, lived as a small boy in Ampfield, where his father was vicar of St Mark's. His earliest recollection is of going down Pound Lane, climbing up the embankment, and strolling along the old London & South Western Railway line.

The two World Wars did not pass Ampfield by. During the First World War a 'holding camp' was established here for horses on their way to France, but one day 20 of them vanished into the bogs of Pound Lane when a noisy train caused them to bolt into the undergrowth. The same area was used as a decoy aerodrome during the Second World War, complete with lights and what looked like a control tower. The Old Thatches public

St Mark's church, Ampfield

house became a First Aid post and the White Horse a mortuary (though it was never used).

Until the 1930s Ampfield was a village predominantly feudal in character, dominated by the Ampfield House and estate, which comprised some 1,600 acres. In 1902 the Faber family took possession of the house and all the surrounding farms. David Faber's death in 1931 led to the final break-up of the estate the following year, when Hilliers, nurserymen, took possession of the house and some of its land.

ASHMANSWORTH

This small village in the north of the county stands on a high ridge very near the Berkshire boundary and has wonderful views of both counties. It is a long scattered village mostly devoted to agriculture and has at least five farms of some size. There is a pleasant mixture of old thatched cottages and Hampshire flint houses.

In the 10th century the ancient manor of Ashmansworth was granted to the Church in Winchester for the maintenance of the monks there and it remained for the most part in Church ownership until the beginning of the 19th century, when it passed to the family of the Earl of Carnarvon. The 12th-century church of St James has some medieval murals although only a small section of these is now visible. In the porch there is a 20th-century engraved window 'A Celebration of English Music' in memory of, among others, the composer Gerald Finzi, who lived in the village for many years. There is a modern, active village hall and the Wayfarer's Walk passes the edge of the village. In August the annual Flower Show and Fete attracts entries from all the neighbouring villages.

ASHURST & COLBURY

Visitors to the New Forest who travel along the A35 from Southampton to Lyndhurst pass through Ashurst village. Some may discover it on a visit to the Longdown Activity Farm. Others come by train to the local station, 'Lyndhurst Road', or stay at the well-equipped Ashurst campsite. All are within the administrative area of the newly formed civil parish of Ashurst and Colbury (1986).

Originally there were four villages: Colbury, Foxhills, Longdown and Ashurst. The name 'Ashurst' does not go back beyond the 1920s; prior to that it was known simply as Lyndhurst Road from the adjacent railway station, built in 1847. As its name denotes, this station was intended to serve Lyndhurst residents, gentry staying at Lyndhurst hotels or with country house parties. This was the nearest approach permitted by local landowners and the line was nicknamed 'The Weymouth Wanderer' from its circuitous route!

Colbury village centres round the church in Deerleap Lane and the Memorial Hall on Hunter's Hill. The name allegedly goes back to the 13th century when land was granted to the monks of Beaulieu Abbey to build a chapel at Colbury. In 1870 Frank Ibbotson built the church at Colbury and endowed the living. He also built two schools at Colbury and Longdown. Marianne Vaudrey Barker-Mill, daughter of Frank Ibbotson, is a local legend. She built the Colbury Memorial Hall in 1928 in memory of her son Claude and other young men who died in the First World War. She made her home in Colbury, building Langley Manor where she administered her estates with charity and charm. She initiated a clothing fund for her estate workers which she personally supervised, and her annual tea-party and fete was a social highlight.

AWBRIDGE

Awbridge's (prounounced Aybridge) main attraction is its lovely rolling countryside. The beech woods and rhododendron-lined roads are a delight in spring. One boundary follows the river Test and there are several trout lakes. The lake at Awbridge Danes was made in the 1920s to provide work for the local unemployed, each man receiving one shilling a day and a loaf of bread.

Roman occupation in the area is suggested by a villa found on aerial survey, and tiles, pottery and coins have been found at Awbridge House dating from AD 307. The Saxons, and later the Normans, had hunting lodges at nearby Stanbridge Earls (whose estates until recently covered large parts of the village) and Awbridge Danes, and the village is still well wooded.

For many centuries Awbridge was a very small settlement. By the 1600s there were only half a dozen substantial houses, of which four still stand. By 1800 there were about 40 houses and a population of some 400, and recent building has raised numbers further. Present inhabitants are mainly commuters to nearby large towns but there are still a few local farms, nurseries and smallholdings, builders and small engineering firms.

The parish itself is relatively modern, having been carved out of surrounding parishes in the 1870s. The church was built in 1876 at a cost of £2,800 and is a pleasant, unpretentious building in pretty surroundings. The village school dates from 1877.

BARTON-ON-SEA

Barton lies on the coast just south of New Milton on the western border of Hampshire, and its cliffs are renowned for yielding flints and fossils from as long ago as the Upper Eocene age. The type of clay that they are made of is known worldwide in geological circles as 'Barton Beds'. Many generations of fossil hunters and schoolchildren from far and wide have visited Barton to seek out its ancient treasure, and today it is a Site of Special Scientific Interest.

Skip forward several millennia and Barton makes an appearance in the Domesday Book as a farm settlement known as Bermintune.

Throughout the Middle Ages and beyond, the village and surroundings known as Barton was a very poor area, and the inhabitants often supplemented their meagre farming income by indulging in a spot of smuggling. The ravines down to the sea known as Chewton Bunny and Becton Bunny, which flank Barton, were clandestine smuggling routes in the 18th and 19th centuries, until the siting of coastguard premises on the cliff top in 1823 attempted to put a stop to the illicit trade. Today's terrace of Coastguard Cottages in Barton Lane was built later in the century to house the station's officers and men.

In 1888, the fortunes of Barton changed dramatically with the coming of the railway to nearby New Milton, and the Victorian fascination with sea bathing. Gentry began to be attracted to the area and grand villas, hotels and a golf course sprang up. Barton's tree-lined avenues exist thanks to Rev John Kelsall, who did so much for the area in the late 19th century. It was also at this time that Barton acquired its 'on-Sea' suffix, lending the village a more exotic appeal.

A few years later the golf course had to be moved from its original picturesque position on the cliff top to avoid slipping into the sea, but it is still a renowned course today. Indeed, in 1989, the redoubtable Dorothy Huntley-Flindt, grandmother of one Sir Richard Branson, ensured that Barton-on-Sea golf course hit the national headlines when she made a hole-in-one there at the age of 90. When she slipped away at the end of her round, most assumed it was because she was tired, but she was apparently later heard to say, 'You have to buy everyone a drink if you get a hole in one, don't you?'

Other famous past residents of Barton-on-Sea include the author Elizabeth Goudge, whose children's novel *The Little White Horse* is loved by many; the

Beach huts at Barton-on-Sea

poet John Heath-Stubbs; and *Stroller*, the plucky showjumping pony who, along with his rider Marion Coakes, won the hearts of the country by taking Olympic silver in 1968. More recently premiership footballer Jamie Redknapp was born in The Grove maternity home (now sadly replaced by flats) in 1973. And paralympic swimmer Alice Tai MBE, who won a gold and a bronze in Rio 2016 aged just 17, grew up in Barton.

The Barton Court Hotel, built in the boom of the early 20th century, is another victim of coastal erosion but before that enjoyed a chequered history. During the First World War it was commandeered as a convalescent hospital, and at one time played host to a number of injured Indian servicemen. Their stay in Barton is commemorated by an obelisk erected on the sea front. Having lost most of its elegant accommodation over the cliff, the remaining Barton Court is now home to a vocal and recording studio which attracts young people from all around the area. It is just six metres from the cliff edge.

In fact Barton cliff top continues to shrink as erosion takes its toll. In Victorian times the grassy promenade was 100 metres wide. Today it is just 20 metres wide in places. Ongoing coastline strengthening has halted the speed of the erosion, but inevitably the cliffs continue to crumble, exposing ever more fossils!

Today Barton-on-Sea is a thriving community with a population of around 7,000 inhabitants. Although many of these are older people, attracted to the area in their retirement by the climate, accessible housing and amenities, the number of young families moving into Barton is on the rise. Visitors flock to the area in the summer months, keen to take advantage of the beach for its swimming and surfing, and of the thermal air currents for paragliding. On many a sunny day the coast is alive with the colourful sails swooping and gliding off the cliffs.

Barton boasts two top-class restaurants and a very popular cliff-top café, the Beachcomber, which has been serving teas, snacks and ice creams to locals and visitors since the 1920s. It is also just a stone's throw from the world-famous Chewton Glen Hotel.

As well as the much-visited cliff top, Barton has plenty of other green spaces, including the common and Long Meadow, both of which are undergoing restoration projects to reintroduce traditional grassland and wild flowers.

The winter months also have their attractions in Barton. The modest street of terraced cottages that is Byron Road is transformed every Christmas into a wonderland of festive lights and decorations. The switch-on brings in thousands of visitors, young and old, gets national newspaper and TV headlines, and raises huge sums of money for local charities. Until recently there was, however, one thing sadly lacking in the Barton-on-Sea community – a Women's Institute! But that was remedied in July 2017 with the inaugural meeting of the Barton Bees WI. A measure of how badly it was needed is that more than 130 ladies turned up hoping for one of the 100 membership places available.

Barton Stacey

The earliest inhabitants of Barton Stacey were a Neolithic tribe who buried their dead in the long barrows on Moody Down – now the army firing range. In Saxon times the village was Bertun ('ber' or barley and 'tun' or place), a royal manor of Edward the Confessor. In 1206 the manor was bestowed on Sir Rogo de Stacy, hence the name.

There are no thatched properties in the village. This is due to a great fire that occurred in 1792 and destroyed much of the village. A spark from the blacksmith's shop set light to some dry litter near a cucumber patch, which in turn ignited the thatch on the adjoining mill house. A strong wind was blowing and soon most of the houses were ablaze. Only Farmer Fred lost his life, he went upstairs to rescue his fortune and died in the attempt.

In the centre of the village is All Saints church. The original church was known as St Victor's and was rebuilt in the 12th century. Almost opposite the church is the Swan Inn which is at least 200 years old. The war memorial inside the church was built during the First World War thanks to donations from villagers (including children and teachers at the village school) and those connected to the village; the total cost of necessary alterations to the church, the shrine and the dedication service was nearly £96. The 'War Shrine' was dedicated on Thursday, 29th November 1917 and by the end of the war the names of 16 men from the village had been added. Candlesticks on the shrine were made from oak over 200 years old, saved from the old bell frame when renovations took place in the bell tower in 1934. It was originally thought that an oak screen would be made through which people would pass to enter the area of the shrine, but this was not added due to the cost. Also in the church, is a book holding the names of all of the residents at the time of the Millennium.

Opposite the church is a fingerpost which was thought to be 'a great convenience to travellers' when it was built in 1900.

The area is a wonderful habitat for a wide range of creatures, including deer, sheep, hedgehogs, trout, pheasants and barn owls.

Barton Stacey has been associated with both the Roman and modern army. There was a Roman camp here, excavated in the 1970s. A large military camp and married quarters were built just before the Second World War and both Winston Churchill and General Dwight Eisenhower visited the camp in 1942 when American troops were stationed there. The area of the village which includes Roberts Road, West Road, East Road and the closes leading from these was also requisitioned at the time of the Second World War. The land was purchased in 1943 and the construction of married quarters for service personnel from the four army camps constructed north of the village on either side of the A303 began in the 1950s. King's Elms was built in stages from 1939 to 1971.

The school was originally on Bullington Lane at the junction with Gravel Lane and had been here in some form since 1819. The then Lord of the Manor had granted land for the 'erection of a National School for the education of the poor'. It was rebuilt in 1896 following a fire. The current school, off Roberts Road, was opened in June 1958, although the school could not reopen for the autumn term as contractors found bombs and shells in the grounds. The bomb disposal team came and found 21 bazookas, seven rockets and countless shells (all expended). The original school is currently being developed as housing along with the rest of the site formerly owned by Goldings.

Our fair was held annually on the Feast of St Margaret, under a royal warrant granted in 1241 by Henry III; our right to a market is even earlier and dates to 1215 from King John. Although the main objective of the medieval fairs was trade and commerce, every fair contained some element of merry-making. Possibly starting from merchants trying to sell their goods, people were determined to attract the most customers to their stalls. Therefore, from a very early date, there were lots of opportunities for fun at the medieval fairs. Our fete today carries on this tradition – stalls where you can buy goods, games of chance, food and drink prepared at the fete and entertainment by players or musicians. We no longer have the cockfights or bear-baiting but the dog show still brings an animal interest into the proceedings.

Knights were an obvious feature of the medieval scene – Sir Rogo and Sir Emery de Stacy being just two. In 2016, groups from around the village decorated the 'Chalk Army' of white knights with incredibly creative results. The knights were displayed at key events both prior to and during the medieval festival which commemorated the granting of the charter, even travelling to the Great Hall and Records Office in Winchester as well as various shop windows in Andover.

The village is a hive of activity with many groups active within the community. Every two years the village has a charity ball on the recreation ground. This began following events to celebrate the Queen's Golden Jubilee in 2002, which proved so successful that it has continued ever since with thousands of pounds being raised for a diverse group of charities both within the village and nationwide.

BASHLEY

The New Forest is to the north of the village, and the sea two miles to the south, past the now large urban area of New Milton and Barton-on-Sea. The Danes had a great battle with the Saxons to the east of the village in the area called Wootton Rough, and the stream known as Danestream, that runs alongside, is said to have run red with blood. The housing to the south-east of the village is called Daneswood.

Road names come from inhabitants who used to live there, for instance Marks Lane from Mark Whitcher who lived in the corner cottage, formerly known as Mark's Cottage. Some roads are named by what went on there, eg Marlpit Lane, where marl was dug for the local hand-made brickworks. At the corner of Smithy Lane and Bashley Cross Road there was a blacksmith's.

On the corner of New Lane and Bashley Cross Road are two cottages. The one known as 'Missioners' was a chapel. The one known as 'Taverners' was a wayside inn. The original village shop was part of the cottage known as 'homestead' by the smithy. It has two front doors, one of which was the shop door. It did a roaring trade whilst the railway line was being built in 1887 to 1888, selling goods to the Irish navvies.

The football club has gone from strength to strength in recent years. They use the recreation ground for matches and training and have built a clubhouse next to the village hall. There are also teams of youngsters who play regularly.

🍁 BASINGSTOKE

Basingstoke has had an interesting and varied history, with well-known celebrities of their time making their mark.

During the Civil War in 1643-45 Cromwell changed the local landscape; although his efforts were mainly directed on Basing House, irreverently, he used St Michael's church as a stable for his horses. St Michael's church itself bears the scars of cannonball fire, with Church Square suffering bomb damage from the blitz in the Second World War.

Jane Austen (1775-1817), who was born in Steventon, just outside Basingstoke, was known to frequent the town for social events and dances and her bronze statue can be seen strolling through Market Square. Coming closer to the modern day, John Arlott (1914-1991), the cricket commentator, poet and broadcaster, was born in Cemetery Lodge. This is at the entrance to the now ruined Holy Ghost Chapel cemetery.

The town even has its own ghost story attached to this cemetery. In July 1674 a Mrs Blunden had been given a prescription of 'poppy water' to help with an ailment. However, this put her into such a deep sleep it was thought she had died. As the weather was so hot the funeral was carried out in haste and she was buried in the cemetery. Following reports from playing children of noises coming from the grave, Mrs Blunden was exhumed. It was obvious she had still been alive and had tried to escape following her burial, but sadly this was all too late or so it was thought. Awaiting the coroner's attendance in the morning, the coffin was resealed and replaced. It is believed that the attending guard must have neglected his duties for in the morning it was discovered that poor Mrs Blunden had been buried alive twice.

At the 'Top of the Town' there is an English Heritage blue plaque showing the site of the original Burberry shop owned by Thomas Burberry (1835-1926). This is where the coats were made for the fated Antarctic expedition in 1901, for Scott, Shackleton and their crew.

As a WI, which has now covered four decades, Basingstoke Afternoon Women's Institute has been very privileged to have their meetings in the historic Barn in St Michael's Church Cottages right in the centre of Basingstoke. Dating back to the 16th century, the Barn has seen many changes over the years. It is believed to have been part of a manor house called Watermartyns back in the 13th century. Through the centuries the building has been added to with medieval wings, huge exposed wooden pillars and beams forming its frame and mullion windows. This substantial frame has been carbon dated, which has shown how the Barn has expanded over the centuries. This past use lends itself to a sense of historic community which comes through into the modern day, from the 17th-century panelling in the Chapter Room, to the deep ridges on the front brickwork where young children sharpened their writing implements while waiting to go through the Tudor doorframes to enter the School Room.

St Michael's Church Cottages, and in particular the Barn, have been a central part of Basingstoke life for many centuries. Many other organisations value the history and community as much as we do, from rousing Burns Night dances to sedate and tranquil afternoon teas – with so much more in between.

With the North Hampshire Hospital site, thriving retail area and large business centre the area of Basingstoke town, along with the bars, restaurants and café culture, and backed by all its history, is a vibrant place to be.

Baughurst

Baughurst, pronounced Borg-hurst, is situated on the north Hampshire/Berkshire border in the middle of the Newbury/Basingstoke/Reading triangle. Baughurst means 'bog wood' and although there are still a number of gravel pits around the surrounding district to account for the excess water, the woods have long since been cleared for housing development. Aldermaston Park became Aldermaston Aerodrome during the Second World War and was used by the Americans. Thereafter it became the Atomic Weapons Research Establishment (later the Atomic Weapons Establishment) employing a large number of people. To accommodate these people, large areas of Baughurst and Tadley Commons were transformed into award-winning housing estates. Although many light industries have since moved into the area, AWE is still by far the main employer.

Baughurst Road is about four miles in length and the village can boast public houses such as the Wellington, a post office and a parade of shops. A derelict bus depot in Baughurst Road was saved from demolition by developers when a local planning officer from Basingstoke & Deane Council noticed it had a unique feature. The timber-framed building had been built in the earlier part of the last century in a style favoured for a great many factories and warehouses, but it featured the largest single-span roof in Western Europe – the roof trusses span some 80 feet from end to end without support underneath.

The present St Stephen's church was built in 1845 on the site of a Saxon church which had burned down. It is Gothic in style with an unusual octagonal tower. The church contains a 15th-century choir screen which is rich in carving and is said to have been the gift of a Lord Chancellor of England, Archbishop Warham.

🍁 BEAULIEU

The Cistercian village of Beaulieu grew out of the abbey, founded by King John in 1204. Its mill, wells and High Street fascinate visitors as they walk on its uneven and ancient stones. The Beaulieu estate came into the possession of the Montagu family in Henry VIII's time.

The 3rd Lord Montagu, who died in 2015, opened his house to the public in 1952 and very much enjoyed meeting his many visitors. Together with the Abbey and the Motor Museum, Beaulieu is well placed in the country's 'league' of stately homes. The famous Montagu Motor Museum was founded in memory of his father, John Montagu, who successfully persuaded Parliament to abolish the 12 mph speed limit, and oblige motorists to register their cars and obtain licences to drive them. It was he who equipped the army in India with mechanical transport during the First World War. Edward's mother, the Hon Mrs Pleydell-Bouverie, lived in the village from 1920 and was a founder member of the Beaulieu Women's Institute.

The village fire brigade was one of the earliest in the county of Hampshire, and before the Second World War was the private fire brigade of the Beaulieu estate. The village shops form the centre of village life and the Beaulieu Chocolate Studio's hand-made chocolates are sold worldwide. The village hall hosts lectures, dramas, bingo, elections, weddings and many other events. A vineyard flourishes on the south facing slopes above the museum.

One could not leave Beaulieu without mentioning the river, with Buckler's Hard so near to the centre of the yachting world, together with the riverside farms, woods, bird sanctuary, and the estuary shores so abundant with wildlife.

BEAUWORTH

Beauworth lies on a sweep of high ground, the Millbarrows Ridge, on the northern side of the Hampshire downs in what has been designated an Area of Outstanding Natural Beauty. Prehistoric long barrows are evidence of early occupation, and, according to charters dating from AD 909, its boundaries lay within the Saxon manor of Tichborne and the village was recorded in the Domesday Book. The earliest cottages, Church Terrace (once three but now two homes), date from the 16th century. In the early 1800s the centre room was used as a school room. A number of cottages are thatched and several had indoor wells.

The Saxon church has disappeared; the only remains are stone heads in Cheriton churchyard. The present church of St James was built in 1833 by Mr H Mulcock, who owned a brick kiln at nearby Shorley Farm, in Cheriton, where local clay was used to make tiles, flower pots and extra-large bricks.

One day in June 1833, some boys were playing near the village pond, now drained and forming part of the garden at Manor House Farm. One boy stumbled over what appeared to be a piece of lead pipe. His companions scrabbled in the ground with their fingers and discovered what they thought was an old metal box full of buttons. They hastily filled their pockets then ran home to tell their parents. The 'buttons' were in fact coins, about 6,000 in all and in mint condition, dating from the reigns of William the Conqueror and William II. They were declared treasure trove and are now in the British Museum. The lead coffer in which they were found is in Winchester Museum.

Another find was made in 1957 when, in an area of heavy undergrowth, Roman tiles and building materials were discovered. These led to the discovery of the site of a Roman villa covering some two and a half acres, further evidence that this has long been considered a desirable place to live.

BEDHAMPTON

Bedhampton is one mile from the town of Havant and, in spite of the growth of the village, retains an attractive look where it lies close to the foreshore of Langstone Harbour.

The manor appears to have existed as far back as the 9th century. A charitable trust set up in 1967, creating an excellent environment for the elderly, preserved the Manor House, but it had to be sold in 2014. Close to the manor is the 12th-century church of St Thomas.

A turreted house named The Elms (18th century) was acquired by Sir John Theophilus Lee and a room within was named the Waterloo Room. Sir John was a friend of the Duke of Wellington, who was reputed to have dined there, and the room was later beautifully restored in white and Wedgwood blue. The house is also owned by the Manor Trust, and has been listed to preserve it for the future.

At the old Mill House in 1819, the poet John Keats stayed with the master baker Mr John Snook and his wife. He had walked from Chichester for a house party, and this is where he finished his poem *The Eve of St Agnes*. He also spent his last night in England here when his ship was delayed in Portsmouth because of a storm. Subsequently he left for Naples, where he died in 1821.

Bedhampton had its share of smuggling in the past. Langstone Harbour was the haunt of smugglers during the 18th and 19th centuries and there was many a skirmish with the Revenue officers. A then nearby inn, the Cat and Fiddle on Bedhampton Hill, is said to have been used by them.

BENTLEY

Bentley is on the A31 between Farnham and Alton. It lies in the middle of an area which has been inhabited at least since Roman times and there are the foundations and floors of a Roman villa in a field at the western end. In the forest of Alice Holt is the site of one of the largest Roman potteries in the country.

In Norman and medieval times the houses clustered nearer to the 12th-century church of St Mary which is on a hill about half a mile north of the main road. The Pilgrims' Way, which led by the shortest route from church to church between Winchester to Canterbury, passes through Jenkyn Place courtyard, where it is said the pilgrims used to stop and drink from a well called 'Jancknes's Well', from which the house gets its present name.

The church itself was much restored in the 14th and 15th centuries and again in the 19th. Jane Austen's brother Henry was perpetual curate of Bentley from 1824 to 1838 and lived at the 'old' rectory on the main road. With others in the parish he subscribed to the setting up of the cage, which was built for the 'temporary imprisonment of the drunk and disorderly'. Nothing of it now remains except the name, given to a row of cottages near the site.

The Eggar family have played a prominent part in the village and its surroundings since the 16th century and at one time owned Jenkyn Place and much of the surrounding land and properties. A Mr Sanderson, who was a director of the White Star Shipping Line, owners of RMS *Titanic*, was holding a dinner party at Jenkyn Place the evening he was told of the disaster in 1912.

Another famous Bentley resident was the Chief Scout, Lord Baden-Powell, who bought Blackacre in 1919 and changed its name to the world-renowned 'Pax Hill'. Since his death in 1941 the house has had various uses but is now a nursing home.

BEREWOOD

Once, the mighty Forest of Bere extended from Southampton to the Sussex border. Included within it were two ancient woodlands, the Royal Forest of Bere Ashley, which stretched from the river Test to the river Itchen, and the Royal Forest of Bere Portchester, which ran between the river Meon and Bedhampton. It was sparsely populated, was densely wooded and had poor soil. Bere, according to the *Collins English Dictionary*, is an old term for barley.

Between 1604 and 1914, there were nationally 5,200 Acts of Enclosure, which allowed common land, previously free for all to use, to be fenced or hedged off. In 1810, 8,000 acres of the Forest of Bere were enclosed and turned to agricultural use. Not far from Waterlooville, Collyers Farm, on present-day Forest Road in World's End, came into being in 1821 as a result of the forest's enclosure. By the beginning of the 19th century, there were 16,000 acres of the forest left. These were the West Walk, situated near Wickham, and the East Walk, between Horndean and Purbrook.

After the enclosure, roads were laid to allow access to the new properties that had been created. One, from the village we now call Denmead, crossed the existing London Road and formed a central crossroads around which Waterlooville grew. The northern quadrant was sold off and this was sub-divided and sold as plots of land for housebuilding.

Over time, Waterlooville expanded and soon was a busy town, but it did not forget its forest roots, which are remembered in Forest End, just off the London Road, a short distance from the new estate that also commemorates the forest that once stood there, Berewood. The allotments in Forest End owe their existence to the 1845 General Inclosure Act, which acknowledged that the poor, owning no land, could not grow their own crops. Provision for field gardens was made in the act and it was this legislation that led to part of the enclosed forest being used for allotments in Waterlooville.

Pockets of the Forest of Bere are still to be seen. The nearest to Berewood are the Forestry Commission sites at Park Wood and the Queen's Inclosure, which are on opposite sides of the old A3 London Road, at the Waterlooville border with Cowplain. These are woodlands that are open to the public and give a hint of the majesty of the old Forest of Bere. It must have been a formidable place in the 12th century!

🍁 Bishop's Sutton

There are many Hampshire villages recorded in the Domesday Book, but the story of each is unique. An Anglo-Saxon hamlet at the source of a tributary of the river Itchen, our village was entered as Sudtone, meaning south settlement. It contained a church with mills along the waterway. Today, it is called Bishop's Sutton, a name incorporating its origins and its ecclesiastical connection to the medieval Bishops of Winchester.

Once held by King Harold, the manor was granted by King Stephen to his brother, Bishop Henri de Blois. Here the Bishop built a rural retreat and replaced the Saxon church with the present Norman building. His successors added to the estate by enclosing a deer park, the pale of which is still visible along Old Park Road. Rabbit warrens were introduced within the park and fishponds were created close by the palace and the Norman church.

Bishop's Sutton became a thriving estate providing crops and livestock to the wealth of the church. The yearly agricultural cycle was underpinned by the feasts and festivals of medieval Christianity. After the martyrdom of Thomas Becket, pilgrims travelling from Winchester to the saint's shrine at Canterbury travelled through the village on the Pilgrims' Way. In the millennium year of 2000, a plaque was placed at the church gate to remind us of the pilgrimage route.

The Reformation saw the church lands sold to the laity while its original dedication to All Saints was changed to St Nicholas and the chapel on the north wall was demolished. Although the manor was later returned to the church, parts had been sold and unofficial enclosure of the common fields began.

In 1644, the Civil War battle of Cheriton was fought south of Bishop's Sutton. Royalist troops lined up on the parish boundary facing Cromwell's Parliamentarians on Cheriton Down. Such was the violence of that conflict, tradition says the lane from Sutton Scrubs to Cheriton 'ran with blood'. Within the parish perimeter, overlooking the battle site, a memorial stone marks the event.

With the coming of a turnpike road through the village, new skills were needed. Richard Andrews, born in Bishop's Sutton in 1798, became a successful coachbuilder and was five times Mayor of Southampton. Next to the Ship Inn was his carriage works where one of Andrews' labourers, William Faichen, worked. He set up an evening school in St Nicholas church offering a basic education to village children and when a school was built in Ropley, Faichen became its first teacher. Buried on the south side of Bishop's Sutton's church, Faichen's grave is decorated annually with bouquets of flowers by the school leavers of Ropley who honour their founder.

The arrival of railways meant that local produce such as watercress, grown in spring-fed beds created from the foundations of the old fishponds from the Bishop's palace, could be sent fresh daily to Covent Garden market. This gave employment to villagers. Today, the Watercress Steam Railway running through the parish brings many visitors to the area while the annual Alresford Watercress Festival attracts thousands.

Bishop's Sutton was changing. The gentry bought property and gave new opportunities to the locals. Lacklands, a large house south of the main road, was the home to Arthur Yates, a gentleman, who became a professional horse trainer. In 1893, one of his stable, *Cloister*, ridden by a local man, William Dollery, won the Grand National. Such was the delight of *Cloister*'s owner, Charles Duff, that he paid for the bells of St Nicholas to be re-cast and re-hung. Where Yates trained his horses, there is a track still called the Gallops.

Before his death in 1922, Arthur Yates wrote his autobiography, in collaboration with a young poet, Bruce Blunt. With his musician friend, Peter Warlock, Blunt led a bohemian existence resulting in fluctuating fortune. In 1927, while living in Bishop's Sutton, the impecunious Blunt decided to enter a *Daily Telegraph* competition for a new Christmas carol. On a star-lit walk between the Plough in Bishop's Sutton and the Anchor in Ropley, he wrote the lyrics to *Bethlehem Down*. With music composed by Warlock, the carol won the competition and has entered the Christmas repertoire. In Blunt's words, the prize money fuelled 'an immortal carouse'!

Bishops and kings, peasants and paupers, death and destruction, innovation and altruism, poetry and music, all have been recounted. During two world wars, the village helped feed the nation. Now, the school has closed and the shop has gone. The almshouses were pulled down. Agriculture no longer relies on intensive labour. Redundant barns and outbuildings have been converted for office and small business use. Inhabitants of Bishop's Sutton dwell in the village but, for the most part, work away.

How does the Women's Institute fit into this village story? The WI in Bishop's Sutton was founded in 1947. On record, there is retrospective recognition of its first president, Miss Kenyon while early minutes show lively meetings with competitions and speakers engaging the members. However, the organisation's original aims of revitalising rural communities and encouraging women to become more involved with food production have been replaced by other priorities. Members of the WI help with the summer garden fete, the Alresford Show, church fund-raising events and occasions of national celebration. A record-breaking tea for over 400 villagers crowned the Silver Jubilee festivities. We are an integral part of our 21st-century community, proud of our past 'but as times change we change with them'.

🍁 BISHOP'S WALTHAM

Bishop's Waltham is known as a small town but many still think of it as a village. It is a nice place to live, but has known hard times, when, to make ends meet, the women went stone picking, pea picking and strawberry picking.

There was a railway station but this has gone to make way for a road across the pond. There were also two brickyards employing many local men. There are now two good schools in the village, three churches and a Gospel hall, the Women's Institute, and many thriving community groups.

Bishop's Waltham House is a care home built in ideal surroundings. The Priory was a seminary run by the White Fathers; after it was sold it became a police college. Cromwell knocked down the Bishop's Palace; the ruins still remain and are a great attraction. The pond once provided fish for the Palace but now the fishing club has taken over and fish themselves.

There are a number of footpaths where one can escape from the busy roads. The old railway track is a public footpath, thanks to the Bishop's Waltham Society who worked hard to make this possible.

🍁 BISHOPSTOKE

The village of Bishopstoke, in the Borough of Eastleigh, is about a mile east of the town centre and on the eastern bank of the river Itchen. It has a long history going back to Saxon times when in AD 948 King Alfred the Great's grandson King Eadred granted land to Thane Aelfric. The original name of the village was 'Ytingstoc', meaning place of the Jutes; later 'Bishop' was added as the land belonged to the Bishops of Winchester. The watermill which was mentioned in the Domesday Book was still working until 1934 but its memory remains as some of the equipment, pictures and information are displayed and locals still call that area 'The Mill'.

The opening of the railway line from London to Southampton in 1840 changed the village. Land was advertised and terraced housing built for railway workers on the green fields with some semi and detached houses. Longmead House, a red brick, 23 bedroom mansion set in 26 acres was demolished in 1938 and the land sold off in sections upon which houses were built. A large council estate, Longmead, was built in the 1950s and Bishopstoke now merges with Fair Oak following the building of many houses and two new schools in the 1970s-80s on the edges of Stoke Park Woods, which are a lovely place to walk and see bluebells in the spring. The former carriage drive to Longmead is now West Drive, bordered on both sides by the original line of trees. Stoke Park Road, which ran along the edge of the estate was a mustering point for American soldiers before D-Day with their field kitchen set up on the site where bungalows now stand. Sadly few of the other large houses remain.

A Victorian mansion with beautiful water gardens is The Mount, later a sanatorium and geriatric hospital and now converted and new accommodation added to become Bishopstoke Park retirement village. Nearby stood a large neo-gothic house, inappropriately called The Cottage. It was later called Itchen House, after the river flowing in its grounds. It was owned by Admiral of the Fleet, Sir Henry Keppel, where he experimented with breeding trout, exporting to rivers in Tasmania.

Two waterways flow through the old village; the river Itchen, a famous trout and salmon stream which in Victorian times had water carnivals held on it, and the Itchen Navigation, one of the oldest canals in England, but the last boat carrying goods between Southampton and Winchester was in the 1860s. Nowadays, the path alongside the canal is a nice walk, called by locals 'going along The Barge'. You might see water voles or even a kingfisher if you are lucky.

There were two pubs facing the river; the Anchor is now flats but the Anglers Inn remains popular. A mix of old and new buildings and housing types make up today's Bishopstoke. A pair of 17th-century thatched cottages stand next to houses built in the 1930s. The late 18th-century manor house has been converted into flats. The Riverside is a conservation area, with trees, running water, wildlife and a small river beach. 'Bishy Beach' is a favourite place for children and families on a hot day.

The old church near the river was replaced in 1890-91 by St Mary's church further up the hill. The ancient yew tree in the old cemetery still thrives.

Opposite St Mary's is the remaining two-classroom building of the old village school of 1880, closed in 1980 and now the community centre.

The inhabitants of the village until the mid 19th century were mostly farmers and their workers. The Lavington family have farmed at West Horton since 1796 and their descendants are still there. A plaque on a house in Church Road shows where Harvey Collyer (grocer and sexton) and his wife Charlotte lived with their eight year old daughter, Marjorie. They had booked tickets on another ship in 1912 but were delayed due to a coal strike and were transferred to the *Titanic*, with all their possessions, to travel second-class to Idaho at a cost of £26 5s. Mother and daughter were rescued but Harvey did not survive. Leonard Knight, a third-class steward, of Spring Lane also drowned that night.

Thomas Garnier, Dean of Winchester from 1840 to 1872 and passionate about plants, helped form the Hampshire Horticultural Society and created a beautiful garden and arboretum at Bishopstoke Rectory (now a private house). Other personalities born in Bishopstoke are Richard Dummer, an early settler in New England described as 'one of the fathers of Massachusetts' and Samuel Sewall, Massachusetts judge, known for his involvement in the Salem witch trials.

Several village roads are named after local families and personalities. Some people have lived in Bishopstoke all their lives, other families originated from Nine Elms in London following the building of the railway works in Eastleigh, while others are incomers finding work post-war in the carriage and locomotive works, printing and at the Ford factory, all of which have now closed.

Today, most people work outside of the village but find it a convenient, happy place to live. The village is lucky to have a small variety of shops, amenities and services. Many societies and groups for all ages run for villagers and each September a two day carnival is held with a parade, big fete and float and duck races in the river. There are excellent schools and most children attend the Stoke Park schools and go up to Wyvern College for secondary education. There is a regular bus service through the village and several takeaway food outlets.

The future of Bishopstoke remains unsure as plans, widely protested, are in progress to build a new road and over 5,000 houses to the north. Whatever is ahead, it is a point of pride with villagers that their history is longer than Eastleigh's. Even the railway station was originally Bishopstoke Junction (for Eastleigh).

Blackmoor & Whitehill

Although Blackmoor is a relatively tiny and quiet hamlet in Hampshire it has had an amazing past. Roman soldiers have passed through the area, with Roman coins found when a local pond dried up in the 1740s and a vast hoard of 30,000 coins dug up in the 1870s.

Gilbert White, the renowned naturalist of nearby Selborne, noted that the area was 'remarkable for timber…the oaks of Blackmoor stand high in the estimation of purveyors and have furnished much naval timber.' In the early 1710s Queen Anne sat on a grassy bank to watch 500 red deer, which were herded by for her delight. However, this same forest was also a refuge for the lawless and destitute in the 13th century and there was known to be a risk of armed robbery. In the 16th and 17th centuries there was also extensive poaching, these poachers painting their faces black to avoid being easily seen at night.

In the 1880s the land in Blackmoor was bought by Sir Roundell Palmer, the 1st Earl of Selborne who created cottages, a school and a church. He started fruit farming which is still carried out to this present day. Apple trees are still grown in Blackmoor and the fruit sold nationwide. The apple farm is the major employer in the village.

Whitehill did not exist until the mid 19th century. In 1860 there was just a pub and one or two houses. The parents of the first person born here were so proud of this fact that they baptised her Alice Whitehill Lemon and her descendants still live in the village today.

With the coming of the army to nearby Bordon and with more traffic on the road running through the village, Whitehill just grew and grew. A military train track was laid through the village to transport troops from Bordon camp to join up with the main line at Liss. It was whilst transporting huts on this railway that one fell off at Whitehill and was used for many years as the police station.

In 1928 Whitehill became a distinct parish of its own after being formed by parts of the medieval royal hunting forest of Woolmer and parts of the parishes of Selborne and Headley. Slowly the nearby village of Bordon grew and Whitehill and Bordon became one town in the 1990s.

After the Bordon army camp left the area in 2015 the proposal is for the area to have a new lease of life with new houses, a new shopping area, many more facilities and a relief road to lessen the traffic through the town.

🍁 BLACKWATER

Situated in the north-east corner of Hampshire, Blackwater takes its name from the river which marks its boundary with the counties of Surrey and Berkshire. In olden times a ford enabled people to cross the river easily, thus making the village an important changing stage for the coaches which ran along the main London to Exeter high road.

As well as two alehouses, there were three large coaching inns, of which one at least had its own brewery at the rear. While the horses were being rested or changed, the weary passengers could enjoy hospitality in the inns, heartened by the sight of rounds of beef, veal pies and hams, washed down with old port, burgundy or ale. Footpads and highwaymen abounded, making these journeys over the wild and desolate heathland, which surrounded Blackwater, extremely perilous. In 1839, 60 coaches a day were passing through the village.

Blackwater's greatest claim to fame must be its great two-day cattle fair. From the 13th century until after the First World War, it was held annually in November on the wide open spaces of commonland round the great crossroads to the south of the village. It was always mentioned in *Old Moore's Almanac* as the largest cattle fair in the south of England. Hundreds of cattle, horses, pigs and sheep were bought and sold.

The pine-scented 'healthy' air attracted many people to settle here and gracious houses were built, each on its individual estate, with attractive lodges for the employees. More new villas and cottages housed the men who worked on the railway line which was laid in 1849, with a level crossing at the station in Blackwater.

Hawley Park is the oldest large house in the vicinity and has a chequered history. It was possibly a hunting lodge in the Middle Ages, then it was enlarged in the 18th century. There is, in the magnificent stable block, a clock dated 1743, still in perfect working order. These stables were used by Sir Francis Dashwood, the founder member of the notorious Hell Fire Club.

In 1860 Wilkie Collins, the author, stayed at Frogmore Park, another house in Blackwater. Did he see the ghost reputed to haunt it? It is said that his novel *The Woman in White* was inspired by his visit there, others say he actually wrote the book during his visit.

🍁 BOLDRE & PILLEY

The parish of Boldre and Pilley is situated in the New Forest National Park, near to the Georgian town of Lymington on the south coast. The name Boldre has been spelt in various ways – Bolre (a plank over the river) and Boulder – but in the Domesday Book is recorded as Bovre, supposedly a Norman clerk's corruption of Boldre, which is Celtic meaning the full stream. Pilley (Pisteslie in Norman French) was originally Pyieley.

Boldre's beautiful, ancient church was built by William I around 1079. Sarcen stones in the foundations, show that possibly the site was a place of worship before Christianity. Known now as St John the Baptist, the church, although rather isolated, is well attended each week; a popular place for weddings and baptisms, it becomes packed at festivals such as Easter and Christmas, maintaining its reputation of welcome and high musical standards.

When a second extension to the choir vestry was built on the north side of the church in the late 1990s, a mass burial pit, thought to be a plague pit, was discovered containing the bones of adults and children. The bones were wrapped in linen and reburied at dawn with a special service for such an occasion.

Boldre and Pilley for all practical purposes are one area, though there is a natural division with the river Lym running between them. In the past this division was more evident with larger houses, and presumably more wealth, in Boldre, and with smaller cottages and labourers in Pilley, although this was not entirely the case. This cultural division has pretty well disappeared with refurbished and rebuilt cottages and houses, and Pilley, verging as it does onto the open forest, is a sought-after area in which to live with most property prices above the national average. The New Forest ponies, donkeys and cows wander the main street and lanes of Pilley, often to be seen in groups outside the village shop, and sometimes making their way into gardens. These animals are allowed to roam freely as their owners will have commoners' rights, one of the many ancient rights awarded to inhabitants of the New Forest to allow free grazing.

The village shop and post office, which is run by voluntary help, provides a much needed service and is an example of the neighbourliness that exists here.

A popular C of E primary school in Pilley attracts children from around the Lymington area as well as locally. The parish can boast two excellent pubs, the Fleur de Lys in Pilley, claimed to be the oldest pub in the Forest, and the Red Lion in Boldre. Lottery funding, combined with a local fund-raising campaign, made it possible for a new community hall to be built in Pilley and opened in the year 2000, replacing the previous one built in the 1920s. The new hall is the centre of the community, always in use by a variety of groups. Boldre Women's Institute celebrated its 100 years in 2017. The Boldre Club in Pilley is the oldest working men's club in the country, celebrating 125 years in 2018.

Boldre has known several notable people, including Rev Richard Johnson, the first chaplain to the Colony of New South Wales at Botany Bay in 1788, but possibly the most well-known is William Gilpin, pastor and polymath who arrived in the parish in 1777 and described the inhabitants as 'little better than a hoard of banditti...exposed to every temptation of pillage and robbery from their proximity to the deer, game and fuel of the forest...[they] presented a picture of savage life, which perhaps was hardly paralleled in a civilised country.' Smuggling was prevalent at the time with barrels being hidden in the river to escape notice. William Gilpin set out, often on horseback, to visit every dwelling in the parish, bringing him to the conclusion that the way forward was to educate the children. He set about opening a school (now a private dwelling at the start of School Lane) educating boys and girls separately in skills judged suitable for their lives and at the same time he improved the conditions in the Pilley poor house.

The word 'picturesque' is closely associated with William Gilpin; he did much to define it in relation to landscape art. He is buried in the churchyard of St John the Baptist in an area where wild flowers are encouraged to grow, with a lengthy inscription on his tombstone which includes 'hoping to meet some of his neighbours'. One might wonder if 'some' might mean not all.

The parish of Boldre and Pilley with its proximity to the delights of sailing in the Solent and walking in the Forest, is a recommended place to visit and a pleasant area in which to live.

BOTLEY

During the Second World War, Botley remained largely unscathed from enemy action but there is still evidence today of the defensive measures undertaken in the village and of the preparations for the D-Day offensive. Civil Defence was organised to prepare for the possibility of an enemy invasion. In Botley a 'War Book' has been preserved which is a handwritten directory of people, equipment and organisations which could be quickly summoned in the event of an invasion.

Contact details such as the fire service, Home Guard, ambulance and police are supplemented with information on the location of fire hydrants, shelters, wells, the mortuary (Maffey's garage in Church Lane, now the Malthouse), sick bay (the Catherine Wheel), emergency fuel supplies etc. Also listed was all the available transport in the village, including eleven tractors, 105 private cars, 46 goods vehicles, 31 horses and 54 carts. Supplies of 50 spades, 50 forks, 24 shovels and five wheelbarrows were stored at Maffey's shop (now the Chinese takeaway), crowbars and pickaxes were stored at Baileys Ironmongers (now Regginas Restaurant), and heavy lifting gear at Botley Garages (now the Funeral Directors). Stocks of blankets were stored at the Catherine Wheel.

Since all able-bodied men were conscripted into the armed services, the working parties for fire guard comprised older men, youths, the disabled and men in reserved occupations. Also listed are the 25 members of the Women's Voluntary Service and it was noted which of them were trained first aiders. The gas decontamination centre was located at the fire station in the High Street (now replaced by a private house).

Provision was made for emergency drinking water by identifying the Hamble River as the source with the stock of chlorinated lime and carbonate of soda for filtration being held at the chemist's shop. Containers for distribution would be milk churns from local farms and dairies with a person appointed as 'Water Warden'.

In the early months of the war the RAF established a decoy site near Marks Farm (near Manor Farm) which was intended to replicate the Northam area of Southampton – the curve of the Hamble River being similar to that of the river Itchen. The site consisted of a control building and concrete-covered Nissen hut which was linked to a series of large bonfire sites. After the first enemy bombers had passed over, these were ignited and the Luftwaffe was then tempted into bombing southern Botley rather than the heavily populated industrialised Northam. This probably worked because a string of seven high explosive bombs fell very close to the decoy site and Marks Farm.

As well as anti-tank concrete blocks being erected in the Square and along the boundary walls of Sherecroft, at the eastern end was a pillbox (a defensive machine gun enclosure). Anderson air raid shelters were constructed in gardens and 86 Morrison shelters were also issued to those who needed bomb protection inside their homes.

Although air raid precautions throughout the country were strictly enforced there was evidence that Botley lapsed at times. Instances at Eastleigh Police Court of residents being fined for showing lights after dark included one referring to a motor cyclist who ran into a herd of cows in Holmesland Lane. Pleading guilty, the herdsman was fined 10 shillings for driving animals during darkness without a dimmed white light behind and in front of the herd, and the cattle owner was fined 7s 6d. In another case, the explanation that she had had a worrying time as five of her sons were in the army did not prevent a fine of 10 shillings being imposed upon a mother for showing a light at night. A more serious event occurred in June 1941 when Hill Farm on the outskirts of the village received a direct hit and five people were killed.

As D-Day approached, the village saw a massive build up of British, American and Canadian servicemen and service vehicles, jeeps, tanks and personnel carriers. The vehicles were parked along many of the roads in Botley and also in lay-bys in Maddoxford Lane (these still exist) which were specially constructed to accommodate the tanks.

A large tented camp was created at Fairthorne Manor for Canadian troops and the manor itself became the headquarters for directing the Canadian assault on Normandy. HMS *Cricket Camp* was constructed in 1943 as a Royal Naval shore establishment in preparation for the invasion of Europe. This comprised 120 individual buildings, including a NAAFI with cinema, small hospital and Nissen accommodation huts. The Hamble river and Hoe Moor creek were dredged and widened to moor scores of landing craft. Three large country houses were also requisitioned to provide officer and WREN accommodation.

On the night of 5th June 1944 armoured vehicles left the streets of Botley and the landing craft moved down the Hamble river to begin the invasion of Europe. The 'War Book' makes one reflect upon the feelings of ordinary village people at a time of uncertainty and shortages, having to contemplate the real possibility of an enemy invasion. We are indebted to Mrs Clare Harding, the granddaughter of Mr Arthur Maffey, for allowing extracts from the 'War Book' to be used.

🍁 BRAMDEAN

If you visit you will see that Bramdean has grown up along the road that runs through the village. A glance at the houses will take you through the centuries, from cottages that date back to the English Civil War to grand private houses such as Woodcote Manor which has stood in its parkland setting since the 15th century. Bramdean House dates from the 18th century and it is well worth visiting the nationally famous gardens which are often open to the public for charity. The 12th-century church up the hill on Church Lane is a place to soak in its peace and quiet and indulge in some quiet contemplation. There is a beautiful tapestry in the church showing some of the old and new houses in the village.

The church in the wood at Bramdean Common

The local pub, the Fox, is over 400 years old and still sports the crest of the Prince of Wales who was crowned George IV in 1820. The oak-carved crest with its three feathers and motto *Ich Dien* was granted to the landlord after a visit by the future king and his entourage.

On the edges of the parish stand the international residential school Brockwood Park which was founded in 1969 by the Indian educator and philosopher J. Krishnamurti, and the Krishnamurti Centre built in 1986 which was chosen by our present Prince of Wales, Prince Charles, for positive mention in his celebrated personal view of architecture, *A Vision of Britain*.

Bramdean Common lies about a mile away from the main village and is an unusual public space in today's fenced-off world. If you venture into the woods you will find another gem of a church with a step decorated with local 'shepherds' crowns' or fossils found in the fields. In 1883 a mail-order church in corrugated iron was erected allegedly to serve the needs of the charcoal burners who lived and worked on the common. Today the 'Church in the Wood' is used for unique Christmas carol services when the congregation usually spills out into the surrounding churchyard, as well as providing some services for the travelling community. The church even achieved television fame by appearing in George Clarke's *Amazing Spaces* in 2014.

Like most places, when you stop to look and find out about those villages that you speed through on your way to somewhere else, Bramdean is a lot more than just a passing blur!

🍁 BRAMLEY

Bramley lies about five miles north of Basingstoke and is divided by the railway line running from Basingstoke to Reading. It is a very busy line for goods and passengers going to and from the south coast and the north of the country. The signal box was demolished in 1977 and half barriers installed but for safety reasons these were later replaced with full barriers and operated by CCTV from Basingstoke.

The census in 2011 showed a population of 4,233 but the village has grown steadily in the last few years, with new estates being built. It is mainly a commuter village with most people travelling to Reading or Basingstoke or to London. There is a primary school, a general store/post office, a bakery, a public house and an estate agent. A few of the redundant barns have been converted into offices and there is a small industrial estate at Campbell Road.

One old building which deserves a mention is the Old Granary. It is situated between Clift Meadow and Stocks Farm. These buildings are comparatively rare outside Hampshire. The Granary was built in the 19th century and is a rectangular timber-framed building with half-hipped tile roof, and weatherboarded walls raised above twelve staddle stones. The grain was housed in this building because the vermin could not climb the staddle stones and contaminate the grain. The Granary was left to the parish by John Clift on his death in 1990. The village is indebted to the generosity of William and John Clift as they also donated land for the building of the village hall in 1972 and later land next to the Bramley Inn for leisure purposes. A pavilion was built on what is now known as Clift Meadow and later a hall for the youth club and they are both well used by various organisations in the village. Over the last few years a St George's Fun Day has taken place on Clift Meadow involving all the villagers with games and races for the children, a dog show, lots of stalls and bouncy castles etc. The Millennium garden at Clift Meadow was made and is maintained by members of the WI. An annual flower show is held in the village hall in August and is well supported. A biennial music festival is held in St James church in the summer with renowned artists performing.

The land to the north of Bramley is part of the Stratfield Saye estate owned by the Duke of Wellington, while the land to the south includes 900 acres of MOD owned land. In 1987 when Royal Engineers were clearing a route for a proposed water main they discovered First World War canisters. Army experts and Basingstoke Council workers evacuated 30 homes and blocked off roads within 550 yards of the highly dangerous mustard gas canisters. Four canisters were safely removed but when more canisters were discovered the evacuation was halted and the water main was rerouted. Today it is used as a training area by the TA and other organisations and is visited by Chinook helicopters from RAF Odiham. Various film companies have also used the area in their films.

In 1967 the Central Electricity Generating Board built an electrical substation in Bramley Frith Wood. The word 'frith' is an ancient English word meaning place of freedom: a place of sanctuary or shelter. Within the National Grid site the Frith Forest School has been set up. Its aim is to give children the opportunity to explore, have fun and learn new skills in a beautiful wood surrounded by mature oaks and hazel copses and carpeted by bluebells in the spring.

BREAMORE

The present village of Breamore (pronounced Bremmer from its original Saxon name) lies along the busy B388 Salisbury/Ringwood road. The rosy brick cottages are mostly 17th-century, built along the turnpike road by families whose descendants live locally to this day. Villagers worked on the Breamore House estate or leased farming land from the estate.

It is a pretty village with colourful gardens and flowering trees by the road, but life is made difficult for residents as the road cuts it in two. The school lies on one side and the village hall and the Bat and Ball pub on the other. Seventeenth-century stocks stand very near their original site opposite the pub. Villagers must have been fairly well behaved as records show the stocks were seldom used.

The original village of Breamore lay to the west of the road across the marsh, where people have grazing rights for geese and cattle and one is often held up while a procession of geese cross the road. It was centred round the Saxon church and is worth exploring to find old hidden cottages, and to take time to visit the church.

Here too is the gateway to Breamore House park. The house is an Elizabethan manor house built in 1583 by Queen Elizabeth's Treasurer, William Dodington.

It stands in a splendid position on the hill slope, backed by sheltering woods and looking out across a stretch of farmland and 17th-century water meadows. The house is still a family home but is open to the public in the summer season. There is much to see, even a ghost, or two, if you are lucky (or unlucky).

You will not find any traces of the major battle that took place in the 5th century near the house but, if you walk up through the woods you come to the medieval maze, known as the Miz Maze.

🍁 BROCKENHURST

There is something unique about Brockenhurst in the New Forest, an ancient, friendly and busy village of about 2,500 people, though with many more visitors during the summer months as there are many campsites, B&Bs and holiday homes. Visitors and residents alike enjoy the glorious countryside with wild flowers, heathers and the yellow gorse, which can always be found in bloom – as the saying goes, 'when the gorse is out it's kissing time'! And of course the ponies, cattle, pigs (during pannage season) and donkeys roam free everywhere, all owned by Commoners and looked after by the New Forest Agisters. There are several donkey families and two in particular, Molly and Mary, play their part in village life, on Palm Sunday and during the village Christmas Celebration Nativity scene.

St Nicholas church, said to be the oldest in the Forest and mentioned in the Domesday Book, has many ancient gravestones, including that of Brusher Mills, the New Forest snake catcher. He lived much of his time in a 'bender' in the forest, the traditional home of a New Forest Gypsy, collecting adders which were sent to a London hospital for research on the venom. There is also a First World War memorial together with 103 war graves; 93 are New Zealanders and there are also three Indians and three Belgians who died of their injuries whilst in the Brockenhurst temporary hospitals. The area is maintained by the Commonwealth War Graves Commission and visited by many New Zealand visitors paying their respect to their family members, especially on Anzac Day.

During wartime local hotels and large houses were taken over by the Army for administration offices and convalescence of troops, while the Balmer Lawn Hotel was the Royal Marine HQ. Many were requisitioned during the Second World War as headquarters for the planning of D-Day in 1944. The village and the surrounding area were on 'shut down' leading up to the invasion, with army vehicles parked in roads, lanes, gateways and every available space ready for 'The Go'.

The village is well supported with independent tradespeople, a master baker and master butcher, among many others, as well as two supermarkets, all with good car parking outside the shops and nearby car park.

The village was included in the National Parks system in 2008 with the necessary authority keeping an eye on planning and new building regulations as well as the local environment.

The village hall is large and modern with a sports games area adjacent, both well used by the local school and organisations, of which there are many. Cricket is played on the open forest and the football club have their own ground. At the end of July, the New Forest and Hampshire County Agricultural and Horse Show is staged in Brockenhurst, a very popular three day event with competitors and visitors coming from far and wide. All in all a splendid place to live, work and visit to enjoy the ambience of the village, the environment and its people.

Brook & Bramshaw

Brook and Bramshaw are two villages situated just inside the New Forest. The villages have changed considerably over the last few years, with the M27 motorway just one and a half miles away. However, the area has certainly not lost its charm and the New Forest ponies still walk along the roads and graze the verges and commons. It is not only ponies that have to be avoided by passing motorists but cows, donkeys, pigs and occasionally deer.

There is still the old forge building in Bramshaw. This has a long history and the cottage adjoining is dated 1793, with the initials 'WH'. William Henbest placed an advertisement in the *Salisbury and Winchester Journal* on 1 September 1794, respectfully informing the public in general 'that he has erected a Foundry to cast iron of every sort'. In 1813 he made numerous cast-iron safes for local churches at £3 13s 6d each. There is one in Salisbury Cathedral, embossed with the initials 'WH' and 'Bramshaw'.

Great attractions in the area are the two golf courses. One is over the open forest with spectacular views, but here the players have the added handicap of the ponies wandering on and off the greens. The main course is the venue for several tournaments, and the complex includes an hotel.

On the outskirts of Brook is the famous Rufus Stone. In August 1100 William Rufus, King William II of England, was shot dead by an arrow whilst he was out hunting in the Forest. The stone marks the spot where William Rufus died. Was it an accident, or was it murder by the hand of the French nobleman Walter Tyrrell? The mystery remains to this day. Very near to the stone is the public house called the Sir Walter Tyrrell.

🍁 BROUGHTON

Broughton has had a very long history, as proved by the discovery of the skeleton of a Saxon warrior, found on Broughton Hill by a ploughman in 1875. The blond hair only disintegrated on being exposed to the air. A 'pig' of Mendip lead, weighing 156 lbs and dated 59 AD, the time of Nero, was found in 1783.

Henry V's soldiers, en route for the battle of Agincourt, encamped in a field near Bossington, part of the parish of Broughton.

As recently as 1829, the owner of Bossington House, a Mr Penleaze, destroyed the hamlet around, and a broadsheet published in 1870 laments this destruction, beginning thus: 'Alas poor Bossington. What is thy village fled? Where are thy natives gone? None left, but sleeping dead?' Before this event, a Thomas South, also owner of Bossington House, and inventor, discovered that by covering a hot air balloon with a net, the difficulties of attaching a basket could easily be overcome. He also invented appliances for raising sunken vessels and keeping damaged ones afloat, and conducted experiments in the river Test.

In the 13th century, John Maunsel, lord of Broughton manor, was granted a charter by Henry III to hold an annual fair. Six hundred years later the reputation of the fair had sunk to 'a nasty mixture of beer and gingerbread'. In July 1871, the fair was discontinued. However, in modern times it has been resurrected and still the ale and gingerbread are present in the form of competition. A procession from the village hall stops at St Mary's church to obtain dispensation and renewal of the charter.

However, the ancient custom of carrying a man on a hurdle and depositing him on the doorstep of newcomers in the parish, when he would start brushing the step and refuse to go away until he had been given food and drink, has not been revived!

🍁 BURGHCLERE

Burghclere was for many centuries a prosperous farming area. Sheep and barley were the chief sources of income with their associated products, wool,

Sandham Memorial Chapel, Burghclere

meat and beer. In recent years the small mixed farms have mostly disappeared, but some dairy cattle, a few sheep and light riding horses can still be seen.

Ladle Hill is an Iron Age earthwork on the southern ridge, and far bigger is Beacon Hill on the western side of the road. These were human settlements 4,000 and 3,000 years ago. They later became look-out posts guarding the important route to the coast, then called the Salt Road, now the busy A34.

In the main village the chief centre of interest is the Sandham Memorial Chapel. It was built in memory of a soldier killed in the First World War, but its main claim to fame is the series of paintings executed by Stanley Spencer on its inner walls. The general effect of the work is macabre because the human figures are stiff and wooden but details are beautifully drawn. The scenes are from behind the Gallipoli war front.

Down in the south-east of the parish is Earlstone House. Its foundations are Norman but the present house dates from the time of James I. Also in the south-east is Watership Down, a pleasant hilltop with literary associations.

Most of the land in the area belongs to Lord Carnarvon, so the village feels it shares in the fame of the 5th Earl who, with Howard Carter, uncovered the wonderful treasure of Tutankhamun.

Burley

Standing on the edge of Cranesmoor and looking up towards the old smugglers' road, it is still possible to mistake sudden movements of a grey or brown forest mare amongst the heather, for the flash of Lovey Warne's petticoats as she ran to warn smugglers of the imminent arrival of the Excise men. At night she would hang a lantern in a tree near Picket Post as a warning, for Burley was the centre of the old smuggling trade.

The Queen's Head Inn is the oldest building in Burley, dating from the middle of the 17th century. The queen of the title could have been Elizabeth I, although no one knows for certain. In 1848 a village smithy and forge were mentioned as being part of the inn, a meeting place in those days for the smugglers planning their 'runs', over jugs of ale.

One hundred and fifty years of Burley history was celebrated in 1989, commemorating the anniversary of the church of St John the Baptist, while the chapel has celebrated over 200 years.

Thomas Eyre (1752-1829) was one of the better known names in the village, and there was old Mrs Evemy who lived to be over 100. The Herberts (family name of the Earls of Carnarvon) came to the 'Old House' in the mid 19th century, and Auberon lived in his beloved forest until he died in 1906. Another long-lived lady who died in 1981 in her 108th year was Constance Applebee, who pioneered women's hockey in America and who, on her 100th birthday received telegrams from the Queen and from the President of the USA. There is now a stained-glass window dedicated to her memory in the church.

Bursledon

Early scribes were casual about spelling, and the place name was written variously as Brixenden, Burtlesden, Bristelden, Bussleton and Brixedone. In 1154 Henri de Blois, Bishop of Winchester, allocated land to the French monks at Hamble, instructing them to build a church at Brixedona, 'to serve it well and maintain it'. By 1230 St Leonard's was completed. When in 1888 Barney Sutton was digging foundations for a new vestry, he uncovered a mass grave which contained the bones of large men thought to have been killed in battle. These were considered to have been the crew of one of the Danish longboats from a fleet defeated by King Alfred in AD 871.

Through the centuries ships were built at Bursledon, the first important launching being that of the man o'war *St George* in 1338. Henry V's *Grace Dieu*, whilst laid up, caught fire in 1439. Whether this was caused by accident or lightning is not known, but when a 'son et lumière' was staged in the church in 1975 the producers took the opportunity to include a very realistic thunderstorm.

With bad roads, and no bridge until 1880, the river was the main highway, and sailing ships carrying cargo moored in the deep water of the Jolly Sailor. The railway came in 1888, blocking the top end of Badnam Creek which formerly gave access to Hungerford, where bolts were made for the wooden ships.

Mrs Shawe-Storey, who lived at Greyladyes until her death in 1937, was responsible for the elaborate brickwork and chimneys around the estate. She also provided the richly decorated Roman Catholic chapel.

John Iremonger Eckless was a notable villager who lived at Upcott from 1790 to 1869. He obtained pardons from William IV and George IV for agricultural labourers sentenced to transportation, and he was highly regarded by Lord Palmerston, who consulted him on such matters. He helped shipwrecked emigrants who were landed at Southampton, destitute. Obituaries in Hampshire newspapers testified to his great generosity and kindness.

Catherington

Imagine standing at the top of Catherington All Saints church tower one fine evening, gazing across the South Downs. Towards the north is Butser Hill, then turning eastwards you see Windmill Hill rising above the A3 from Petersfield. Across the fields in a southerly direction lies the silver stretch of the Solent towards the Isle of Wight. Finally the western pinks, oranges and reds fill the sky with a spectacular sunset over the slopes of the Downs, with buzzards circling above.

No wonder archaeological diggings have found signs of ancient civilisations settling here. Catherington, or Cateradaune (People of the Hill Fort), has been a close-knit community through the centuries. To this day the bells ring from the Norman church tower. There are still remains of a Saxon cross and a medieval wall painting.

The village itself is compact and picturesque. Bordering Catherington Lane there are thatched Tudor cottages, brick and flint Georgian and Victorian houses, a converted forge and even a colonial style early 20th-century bungalow with veranda. For many years, Kinches farm had a rare man-operated treadmill mentioned in a deed of 1692, now restored at the Weald and Downland Living Museum, Singleton. The farm itself has belonged to the same family for 300 years. No longer farming, they specialize in car radios.

The 18th-century Catherington House, a mansion with a large secluded garden, was the home of Admiral Lord Hood (1724-1816), who became

Catherington village sign

Commander-in-Chief, Portsmouth. He used the roof to watch his frigates entering Spithead. Lord Nelson (for whom Hood was a mentor) was a well known visitor, as was Queen Caroline, the wife of King George IV. The house later became the Retreat House in the Diocese of Portsmouth and is currently a thriving private school.

There is no village green as such but one pond still remains along with a playing field near the Church of England primary school. Back from the road on either side, the gentle downland slopes are popular open spaces for grazing horses and walking dogs. In a snowy winter, tobogganing is great fun too!

Catherington Down itself is a designated Site of Special Scientific Interest, with several rare wild flowers, including orchids. Catherington Lith, the woodland towards Horndean, is a local nature reserve where a sea of bluebells flourish in springtime.

As throughout Britain, agricultural life changed little for many years and the Downs were more intensely farmed with cattle and sheep, but in the First World War Catherington suffered the loss of a quarter of its men of military age. They are remembered by name on the churchyard lychgate. The development of machinery and transport changed village life and farming for ever.

During the Second World War Catherington suffered very little, but because of its proximity to Portsmouth, a number of service personnel were living locally. One of these was Lieutenant Colonel H.G. 'Blondie' Hasler, DSO, OBE, CdG, Royal Marines (he hated the film title *Cockleshell Heroes*). He famously led the commando raid by canoe on German shipping in Bordeaux in 1942. A blue plaque at his former family home in Catherington commemorates his exploits. After the war he became an international yachtsman who invented the 'Hasler self-steering gear' for solo ocean yachtsmen.

Prior to D-Day in 1944, the local lith (woods) served as camps to the Canadian soldiers waiting to embark at Portsmouth. Many local householders provided the troops with washing facilities. During the war of course, everyone contributed as far as possible to the war effort; growing extra potatoes, preserving fruits and vegetables, bee-keeping and acting as our own ARP warden and Home Guard.

From the 1930s Catherington had a post office and shop, Fletchers' newsagents and wool shop, Tremlett's butchers and the Queensferry Stores: these were all housed in private residences. Milk, bread, meat and fish were all delivered. Village life thrived as wartime bonded people together in a small community. However, there was no bus service until the 1950s. Peacetime saw the expansion of housebuilding and private car ownership. Unfortunately, these advantages have now partly led to the closure of local shops and cancellation of the bus service. Fortunately, though, despite the growth of the village, the existing friendly atmosphere within the community is intact and thriving.

Nowadays, both the church and the village halls have busy nursery groups, fitness classes and special interest groups. The Farmer Inn hosts monthly village residents' evenings and the popular annual village picnic. Catherington WI, which was formed in 1954, now has upwards of 60 members.

With its roots and early beginnings as a small hill fortress, throughout living memory Catherington has continued to be close-knit but outward looking. In the words of the late and popular resident, character actress Charmian May:

> High on a hill stands a village called Catherington
> Blown by the winds for a thousand years.
> Blessed by the rain and warmed by the summer sun
> Clothing its people in their hopes and fears.

Chandler's Ford

In the early 1920s Chandler's Ford was a small village surrounded by beautiful woods and fields. The main road running through the centre, linking Southampton to Winchester, was quiet and traffic free. Now the village has grown in all directions and is a very busy place.

There were many groups of thatched cottages, interspersed with large properties set in several acres of land, and a number of market gardens and dairy farms. The springs and little streams have mostly been piped, converging where the railway station used to be, under the name of Monks Brook. The whole area was densely wooded, chiefly oak, yew and sweet chestnut. In the autumn lorries used to come to gather the fallen chestnuts to take to town for sale.

Before the railway works came to Eastleigh providing employment, the main industry was brick making. Bricks were taken from here by rail to London to build the Law Courts in the Strand.

In the 17th century, cherry trees grew in abundance throughout the village and each year people came from surrounding places to buy cherries (or merries as they were called). Oliver Cromwell's son Richard brought his wife from Hursley to enjoy the Merrifeasts.

During the Second World War, American troops were stationed in Chandler's Ford before D-Day. The men ate and slept with their vehicles which were parked under the trees along the roads. Many friendships were formed with local people and the children were given food they had never seen before, such as white bread, tinned peaches and tinned ham.

Charlton

Charlton village sits to the north of Andover in Hampshire; it has a thriving pub, a family-friendly church which is also the village community centre and two convenience stores. It also benefits from a large recreation area, a private fishing lake and close by there is a small pretty cemetery.

The earliest mention of Charlton and Foxcotte (which was a nearby hamlet but is now part of Charlton) is as a small Saxon settlement two miles outside Andover. With the growth of Andover, Charlton now abuts the town, and as with most villages near small towns, the residents fiercely defend their village status.

Charlton has quite an eclectic mix of housing. There are some quaint thatched cottages and older houses along Hatherden Road and Foxcotte Road, the two main roads through the village, which are separated by more modern houses and developments where home owners have sold off their land.

Rapid development of Charlton began in the 1970s when larger housing estates started to be built on farmland around the village. This continued the expansion of Andover town which had started in the 1960s as the result of many companies moving from London with their employees; the Ministry of Defence moving some of their departments from London to Andover which contributed to large numbers of ex-military and civilian personnel being relocated; and other large companies, including Lloyds Bank and Simplyhealth relocating to the town with their staff.

The church was originally at the Foxcotte end of the village, then over 100 years ago it was moved brick by brick and rebuilt in the centre of Charlton, but for some reason the church tower was left behind. Foxcotte Tower has had a number of uses over the years; 30 years ago it was a Montessori nursery and it is now a private residence as is the old school in the village. The church is also a community centre and is home to the playschool, Brownies, WI and other friendly groups.

Opposite the church there is the Millennium Stone, which is used as a memorial. Also to be seen is the old red telephone box; as in most villages this is now the mandatory book exchange.

There are fantastic recreation facilities in Charlton. We have a huge park area including Charlton Lakes, Charlton Leisure Park and Charlie's Lake (a private fishing lake). Charlton's two lakes were

Foxcotte Tower, Charlton

once gravel pits, and are now filled with water from a small river. Adjacent to the lakes there is a large field with rugby pitches which is also used for leisure activities and by the local dog walking community, a very sociable daily event.

The small river runs through Charlton into Anton Lakes and through to Andover. In the village centre you will see a marble bench sited by the river to commemorate the Queen's Diamond Jubilee; it is shaped to reflect the movement of the river and also shaped to seat bottoms! Next to the seat is a history board of the village.

In short, Charlton village is a lively community which fights hard to retain its status as a village; its residents enjoy living in a semi-rural location which benefits from its close proximity to the local town and is surrounded by the countryside. Not so much the picture-postcard thatched Hampshire village, Charlton may be better described as a 21st-century village.

CHILBOLTON

Visitors to Chilbolton are intrigued to find a large 'Stars and Stripes', topped by a gilt eagle, adorning the village hall wall. A proclamation beside it declares that the citizens of Chilbolton have 'Honorary Citizenship of Montville, New Jersey'. What could they have done to have earned this honour? What connects this Test valley village with a town so far away?

The story began at the outbreak of the Second World War when Chilbolton was chosen as a suitable site for an airfield. In 1944, new craft were brought in, in preparation for the invasion of France. These were troop-carrying gliders, and the men who would use them were the 17th Airborne (US) paratroopers and glider-troopers. In December, in atrocious weather, they were towed into the air, the men inside crammed in like sardines, and they crossed the Channel into France. There they took part in the Battle of the Bulge in the Ardennes mountains.

In June 1984 a large contingent of ex-servicemen and their wives and families, numbering over 100, came to the village at the start of their 40th anniversary celebrations commemorating the D-Day landings. At the end of their visit, the veterans presented 'the citizens of Chilbolton' with an American flag, and a proclamation. The flag had been flown for a day from the Capitol in Washington in Chilbolton's honour, sponsored by the town of Montville, New Jersey (home of the 17th Airborne Division), and Honorary Citizenship of Montville bestowed on all citizens, in 'the interests of world peace'.

The flag now hangs in the village hall. An American lady, who had lived in the village some years previously, saw the flag during a return visit and on her return to the States, sent over a gilt eagle to top it. This transatlantic link is treasured by many in the village, and the striking emblem of the 17th Airborne has been incorporated into the Chilbolton panel of the Test Valley Tapestry.

Chilworth

Chilworth, referred to as Celeworda in the Domesday Book, is a leafy village on the A27 between Southampton and Romsey. Administratively, Chilworth comes under Test Valley Borough Council, rather than the unitary authority of Southampton.

The village includes the highest point in the landscape for many miles, so that in the Iron Age it was considered to be the perfect place for a fort. The fort's defensive earthworks, nowadays known as Chilworth Ring, are marked as tumulus on Ordnance Survey maps and their remains are still clearly visible at the bottoms of the gardens of the houses built there in the 20th century. The defensive topology of the Ring was not lost on the Romans, who used it for an encampment. Because Chilworth Ring is now a Scheduled Monument, today's residents have to apply through Historic England for consent in addition to the normal planning constraints.

At the other end of the village, still on high ground, there is reputed to be the site of one of the beacons that were used in a communication chain used to convey news of significant events such as the defeat of the Spanish Armada.

Once part of the Chilworth Estate, the village is now in two parts. Together they form a crescent around the north-eastern border of Chilworth Common, which is managed by the Forestry Commission. The more modern part of the village straddles the A27 while the Old Village, a conservation area with some buildings dating from the 16th century, is built around the old Roman road that runs past the Saxon church of St Denys, which is also mentioned in the Domesday Book. In the 18th century the church fell into such disrepair that it was unusable, until in 1812 the then Lord of Chilworth Manor, Peter Searle, rebuilt it at his own expense.

The whole place was once densely wooded, and there are still many areas of ancient woodland dating from the Middle Ages with mainly oak, beech, birch and pine trees. Many significant old trees border the roads or are found in the gardens of Chilworth's substantial homes. In front of the old Chilworth

Manor there is a huge Cedar of Lebanon thought to be 250 years old. It is known to be one of the largest specimens in England. In spring the whole village becomes a riot of colour when the many varieties of rhododendrons and azaleas start blooming. There is an abundance of wildlife, especially deer (roe and muntjac), foxes and badgers. As in many suburban areas, the bird population is today much diminished, but there are still numerous species of both woodland birds and birds of prey.

Chilworth Manor was home to the Willis Fleming family until the middle of the 20th century. Prior to that, many local residents would have worked on the Chilworth Estate which surrounded the manorial home. The Willis Fleming connection is still evident in many road, park and building names in and around Chilworth. The Manor is now a successful hotel, with a sports club and conference centre, although these days a large part of its former grounds are owned by the University of Southampton, for its Science Park, which opened in the mid-1980s and which is now home to a large number of mostly technology-based businesses. The Science Park grounds include an important Conservation Area that the university established in 1989, which is now home to many rare and protected species. It is a beautiful and peaceful place to explore, especially in spring when the shrubs are blooming and the trees are coming into leaf.

The village hall provides a meeting place for various clubs, societies, classes and events and is one of the focal points for the community. The local pub was originally called The Clump, but after it was acquired by a national brewery it was renamed the Chilworth Arms. It is popular with both locals and passing trade, of which there is plenty on the A27. Behind the pub and the hall is the village green, owned and well looked after by the parish council. It has outdoor exercise equipment, a children's play area and it's also a good exercise space for the local dog population.

Chilworth is exceptionally well connected, with easy access to two motorways, two mainline railway stations, a major cruise terminal and one of the busiest regional airports in the country. Access to the ground transportation network means that residents are able to commute long distances, although many professionals have moved to the village for careers on the Science Park or in the various hospitals, universities and colleges in southern Hampshire.

CHINEHAM

To describe our Chineham village
Is very hard to do.
Those Red Men are so famous now
We must give them their due.

Some of Chineham's very old.
Bronze Age man lived here,
Then along came Iron Age man
Did they invent our beer?

And Romans roamed around the place,
An agger* cost them dear.
Anglo Saxons and Normans both
Named Hampshire –'Hantescire'. Clear?

On Binfields Farm now Tesco's realm,
Was Becmnit Feldas stood**
In AD 945, no shops
What did they do for food?

In William's Domesday Book we see
The 'Basingestoch Hundred' appear.
The scribes wrote down on parchment
Thus Hampshire did appear.***

It's possible our name derives
From farm or enclosured land
Some say 'tis Old English 'Cinu'****
That does sound rather grand.

---

* A type of ancient Roman rampart or embankment (wikipedia)
** open land with bent grass
*** AD 1086
**** means a 'ravine or rift' in Old English.

The names in the archives start with
Aghemund, then Hugh,
That's De Port, with de Chineham
and wouldn't you know
There was a Warblington too!

And a Brocas and a Puttenham
They're just a few
Of those Lords of the Manor
Who did Chineham subdue.

What happened next's a little foggy
Till the mists of time they clear
Until in 1848
The railway was here.

But only 34 inhabitants
To gaze upon the train,
Going off to Reading
Back to Basingstoke again.

Nineteen Sixties things increased
Now there were 70 dwellings.
A wooden church, a village shop
The numbers they were a'swelling.

Now Chineham's divided into thirds
By railway and by roads,
Neighbouring to villages
Whose names you may have heard*

Light industry and silicone stuff
The commercial area supports
And there's a gym, and more Red Men
And a running club for sports.

---

* Old Basing, Bramley, Sherfield on Loddon and Sherborne St John.

Round Crockford Lane to Hanmore Road
You'll find the Chineham Arms
Which serves a pint to thirsty folk.
It has its little charms!

Most folk live in closes here
With names like Long Copse Chase
Herbs are represented too
And Catkin Close sounds ace.

A Mongers Piece and a Pettys Brook
An Alderwood and such;
While Farm View Drive's got history
Some ancient bricks to touch*

Chineham has grown extensively
From a hamlet hardly known.
Bypassed by the 'A three three'
But the residents do moan,

'Cos at the village edge
Just passed the Toll House quaint
Is a very large incinerator
And popular it ain't!

They say there's a Goat Man in Chineham
Who walks his two goats on a lead
Conan and Doyle he's named them
But sceptical I am indeed.

So that's just a bit about Chineham
I belong to their WI.
And we chat and we talk about Chineham.
Oh! Look there's two goats passing by.

---

* Farm View Drive is the position of a medieval moated site.

CLANFIELD

The village of Clanfield has existed since the Middle Ages when it started as a tiny farming settlement. Its name comes from the Saxon meaning 'cleared or clean field', an area of cleared open land amidst woodland. A parish church existed in Clanfield by the 14th century. The church of St James was rebuilt in 1875 and was constructed of brick faced with local flint; both bells, the font and stone for the west window came from the original church. The village was centred around it with the thatched village well head, village pond and Mill House. A few of the original thatched cottages remain at this end of the village. At the first census in 1801 the population was 153, by 1901 the population was 213. The first school, a church school, was built in 1857 and then the first state school, now Clanfield junior school, was opened in 1890 with 36 pupils.

During the Second World War, when Portsmouth experienced heavy bombing, people moved up to the Clanfield area to escape, sheltering in shacks and old railway carriages. By the late 1940s the population was 500. Then, during the mid-20th century the village started to grow rapidly, and development and infilling has continued steadily; recently two large new

St James church, Clanfield

estates have been added to the village. The population in the 2011 census was 4,600 and it is now estimated to exceed 6,000.

The village is divided roughly into two sections: Old Clanfield, comprising the church of St James and some of the historic buildings and landmarks of the village, and New Clanfield, centred around Green Lane and Drift Road, the main village shopping area and village GP practice. The village has two schools, Petersgate infant school on Green Lane and Clanfield junior school on Little Hyden Lane. The schools are two and a half miles apart, which accounts for some of the traffic surges in the village with families trying to access two schools in a short space of time. Older children attend secondary schools outside of the village in Horndean or in Petersfield. We have two parks with play areas: Peel Park and the new South Lane Meadow. The north of the village is bounded by the very busy A3 motorway. The village used to be surrounded by fields, even as recently as the 1980s, and the agriculture was mixed rather than arable as now. New and rapid development has changed this. There are still fields and woodland to the south and north of the village, with a smaller area between Clanfield and Catherington and Horndean.

The village is situated just outside the boundary of the newly formed South Downs National Park and has good transport links to major conurbations as well as easy travel to the south coast, South Downs and Queen Elizabeth Forest. There is a good bus service to Waterlooville and Havant and a sparser service northwards to Petersfield. The growing number of houses and increasing population help to keep local shops and business running and vibrant, but have also caused problems of speeding and heavier traffic along the narrow lanes and roads, as well as parking problems near the schools.

The village is a thriving community with many activities and groups available locally for both adults and children. The Memorial Hall and St James church hall are where most functions and meetings take place.

For a semi-rural area, parts of the district are surprisingly prone to air pollution coming from the motorway which is now heavily used by heavy goods vehicles, and occasionally there is pollution carried by prevailing winds from Fawley Oil Refinery. In earlier times, the village had a higher than average number of asthma cases, in part due to pollen from the surrounding fields and crops, and to the use then of agricultural chemicals. The village often seems to have its own micro-climate: it is often very breezy – when I moved to the village in the early 1980s I was told I would always need to wear a cardigan! You can travel five or six miles away and find a completely different weather picture.

Compton & Shawford

Nestling in the chalklands approximately four miles south of Winchester, are the twin villages of Compton and Shawford. In this area of outstanding natural beauty, despite the intrusion of the M3 motorway in their midst, they have much to commend them, centrally placed as they are to take advantage of good road and rail links, schools and hospitals and many of the appurtenances attached to modern life.

Traditionally environment has shaped its people, their lives and their work and for centuries the huge chalk hanger of Compton Down versus Shawford Down must have influenced how the folk worked the landscape. History rests well in this chalk valley. Travelling south from Winchester we descend into Compton along the ancient Roman road ornamented with fine, towering beech trees. This is a place of brave deeds and martyrs, skirmish and romance; where kings travelled incognito, and the Civil War was never far away. The Normans came here and built a church, the parish church of All Saints situated in Compton Street, unusual now for its two naves and chancels. Here it was that the village school was opened in 1838 and remains a thriving educational establishment today.

No worthy village is without its ghosts and the occasional sighting of a hooded apparition in Compton Street is not unusual. It is reported that the Old Manor House situated in Place Lane has its fair share of ethereal 'visitors' too, and it is not unknown for guests to be startled by the sudden appearance of a 'dark lady' in their rooms. The Old Manor House was home to the Goldfinch family from the mid 1200s until 1888, so perhaps it is their heavy footsteps which have been reported by the present incumbent, ascending the stairs at odd times. Perhaps too the ghostly form of the Rev John Philpot, Archdeacon of Winchester Cathedral, who was burnt at the stake in the time of Catholic Queen Mary for his Protestant religious beliefs, in December 1555, still remains an unseen presence in Compton. Today all that is left of the Philpot home, Compton Place, is an old gateway set in a length of Tudor wall near Place Lane towards the Navigation.

For those visitors keen on walking, the parish is crossed from north to south by the Itchen Way along the river Itchen Navigation, and from east to west by the long-distance path known as The Monarch's Way. This latter path was the route most closely followed by King Charles II in 1651, fleeing to France after his defeat at the Battle of Worcester. He is said to have crossed the river Itchen at Shawford, a daring passage as the area would have been crawling with Cromwell's men all searching for him.

Another monarch remembered in Shawford is King William II, known as King William Rufus. A paved mosaic outside the parish hall chronicles the circumstances of his death in 1100 in the New Forest and the hasty conveyance of the royal body in a cart along the road to Winchester for burial in the Cathedral. A decade later masonry is said to have collapsed onto his tomb! The mosaic is well worth a viewing, and more information is available inside the hall.

Shawford parish hall is an important village venue which underwent a renaissance at the time of the Millennium, thanks to much hard work and fund raising by many dedicated people. It attracts a variety of groups and activities and has been the regular meeting place of Reeves Compton WI since the mid 1970s when the institute was formed.

Shawford has become known in more recent years as the place where Victor Meldrew met his untimely death in the TV series *One Foot in the Grave*. A red plaque to his memory was installed near the Bridge Hotel.

Just beyond here Shawford Down rises steeply, its crown surmounted by a fine stone cross dedicated to those from both villages who gave their lives in the First and Second World Wars. A short distance from here and overlooking the road to Southampton, stands the 'Wayside Cross', its very simplicity an emotive presence and reminder of the troops from both World Wars, bound for France, who paused at this point before marching onward.

Countless generations have made Compton and Shawford their home. They have worked the land, filled the tithe barns, raised families and fought for their monarch, perhaps known times of starvation, plague and pestilence, but hopefully prosperous times also. Undoubtedly countless generations will continue to make this place their home and work hard for their community, continuing to foster local potential and traditions; to safeguard open spaces for sport and leisure activities; to care for the precious chalk downland, and fragile wildlife habitats for the coming generations. For what is a village, heart and soul, but its people?

COPYTHORNE

The parish of Copythorne is situated at the edge of the New Forest National Park and consists of the six villages of Bartley, Winsor, Ower, Copythorne, Newbridge and Cadnam. Copythorne was originally known as Cropped Thorn because trees were pollarded to provide animal feed. The site of an ancient burial mound is at Barrow Hill. Bartley Regis was part of the Royal

Sir John Barleycorn inn, Cadnam

hunting grounds and when King Rufus was killed by an arrow in 1100, his body was taken on a cart to Winchester by a local charcoal burner named Purkis.

The Sir John Barleycorn public house at Cadnam is one of the oldest pubs in the forest and the White Hart began as a 14th-century coaching inn for the London to Plymouth stagecoach. The Vine Inn at Ower dates back to the 16th century. The cellars were used by local smugglers to hide contraband goods but their escape tunnel collapsed.

The majority of men and boys worked in agriculture, forestry or as estate workers. Many girls went into service in one of the manor houses or helped on the family farms. From the 1700s to early 1900s the Cadenham Oak was famous for breaking into leaf in January, on the old Christmas day. Copythorne had large plantations of pine trees and the commons were sometimes used for military training. Now they are Sites of Special Scientific Interest, with areas owned and managed by the National Trust and the Hampshire and I.O.W. Wildlife Trust. An old oak tree known as the Bartley Spire was used as a local meeting place and an interesting feature of terraced land still stands alongside the road to Newbridge. The first local Flower Show was held in 1899. Ladies seized the opportunity to become members of the Women's Institute and it was so popular in the area that the separate Copythorne group was inaugurated in 1921. In the same year the first New Forest Show was held at Bartley Cross, attracting 1,500 visitors to the one-day event. Bartley Nurseries achieved worldwide fame for the freesias and auriculas developed by Cyril Haysom. They won many medals, including a Gold at Chelsea Flower Show.

Sir Charles Lyell spent much of his childhood at Bartley Lodge, developing his interest in the natural world. He became a famous scientist, geologist, author and barrister. The novelist and playwright Horace Annesley Vachell lived at Beechwood House in Bartley and Sir Arthur Conan Doyle often drove through the villages in his open-topped sports car. Major R.C.H. Sloane-Stanley inherited the Paultons Estate at Ower, now home to Paultons Park. He became a generous benefactor to the parish and in 1910 formed the Stanley's Own Scout Troop which still thrives with Beaver, Cub and Scout Troops. The 1st Copythorne Guide Company was formed in the 1920s and, with Rainbows and Brownies, they all meet in what may be the oldest Scout headquarters still in use in Hampshire.

The parish of Copythorne lies within the boundary of the New Forest but has easy access to the motorway at Cadnam. The village centres around the parish hall, Copythorne infant and Bartley junior schools, the Winsor Mission, Cadnam Methodist and St Mary's Church. This is an area with a very strong sense of community, with many long-standing clubs, societies and annual events such as the church fête, history exhibition, horticultural show, carnival, steam and vintage rally, Women's Institute show day and theatrical productions. The community spirit of supporting families, friends and neighbours still noticeably exists today and many generations of families have happily continued to live here.

CRONDALL

The village church is in the centre of Crondall and is over a thousand years old. It is a Norman building, built on the site of the original Saxon one, which has had many modifications over the centuries including a fine lime tree avenue leading up to the entrance through the churchyard. The only Saxon element which remains is the font. The bell tower has eight bells, which a very enthusiastic team of bell ringers ring every Sunday and whenever needed, perhaps to celebrate one of the weddings for which the church is in great demand as it is so attractive. Apart from local bell ringing, the team also travel to churches around the country to experience other bells. There are always people in the village willing to learn the art of campanology.

Crondall was mainly agricultural. Most of the men were employed on the farms and many of the houses were tied cottages. Over the years, the farm workers retired and their children did not want to work on the land, so the small cottages were sold and inevitably were redeveloped. In some cases where two joined workers' cottages were sold together the buyer would make them into one house. Some of the old properties in the village are Tudor, Georgian or Victorian and there are also a number of country houses. The Borough in Crondall was used for filming an episode of the popular TV series *Foyle's War*.

Many years ago, there were eight pubs or inns here and you could take your jug to the public bar to get it filled up and go back home to enjoy the beer. Nowadays there are only two pubs left, one of them being the Plume of Feathers, thought to be one of the oldest pubs in Hampshire and where Oliver Cromwell is said to have stayed during the Battle of Basing House in 1645. His ghost, called Ollie, is still seen some nights, so they say! Also, a ghost of a Cavalier soldier may roam around the pub garden and the churchyard.

The village had many rural industries in the past. There were watercress beds, hop fields which provided hops to the village brewery, brickworks making bricks and roof tiles for the local area and osier trees for basket making, some of which were used for hot air balloons at the nearby Farnborough airfield by Samuel Franklin Cody in the early 1900s. A blacksmith shod the carriage horses of the gentry, the cart horses that pulled the farm implements, and horses owned by anyone travelling through or staying at one of the many inns.

Descendants of a number of original families still live in the village though there has been such a change in the village in the last 60 years. The increase in car ownership is one. Most of the old houses in the main streets were not built with garages or drives, so the cars nowadays are parked on the road. There used to be many bus services coming through the village though this has changed as the demand is lower and the roads are so narrow. So if you wish to shop in the larger towns or cities like Basingstoke or Guildford you must either see if a kind neighbour will take you or get a taxi. The only daily bus goes between Fleet and Farnham these days. At one time, there were also many shops here including a butcher, baker, two greengrocers, a post office and a cobbler – now there is only one village store with the post office inside.

If you are an energetic outdoor person then there is much to interest you. A cricket pitch, tennis, boules and bowling clubs, and football field are available for the sporty and many horses can be seen being exercised every day. There is a very popular golf course, a private hospital and a splendid retirement home at Clare Park, a stunning Georgian manor built by a retired West Indian sugar plantation owner in 1725. A village doctors' surgery with pharmacy is on hand to keep the villagers well. For the children, scout and guide troops keep them occupied. To make sure they are also well educated, there is an exceptionally good primary school as well as St Nicholas', a very good private school. The church, the primary schools and the cricket pitch are in the centre of the village, and the jewel in the crown is the village hall with its own car park.

As there is countryside all around the village and there are many public footpaths it is not surprising that walking is popular. For the more active, the Plume of Feathers pub organises an annual triathlon which is very well supported and enjoyed by many locals.

In the near future things will change even more. The government wish to build so many houses and the plan, at the moment, is that over 65 homes should be built in the charming village of Crondall, increasing the number of parish homes by 5%. C'est la vie.

Crookham

The pretty village of Crookham is located to the south-west of the town of Fleet in the north-eastern corner of Hampshire. The village dates back to 1200 and now forms part of the local government district of Hart. To the east of the village is Malthouse Bridge, built in 1798, which now marks the boundary with neighbouring Church Crookham. The two areas were once combined and known as 'Crokeham'.

Malthouse Bridge crosses the beautiful Basingstoke Canal, which is used nowadays for pleasure boats and enjoyment whereas in the past it was used for ferrying timber, bricks and coal. The canal is a Site of Special Scientific Interest and is protected as a conservation area, as are parts of the old village. Crookham village is in a much more rural setting than next-door Church Crookham.

The old village is mainly set along one main road, The Street. Approaching from Malthouse Bridge, along the left-hand side of The Street are the majority of the houses – well established and with a scattering of ancient cottages, many of which are timber framed and extremely attractive. There is a local village store (with coffee shop!) as well as a much needed post office.

At the other end of The Street you come to the junction of the Crondall and Pilcot roads. It was here that the Jessett family established their village shop in 1836, the earliest business to open in the area. The shop catered for everybody and sold everything from food to clothing and tools. It also housed the then local post office with Mr Jessett as postmaster. There was a bakery behind the stores, and all goods were delivered by horse and cart. The Jessetts were a well-known family in the village and local community. Outside the shop was a small village green where meetings and gatherings of all kinds were held, including a fete to celebrate the Coronation of King Edward VII and Queen Alexandra.

Almost opposite Jessett's store were hop kilns where locally grown hops were processed and dried. The last remaining kiln is now a listed building and is used for small local businesses. Hops were grown in the village on three farms, the last crops being harvested in 1974 by Mr White at Grove Farm. The White family are still very active residents of the village. The crops were harvested by hand in September with everyone helping with the picking over a very short period of time. Once the contents of the baskets had been weighed, they were taken to the kilns and dried before being sent off to the brewery.

The area has rich soil which means that agriculture and horticulture are important industries. In earlier years Crookham was also famous for its brick-making and potteries which produced the coarse red flowerpot clay.

Turning back along The Street, just along the road on the left is a pair of 17th-century brick and timber-framed cottages, next to the social club. Today, also next to the social club and set back a little is our very own WI hut sitting on White's land and very kindly leased to us by Mr White. Another ladies-only group was the ladies' cricket club. The daughter of Mr Barnard at Cross Farm persuaded her father to lay out a pitch and here, in a field opposite the social club, from 1928 to 1936 the team played against other ladies' teams. The men soon followed suit! An empty barn served for changing in and the ladies' team named themselves the Barn Owls.

A little further along the road is the Black Horse public house (now renamed the Spice Merchant) where every year on Boxing Day the local troupe of Mummers perform their play. This play has been acted out in the village for over 100 years, and another local family is very much involved in its production. The cast wear outfits made from strips of paper, and some of them look very threatening with their sticks and blackened faces! People come from miles around to enjoy the spectacle.

Next comes Grove Farm, a large area of open land but also a small community of local businesses housed in individual buildings. These include furniture makers, carpet suppliers, curtain makers, fireplace installers and many, many more. A welcome set up in the quiet surroundings of the village.

A little further along the leafy road you again meet up at Malthouse Bridge, and the road carries on to Church Crookham – or turn left and you are heading back towards Fleet.

🍁 CRUX EASTON

The hamlet of Crux Easton appears in records as far back as the 11th century as Estune. Then it became Eston Croc when it was given by William the Conqueror to Croch the huntsman (warden of Chute forest), from whom the present name probably derives.

A church is recorded in the Domesday Book. A Norman church, standing in the 12th century, was replaced in 1775 by the present St Michael's which was restored in 1894, when a commemorative tree was planted at the crossroads.

The wind pump is said to be unique, being the only one of its kind remaining in Hampshire, if not the whole of southern England. It was certainly in use at the beginning of the 20th century, pumping water into a reservoir opposite where the Porchester estate cottages now stand, supplying only the present manor house. The original blueprints for this still survive.

In about 1692 Edward Lisle bought the estate and made copious notes of agricultural practices in the district. After his death his son Thomas, then rector of Burghclere, published these as the best-selling *Observations in Husbandry*. Edward Lisle had 20 children and his daughters built a grotto in what is now called Grotto Copse.

In 1897 when the Rev Charles de Havilland took the living, the village consisted of the rectory, church, school, farmhouse, pub and a dozen cottages. His son Geoffrey, who 'tinkered' with machinery, installed the first electricity into the rectory. Since the Rev de Havilland's day the village has changed. The village policeman left in 1930, the school closed in 1945, the pub in 1950 and the generations of rural families who lived in the cottages have gone, but their names live on in the names of the properties.

🍁 DENVILLES & WARBLINGTON

Warblington Castle and the church of St Thomas à Becket have long been historic landmarks overlooking Emsworth harbour.

The then moated castle was destroyed by Parliamentarian forces during the Civil War in 1642 leaving only the tower and one side of the gatehouse. Warblington church (13th century) was at one time in the centre of a village which was wiped out by the Black Death. The houses fell into dereliction leaving only the church. The church has a partly Saxon tower and a fine 15th-century timbered porch. Standing in the churchyard is a grand old yew tree which is reputed to be at least 1,500 years old. At the west and eastern ends of the churchyard are huts built to accommodate watchmen who were employed to prevent 'body snatching' when medical men, mainly students, desperate for cadavers on which to practise their profession, were willing to pay for a dead body.

Prior to the Second World War, Warblington House stood in its own grounds bordering Pook Lane and was occupied by the Marquis of Tavistock. Within the estate, enclosed by high brick walls, was a small wildlife park kept by the Marquis, specialising in parrots. The secretary to the Marquis was none other than the notorious traitor, William Joyce, who, having absconded to Germany, regularly broadcast enemy propaganda as Lord Haw-Haw. Denvilles, by comparison, is more recent development. In all probability the first houses were constructed in the late 19th century, the residents being mainly naval officers and businessmen.

East Boldre

Along the main road between Beaulieu and Lymington, lies the well known beauty spot of Hatchet Pond. This serene stretch of water reflects pine trees and is often marbled at sunset with pink, gold and the blood-red of a dying day.

When tired of idling here, take the turning sign-posted 'East Boldre'. The village is a long straggling one – a rural ribbon development, and the road leads eventually to East End, South Baddesley and the Lymington to Yarmouth ferry.

Most of the houses are built on the left-hand side of the lane, with open forest and grazing animals on the right.

Further on is the old schoolhouse and the village school which are situated on the right, between clumps of pines trees. The school was built in 1842, on four and a half acres of land presented by the young Queen Victoria, together with money from the Crown and the Church of England. The logbooks of these early times bear witness to the strict discipline enforced by the use of the cane for such offences as untidy arithmetic, loitering outside the school, kicking a dog, and having dirty boots!

This, the smallest and oldest school in the Forest, was a sad loss when it was closed in 1985, but there was one happy outcome. When closure was first mooted because of falling numbers, a sub-committee of the Parish Council was formed and, after valiant fund-raising efforts, the playing field and infants' classroom were purchased for the modest sum of £9,000. This amenity is now used by the Scouts, Beavers and Cubs, the under-16s football club, and the Mothers and Toddlers Club, not to mention the annual church fete and countless other activities.

🍁 East Meon

East Meon is a picturesque village, four miles west of Petersfield. There have been Bronze Age finds near Westbury House, and Old Winchester Hill, now a nature reserve with extensive views over the countryside, was originally an Iron Age fort.

All Saints' church was built between 1075 and 1150 by Bishop Walkelin, who also organised the building of Winchester Cathedral. It is magnificently situated at the base of steeply rising, green Park Hill, overlooking the village. The most famous feature is a black marble font, from Tournai in Belgium, carved about 1150, depicting the Garden of Eden.

The river Meon rises behind South Farm and wends its shallow way through the village. During past centuries flooding of the river became a worsening problem, with streets and houses annually under several feet of water, even preventing children attending school. As there was no mains drainage or piped water, this brought additional problems from privies. In 1955 the course of the river was changed and widened. It now flows over a concrete base with many small bridges.

There are two lovely Tudor houses in Workhouse Lane (where there was a workhouse between 1727 and 1910) and several Georgian and earlier houses and cottages in the village centre. The Court House, now a private residence, has a large medieval barn from the same date. This was used by the Bishops of Winchester for the local manorial court and residence for the visiting bishop. It has 5 ft thick flint and stone walls, which are 50 ft high.

To the south of the village HMS *Mercury* – a naval communications school – occupies a sprawl of buildings over the hilltop by Leydene House. This magnificent mansion was the home of Eleanor Countess Peel, who, with her politician husband, built it in 1924, probably the last 'stately home' to be built in England. When Lady Peel died in 1949, the Navy bought the house and some of the land.

EAST MEON · 65

View of All Saints' church, East Meon

East Tytherley

If you drive from Lockerley to West Tytherley, you will pass through one of the smallest villages in Hampshire – East Tytherley.

In 1335 Tytherley was given to Queen Philippa by her husband, Edward III. She loved the peaceful village, and when the appalling Black Death spread to London, she brought her court here for safety. Tragically, two of the young courtiers had already been touched with death's finger, and within a few days 70 per cent of the village died. Flemish weavers, who had been given sanctuary by the Queen from persecution in their own country, helped prepare the shrouds. Philippa created a semi-permanent court here, and names such as Queenwood and Queen's Croft remain.

After the Civil War, the Rolle family became lords of the manor and until 1800 lived in the village. Each generation added something to the history of the place. In 1736 Miss Sarah Rolle founded a charitable school, which exists to this day, and the beautiful old trees in the churchyard of St Peter's were planted by Dennis Rolle. Built in 1250, the church remained unaltered until 1863 when a porch and bell tower were added.

Of course, East Tytherley has had its share of eccentrics. Sir Robert Peel's uncle, General Jonathan Yates, became tenant of the manor house, and was much admired by the village in spite of rather dubious morals. Amongst his hobbies was cockfighting, and in the grand salon of the manor, turf was laid instead of carpet for matches between his birds and those of other landowners.

In 1849, a Mr Cooke bought half the estate, and while living in Tytherley he invented the electric telegraph. Telegraph Hill, and Telegraph House are reminders of those times.

Today, the village is as peaceful and happy as it has ever been, though of course the cricket pitch sees some good battles, and the skittle alley in the Star Inn is a popular rendezvous.

Enham Alamein

Enham was a tiny hamlet at the turn of the 20th century. Enham Place was a large house owned by Lord and Lady Earle, and there were two smaller houses, Littlecote and the White House, each with a few servants. Some villagers lived in their place of employment, others in lovely thatched cottages, or chalk and flint cottages with tiled roofs dotted along the Newbury to Andover Road

Enham Alamein Museum

which ran through the grounds of Enham Place.

In 1919, a consortium of London businessmen purchased Enham Place and started a rehabilitation centre for disabled men from the First World War. In 1939 Enham Place was demolished, and in its place Enham Industries was built, thus enabling victims of the war to help in the manufacture of Nissen huts and barrage balloons. Over the years several houses have been donated to the village by outsiders who have appreciated the work being done by the Enham Village Centre.

In 1942, after the battle of El Alamein, one of the turning points of the Second World War, some prominent Egyptians gave £100,000 to the Enham Village Centre as a mark of their gratitude to the men who had saved Egypt from occupation. It was then decided to rename the village Enham Alamein. Plans were made to build 100 cottages, a hostel for the disabled, a church, a school and an inn. The houses were to be specially adapted for disabled personnel. The school and inn did not materialise, however, there being an excellent school in nearby Smannell.

Every year on Alamein Sunday in October, the young men of 1942 who turned the tide at the battle of El Alamein are remembered with a parade and service at St George's chapel.

Enham Trust has now diversified its products. Engineering, furniture-making, book-binding, candle-making and wax items, electronics and horticulture give work for over 300 disabled men and women.

🍁 Eversley & Bramshill

Set in North Hampshire two miles from Blackbushe Airport, and on the boundaries of three counties, Eversley was once long ago, covered by the Bramshill Forest. Over centuries, large swathes of the forest have been felled and the land altered. For many years now it has become a major source of gravel extraction, but there are many footpaths and bridleways remaining so everyone has the opportunity to enjoy the freedom to walk or ride. There are even the occasional paintballing activities!

One of the things that defines Eversley as special is its greenness. Being surrounded by farmland and forestry, it is one of the first features noticed by people new to the area and the reason many want to live here. A public footpath through fields near Eversley Centre leads to an ancient bluebell wood, where many local people walk their dogs. In simpler times the local children used to play in the woods all day during summer holidays, climbing trees, making camps – simple pleasures!

We have a very old established Cricket Club at Eversley Cross where matches are played throughout the summer, attracting large crowds. Many folk bring picnics and the Clubhouse bar, Frog and Wicket and The Chequers pubs do a roaring trade as they are opposite the Green.

Over the years, lots of subtle changes have taken place in the village including the building of quite a few new homes. Several small but carefully planned developments have given the village new life without spoiling the semi-rural feel.

Source of much pride is the Junior School at Eversley Centre. Founded in 1853 by the Rector of Eversley, Charles Kingsley, the school still upholds his ethics and aspirations.

Just across the road from the school, the village hall has been the meeting place for Eversley WI since it was built in 1953 and gifted to the people of Eversley by Mrs Humphries Owen. Major refurbishment over the last few years makes it a very popular venue for many local groups and clubs to enjoy the modern facilities. The pre-school uses it daily during term time. Last

Bramshill House

autumn, members of Eversley WI planted 100 daffodil bulbs in the grass triangle fronting the hall, to celebrate the Women's Institute Centenary Year and they are just coming into flower as I write.

St Mary's church, with nearby original rectory where Charles Kingsley and his wife Frances lived, is half a mile from the school. They are buried together in the churchyard to the left of the footpath with a white cross on a circle marking their grave. After her father died, Rose, their eldest daughter, took a seed from the cone found on his desk and from that, grew the huge sequoia tree near the lychgate. Opposite the church across the field beyond the new burial ground is a wooded hillside. In the centre under the trees, looking towards the church, there used to be a summer house where Charles Kingsley wrote *The Water Babies*. I believe there is only one remaining photograph of the summer house in existence now.

In conclusion, there is nothing lovelier than Eversley on a quiet Sunday morning, when the bells from St Mary's church float down across the fields calling the congregation – village life at its best.

Ewshot

Ewshot is small and consists of five hamlets: Ewshot Village, Beacon Hill, Warren Corner, Doras Green, and the next complex, now known as Ewshot Heights, built by the late Charles Church. The postal address is Farnham, Surrey, the postcode is based on Guildford, the telephone is via Aldershot, rates are paid to Fleet in Hart District, and the County Council is Hampshire at Winchester!

Many of the older houses were built with bricks made at the local brickworks, which no longer exists. Bricks were also supplied for the building of Ewshot Camp in 1900. Gravel from the local pits was used, much of which was transported on tramlines laid for that purpose, down the hill and through the woods and across fields. Sand too was required, and Sand Pit Cottages in Tadpole Lane mark an area where much sand was extracted.

The camp, when finished, was occupied by the Royal Artillery, and for many years the horses being exercised were a familiar sight in the village lanes. When Aldershot Camp was built in the 19th century, land known as Bourley Bottom became a catchment area. Five reservoirs were dug and water from the surrounding hills ran into them and was piped to form the water supply for the camp. It still does so today. The water bailiff's house is on the far side from Ewshot and in days past, the Ewshot postman had a long and bumpy ride across the common to take letters.

In the early 1920s, a local man started a bus service to Farnham, three miles away. If the passengers were lucky they rode all the way, but alas, they often had to get out and walk up the steep hills, as the bus couldn't make it when loaded. Later the Aldershot Traction Company took over.

🍁 EXBURY

Exbury must surely enjoy one of the most favoured situations in Hampshire, being on the edge of the New Forest, just one mile from the Solent coast and having its fields and woods overlooking the Beaulieu River. Its fortunes have been much tied up with the owners of Exbury House, a fine neo-Georgian mansion which stands in Exbury Gardens, now famous for their collection of azaleas and rhododendrons. In the 18th century Exbury House was owned by the Mitford family. The next owner was Lord Forster who, in 1919, sold the estate to Mr Lionel de Rothschild, whose son, Mr Edmund de Rothschild took on the enormous task of restoring the gardens after the war and opened them to the public.

All the cottages in Exbury village were built for workers on the estate. The earlier ones are built of distinctive yellow bricks made at a brick kiln on the estate. Later when the gardens and greenhouses were being established, a large army of labourers and gardeners was recruited and houses were built for them in the 1920s in red brick. Mr de Rothschild also built an attractive bow-fronted shop and post office and a village club.

Exbury church was built in the early 19th century using some of the stones from a monastic chapel which had existed at Lower Exbury. Several members of the Mitford family are buried in the churchyard.

The most impressive monument is the Forster memorial bronze in the Memorial Chapel. It depicts Alfred Forster, son of Lord Forster who died of wounds sustained at the end of the First World War. A young sculptor, Cecil Thomas, was wounded at about the same time and for four months the two young men were in the same hospital and became great friends. After the war, Lord and Lady Forster commissioned Cecil Thomas to design a memorial to Alfred and his elder brother, John, who also died in the First World War. The bronze was so impressive that it was exhibited at the Royal Academy in 1924.

🍁 FAIR OAK & HORTON HEATH

The village of Fair Oak and Horton Heath came into existence in 1983 when Fair Oak incorporated the adjoining area of Horton Heath into the name. Fair Oak was established as a civil parish in 1894, although there is documentary evidence of a settlement here in AD 901, called Cnolgette. The village is mentioned in the Domesday Book (with a population of 22 households and a tax assessment of 1 geld unit). The name Fair Oak is derived from the original fair which was held on 9th June each year beneath the oak tree in the village square. This fair was held until 1918, so lasted throughout the First World War.

There are several historic buildings still in the village, including a Wesleyan chapel (now used as a house), the George Inn (18th century), the Cricketers Arms (1910) and Fair Oak Lodge (originally pre-Tudor) which became St Saviour's Catholic convent until the last nuns left to live in a house in the village in 1989 and it became the independent King's School.

The parish church of St Thomas was originally built as a chapel of ease for Fair Oak cemetery. There is also a Catholic church (St Swithun Wells), a Gospel hall, a Baptist congregation and there is a Christian congregation who worship at King's School. So the moral well-being of Fair Oak is well served.

Fair Oak has a reasonable selection of shops and takeaways and also has several pubs (some of which serve food) and an excellent Indian restaurant, so shopping and eating out can all be done locally. It still has a post office and small supermarket and garage. Unfortunately the last bank closed a few years ago.

There is a village hall in Fair Oak itself and in Horton Heath, where there is also a local working men's club – the Acorn, and a squash club. Fair Oak Cricket Club is one of Hampshire's largest cricket clubs and was established in 1947. There are several active clubs/associations including the Fair Oak Women's Institute which celebrated its centenary in 2018. Three schools (infant, junior and senior) serve the village and there is a good bus service to many areas. There is a local doctors' surgery, two dental surgeries and two pharmacies. Past residents would be amazed to see how local amenities have grown.

There is reputed to be the ghost of a horseman who rides through the woodland near a pond just off Allington Lane, and on 15th November 1981 there was a well documented UFO sighting on open ground behind a house in Horton Heath for which no logical explanation has ever been put forward.

The population of the village is evolving constantly. There are still several farms. Many new houses are being built and two extra community halls have also recently been erected. The village caters well for all the generations who live here, families young and old. There are pre-school and toddler groups, groups for the elderly and not so elderly and Fair Oak has a strong scouting tradition.

All-in-all Fair Oak and Horton Heath has a fascinating history and is still flourishing today. Although like many modern villages it is expanding constantly, it has managed to maintain the feel and friendliness of a true community, where people still look out for and care about each other.

🍁 FARRINGDON

Farringdon is a small village in the fold of the Downs between Selborne and Chawton. In his journal dated 13th February 1774, the naturalist Gilbert White mentions 'Great flocks of buntings in the fields towards Farringdon'. At the time he was curate of the 12th-century church of All Saints at Farringdon as well as curate at Selborne. There are still many beautiful thatched cottages which Gilbert White must have seen on his rambles round the village and certainly the present yews in the churchyard were already old by that time.

Later, about 1877, the eccentric rector Rev Massey bought an old boarding school opposite the church and, with only the help of one bricklayer and his labourer, proceeded to add a tower and a wing and gradually covered the building with red brick, ornamented with beautiful terracotta work of pomegranates and other fruits. Work went on for the next 20 years and when the puzzled villagers pressed the rector for an explanation of what he intended the building to be used for he would tease them by saying confidentially: 'I believe I shall make a tea house out of it. Do you know of a secondhand revolving light for sale, such as they use in lighthouses? I want one. When it turns green it would be tea time!'. 'Massey's Folly', as it is now called, was divided into the school and village hall. Sadly the school closed in 1988, but the hall is still used by village organisations.

An unsolved mystery in 1785 is recorded in the churchyard where the tomb of Mary Windebank, aged 75, appears to tell of a murder in what is now Gilbert's Cottage. The top part of the stone is carved. It shows the old lady in a large four-poster bed, with a row of money bags underneath. A thief is seen coming up the stairs and behind him is a curious winged figure thought to portray the Devil. Simon Windebank married Mary in 1700. When he died he was quite well to do. The heir to the property was a certain John Heath. A stipulation in Simon's will stated that his widow was to be provided for and so, following the usual practice of the time, Heath mortgaged her house and its grounds. Mary's death is recorded in the burial register with no mention of murder. It is speculated that perhaps John came up the stairs simply to take charge of his own money and explain the new arrangements about the mortgage. But who put up the tombstone? Was it indignant Windebank relatives? John Heath lived comfortably in Farringdon until his death and the mystery was never explained.

Nationwide interest has been sparked by the discovery of a 14th-century 'Doom and Last Judgement' wall painting in the church, dated about 1380, with another dated about 1400 painted on top, no doubt when a new patron commissioned it. It is the older of the two that is causing the most excitement, the blue pigment of the Saviour's robe making it a rare and very special find.

FORDINGBRIDGE

Fordingbridge sits on the edge of the beautiful New Forest, and its outstanding feature must be the River Avon, one of the best fishing rivers in the country. Salmon, trout, pike, chub and other coarse fish are plentiful and record catches have been made. The river flows alongside the recreation ground (as well as meandering round the houses) making this area a very pleasant place to wander.

The old medieval bridge has seven arches and the centre one is 14 ft 6 inches wide, possibly constructed about 1362. From 1870 until the First World War, a regatta was held each year. The boats and riverside gardens were illuminated, trainloads of people came down from London to 'Hampshire's Henley' and much fun was had by all.

During the Second World War the 3rd Royal Tank Regiment was stationed in and around Fordingbridge and from here dashed to Calais to cover the retreat from Dunkirk. Under the threat of invasion, the Royal Engineers were asked to drill into the foundations of the bridge to place charges of explosive so the bridge could be blown up if necessary. The men found it extremely difficult to drill into the stonework placed there in the 14th century. Later, during the war, the 7th Corps of the US Army were just outside Fordingbridge and General Patton stood outside Locks, the chemist, watching his troops march through.

In the 14th century, St Mary's was a very important church, Fordingbridge being the head of the Deanery which included Ringwood, Christchurch and the Forest parishes. It is very important to its parishioners today and the building itself is beautiful and such a peaceful place to worship.

Four Marks

The first mention of Four Marks was as Fourem'kes in a document dated 1550, denoting the place where four parishes met. Evidence of settlements from the earliest times have been found during excavations, such as when digging out the railway line and ploughing. A small stone coffin from a Saxon burial, a Neolithic axe head, and a Bronze Age bracelet are among the artefacts found locally. There was also evidence of a bowl barrow which was largely destroyed by ploughing in the 20th century.

The modern name is believed to be derived from a 'land grab' in the 19th century made by the Bishop of Winchester who wanted to claim the fees paid by the government to maintain a beacon at what is now Telegraph Lane. This was one of a chain of signal lights from Portsmouth to London during the Napoleonic Wars. Four marker stones were placed around the beacon, and the site designated as extra parochial and the fees were duly paid to the Bishop instead of the neighbouring parishes. The area is sited along the Pilgrims' Way from Winchester to Canterbury.

The village as we know it came about in the later 19th century as a settlement area for veterans of the Crimean War who were given a plot of land and the chance to build a home, raise crops and keep animals in order to support their families. For many years this very rustic area was a little like the Wild West and people

Medstead and Four Marks railway station

today still remember that Four Marks was to be avoided whenever possible! Chicken farming was very popular and many businesses started out full of hope but soon failed due to lack of knowledge of chicken husbandry. Then rearing beef cattle and fattening pigs became quite widespread. There were several dairy outlets in the area and before the 1950 pasteurization rules came into force, milk seemed to be obtained and stored in some very imaginative ways. The milk deliveries were by pony and trap, motor cycle and eventually motor van.

However, like most settlements the village developed, and by the 1930s there were many small shops selling a range of goods and services unknown in the village today.

Despite Four Marks being a modern day busy and vibrant village, there are few modern amenities. A row of small shops, two mini supermarkets and a garage form the major commercial centre with a few older businesses sited in Lymington Bottom Road. However, there is a wonderful sports centre with cricket and football fields, tennis courts, bowling green and outdoor adult gym. The children's activity park is very well used and the younger local children are well served by an excellent primary school and a selection of pre-school establishments.

A major attraction for visitors is the Watercress Line running through Four Marks from Arlesford to Alton. The station is used for many films and television programmes that require a vintage/period setting. The steam engines and the maintenance of the lines and stations keep a lot of local folk very busy and there is the almost daily thrill of seeing the engines puffing along the skyline alongside the A31 or even at the bottom of many gardens in the village.

Another great asset is the monthly publication *Four Marks News* which started in March 1973. Mrs Elsie Stevens was the first editor and the whole enterprise was the brainchild of the Four Marks Afternoon WI.

Fritham

In the north of the New Forest, a stone's throw from the Wiltshire border, nestles the ancient village of Fritham, a hamlet of fewer than 200 people, and mentioned in the Domesday Book as Thorougham or Truham. For generations this Hampshire village slept happily at the end of a track which dwindled into the silent forest. Most farmsteads had a few cows, pigs and hens and an acre or two which supplied their needs, and villagers teamed up and helped each other with the harvesting at the end of the year.

The village shop with its clanging doorbell and indescribable smell of freshly baked bread, shoe polish and smoked bacon, was the main shopping centre and post office, and as the towns of Ringwood and Lyndhurst were a fair old pony and trap ride away they were not journeys to be undertaken lightly.

At the top of the lane, the banks of which are still dotted with primroses and bluebells in spring, stood the Royal Oak, one of the oldest pubs in the forest. It was renowned for its beer from the barrel, drunk in the little front parlour, often in the company of a pony or cow's head peering in through the open door, and to the accompaniment of the grunting pigs in the adjoining sty.

The other main meeting point in Fritham was the little tin chapel where services held twice on Sundays were attended by everybody in the village. Every child, willing or reluctant, was washed and scrubbed for the weekly visit to the Sunday school in the hut beside the chapel, which served as the junior school during the week and meeting place for the Band of Hope, sewing circle and socials most evenings.

Many of the old cottages had Forest Rights, which entitled the owners or tenants to collect wood and turf, and to pasture their cattle, ponies and donkeys on the forest. Pannage rights also allowed pigs to forage and root for acorns from 25th September to 22nd November, thus preventing the ponies from eating too many, a practice which is too often fatal. These rights belong to the chimney and hearthstone of the cottage, not to an individual, and several cottages in Fritham still hold on to them.

When the Schultze Gunpowder factory was built in an isolated glade by Eyeworth Pond, life for the village changed overnight. The factory, making ammunition for sporting guns, provided work for most of the men and many women in Fritham and surrounding areas. The grass tracks, unchanged for decades, were strengthened with gravel from the forest, and huge carts drawn by teams of heavy horses trundled along the once deserted lanes. The tin chapel was 'adopted' by the factory owners, and a handsome brick building was erected. The village had never been so prosperous.

In 1912 disaster hit this tiny hamlet when five of its young men perished in the *Titanic* and, when the factory closed a few years later, Fritham returned to its sleepy isolated existence. Today, although much is unchanged deep in the glades and marshlands, and animals still graze the green and wander down the lanes, life in Fritham has changed considerably.

The shop and post office closed a few years ago, the Royal Oak has never been busier, but the little chapel holds only two services a month for a handful of people and sits silent and withdrawn, remembering perhaps the days when its congregation spilled out on to the forest.

🍁 Godshill

The village of Godshill is tucked into the north-west corner of Hampshire, at the edge of the New Forest, overlooking the Avon valley: it was first recorded by its Latin name, Godeshull, in 1249. While the village might not have a traditional green at its centre, it has several other attributes. Its pond, for instance, has no ducks swimming on it but it is home to the fairy shrimp, a primitive crustacean of great interest to biologists, which entitles the pond to SSSI status.

Opposite the pond is the village pub, the Fighting Cocks. Cockfighting took place in the village until 1849, when it was prohibited by law. The pub stands on land adjacent to what was the cockfighting pit, the outline of which is still in evidence today. The present building was erected in 1929, and today welcomes both locals and visitors to enjoy its food as well as its ales. Outside, there is a play area for children: inside, customers can enjoy the mural of forest life painted by talented villager Amanda Bowles. New Forest ponies loiter at the fence, to the delight of diners eating al fresco on a fine day.

The third point of the central triangle is the village hall, built in 1923 and extended in 2003. It is here that the village's organisations meet. West of the village centre is St Giles' church, built in 1913. St Giles is the patron saint of beggars and blacksmiths: he is famed for his devotion to a wild stag, his gentleness and affection winning the animal's trust. Those who admired Amanda's mural in the pub can follow their meal with a short walk to the church, where they'll see her painting which illustrates this tender scene.

Beyond the church is Sandy Balls Holiday Village, developed from the original piece of woodland purchased by its founder Ernest Westlake in 1919. With its lodges, camping 'pods', gymnasium, swimming pool, riverside walks, restaurant and shop, it is now recognised by the English Tourist Board as one of the finest holiday centres in the south of England.

Belying its tranquil location, a bombing range was established at Godshill during the Second World War. In March 1945 villagers were warned that a large device was to be tested: it was not until after the event that they learned it was the biggest bomb ever developed, nicknamed the Grand Slam and designed by Sir Barnes Wallis, inventor of the 'bouncing bomb' of Dambuster fame. Fortunately today's residents, three of whom enjoy the status of Commoner, need fear no such traumas disturbing their peaceful New Forest lives.

🍁 GOODWORTH CLATFORD

If travelling west on the A303 in north-west Hampshire you will pass within a couple of miles of this village, just south of Andover. However, you can no longer approach Goodworth Clatford by way of the Andover-Redbridge canal (1794-1859) or by its replacement, the railway, which ran from Andover to Southampton and was commonly known as the Sprat and Winkle line, possibly named after the seafood carried from Southampton to Andover. This closed to passengers in 1964 to the disappointment of many villagers who would travel from the village station to Romsey or Southampton. The river Anton, a clear, chalk headwater feeder to the river Test, still flows peacefully through the village and provides a great recreation facility for walkers, summer picnics or those who just want to sit and watch. A network of footpaths and bridleways provides the opportunity to walk by the river or to Upping Copse and Harewood Forest where you can join the Test Way.

The discovery of flint tools and the name of an ancient route into the village, Barrow Hill, indicate that this area has been lived in and farmed for thousands of years. Over the centuries the village name changed from South Clatford to Lower Clatford to Goodworth Clatford. The meaning of Clatford is 'the ford where the burdock grows' and Goodworth, 'the enclosure of a woman called Goda' and is believed to be of Anglo-Saxon derivation.

Goodworth Clatford is now a thriving community of about 750 people. Although farming is still carried on around the village the occupations of the villagers have changed. In the 1851 census 103 people, about a quarter of the villagers, were agricultural labourers, another 30 were servants and there were six shepherds. There was also a corn mill and a small brickworks in the village. In the mid 20th century Grace & Sons, builders, employed a number of people. Today the occupations of villagers are varied with people working both locally, in Andover and commuting further afield. The village still prides itself on its sense of community. There is now just one post office and community-owned village store run by a committee and an army of volunteers. The primary school is thriving, as are the two pubs, the Royal Oak and the Clatford Arms. There is also a garage. In 2005 more than 50 volunteers were involved in the restoration of the river banks for conservation and the Riverside Walk and Riverside Rest created are now cared for by a group of conservation volunteers.

The 13th-century St Peter's church was built on the site of an earlier structure. Goda's Enclosure was a Saxon pagan site until it was visited by missionary nuns from Wherwell Priory when it became a dependency of

Wherwell Abbey up until the time of the Reformation. The church contains no ancient monuments but does contain much early Norman architecture. The eight church bells are regularly rung by a group of enthusiastic volunteer bell ringers.

In July 1944 the war came to Goodworth Clatford. A flying bomb (doodlebug) fell on the village destroying the original Royal Oak pub, the village school and several properties including the old forge and a shop. One lady still living in the village remembers the windows of her home at Yew Tree Farm being blown in by the blast. This happened at night so fortunately the school and pub were not occupied. There were several fatalities and sadly those who died were evacuees from London who thought they were escaping the bombing there. The schoolchildren joined Upper Clatford School until a new school was built in Goodworth Clatford in 1963 and both schools relocated here.

Goodworth Clatford once had two mills, the fulling mill which was still in existence in the early 19th century and the corn mill at Green Meadows, close to the present ford. The corn mill existed until the early 20th century. In the early 1920s the mill was converted into a private house for Sir Alfred Yarrow and remains a private residence to this day.

Sir Alfred Yarrow was a marine engineer and shipbuilder. Growing his business in east London from small beginnings he built boats, from small steam launches to being credited in 1876 with building the first specially designed torpedo boat and eventually warships for the Royal Navy. In 1907 he moved his shipbuilding business from London to the Clyde and started another in British Columbia. Sir Alfred donated much of his fortune to worthy causes throughout his lifetime including large endowments for medical and educational establishments. He was created a baronet in 1916. Sir Alfred was around 80 years old when he moved to the village of Goodworth Clatford shortly before marrying his second wife, Eleanor. He died ten years later aged 90.

The Goodworth Clatford Village Club, incorporating the village hall, is the social hub of the village. It was built following a generous endowment in 1922 by Sir Alfred and had public bathrooms and a library of 700 books. This was his third village club endowment, the others being in Blanefield (Scotland) and Hindhead, both places in which he had previously lived. Every resident of Goodworth Clatford is automatically a member of the Village Club, there are no fees and the club is run by a management committee. There are tennis courts and a snooker room and many groups and societies meet there. The committee also arranges entertainments and quizzes, and every August the grounds are used for the popular village show and fete.

GRATELEY

The name Grateley derives from Saxon times, namely Great Lea or Meadow. To the north lies the smaller village of Quarley and both are dominated by the highest point, Quarley Hill, an ancient Iron Age fort, smaller than the better known Danebury hillfort a few miles south. In the 1950s it was a favourite playground for the village boys and from the top it was possible, most days, to see the Fawley flame on Southampton water. In late spring the green corn blown by a strong breeze undulated and looked more like gently rolling waves. The gorse and heather southern slopes were cleared in the 1960s and there is now a small grass landing strip lower down for the local farmer's light aircraft. During the Second World War there were large ammunition dumps on the top and on the Green Drove, once used for extensive sheep grazing. Green Drove was part of an old Roman road running from Hampshire Gap towards and beyond Andover. A narrow-gauge railway ran from Grateley station up to the top of Quarley Hill to move the ordnance. Water from the reservoir on top of the hill supplied many of the houses in Grateley even though there were at least eight wells in the village. In about 1954 a Hawker Hunter jet crashed on the field below the hill, slid through a barbed wire fence and came to a halt halfway up the hill. The pilot had safely ejected earlier.

The population of Grateley village and station in the 1800s was about 700. Mains water was provided in the 1950s. The Plough inn in the village is largely chalk built and the original was burnt down in 1875, the cause apparently dirty ovens! The landlord then was described as a publican, grocer and whitesmith, a person who worked with metals like zinc and tin. At Grateley station was the Railway Hotel which became known later as the Denbigh and lastly as the Shire Horse before its closure in 2014.

At one time there were four dairy farms and a fifth rearing Hereford beef cattle. Quarley Hill, part of Manor Farm, was owned by a Scotsman named Mr Baird who had a workforce comprising five sons and four daughters. The second eldest daughter, Isobel, was well known for visiting the village shop, now also closed, with her pet lamb in tow.

Mr William Nelson Shearing, succeeded by his son with the same name, farmed at Grateley station in the 1930s but also had a large business as a coal and corn merchant. Six lorries delivered solid fuel within a 15 mile radius and the same number of lorries hauled animal foods from Ranks at Southampton docks and Avonmouth. The coal came in by rail and the sidings were full of trucks waiting to be unloaded by hand. Today Grateley station car park, enlarged several times, still struggles to accommodate all the commuters' cars from villages around.

The church, St Leonard's, was built in the 11th century. Farmer's wife Mrs Crook was a long serving organist and a succession of vicars often found the choir of sometimes only three outnumbering the faithful few. However, children attended Sunday school in larger numbers both in church and chapel. They needed to attend both to qualify for the annual free trips to Hayling Island or Sandbanks. Mr Razey provided a regular bus service all year round and also took the families to the seaside. Inside the church recognition is given to the village men who gave their lives in two world wars. Two brothers (twins) were killed in the Second World War, one in Germany and one in Holland. A former rector, Mr Dobson, was also the main custodian of the infamous Andover Workhouse of the 1800s.

Grateley House, now a special needs school, was the home of Mr William Boucher West who dealt in furs and leather. He founded a school in Southwark which still bears his name. Another famous resident is buried in Westminster Abbey, a gentleman titled Lord Lawrence of the Punjab and Grateley who gave his name to the council houses built in the 1950s.

At one time Grateley had both football and cricket teams and allotments, now all no more. The cricket field was also home to two Jersey cows who always managed to foul the main wicket strip. The present village hall, built in the 1980s, replaced an old wood and tin hall which stood on many staddle stones.

When most villages had no transport, residents were serviced by Mr Moon, the grocer, Tambling & Denton, the butchers, a mobile fishmonger and a Corona man carrying fizzy drinks. There was also Mr Threadgill, the village baker. There are no shops in the village today.

Villagers often went to watch the *Devon Belle* steam train, with its observation carriage, and the *Atlantic Coast Express* go roaring through the station. Mr Burden, a porter at Salisbury station, would throw meat or fish into his garden from the train on the way back home, so that his wife could prepare and cook it while he walked the couple of miles back from Grateley station.

Nowadays many of the residents are retired but younger families keep the school well attended. New building is carefully controlled and the balance between inevitable progress and keeping a rural atmosphere is maintained.

🍁 HALE

Few places can claim to have witnessed the 'seizing' of their village green, but such was the ritual performed on a bright Saturday afternoon in February 1975 in the presence of some 200 villagers. Hatchett Green, as it is known, is one of the main attractions of the small village of Hale, which lies in the northern corner of Hampshire. The picturesque green, surrounded by fields, houses, the village school and the village hall, extends to about 13 acres.

The Hale Cricket Club have used it for many years and some exciting matches have been played on it, much to the delight of local spectators, who sit around the green every Saturday afternoon during the summer months.

For many years, in the absence of any indication of a legal owner or title to the land, Hale Parish Council had exercised a form of guardianship over the green. This ensured a degree of protection, but not being the owners of the land, the Council were unable to enforce their edicts. They therefore gave formal notice of their intention to 'seize' Hatchett Green and to hold it in perpetuity for the benefit of the inhabitants.

No-one came forward to oppose the 'seizing', but it was considered advisable to enact an ancient ceremony by which a person who had entered into possession of unclaimed land made it clear to his neighbours that he was the legal owner. So, on 22nd February 1975, the villagers assembled on the green to see the ritual performed. The chairman of the Parish Council cut a sod from the green, held it up at arm's length, replaced it and solemnly proclaimed that the land was now vested in the parish. Registration of the Council's 'possessory title' at the Land Registry followed. An historic day for the village of Hale.

🍁 HAMBLEDON

Hambledon has a long and distinguished history, stretching from evidence of a settlement 2,500 years ago, through a Saxon hamlet and a busy market town in medieval times to a prosperous village, although in 1830 William Cobbett in his *Rural Rides* describes it as a 'tumbledown, rubbishy sort of place'. Now it is part of the South Downs National Park, and home to about 950 souls. It is, of course, famous for its cricketing links, its soft drinks, its beautiful old church, its vineyard making excellent fizz, and its propensity to flood when the water table is high.

The village has always been the centre of a farming community and still today it is surrounded by many arable and some dairy farms. The Hambledon vineyard is a thriving concern with many acres laid down to vines. These produce several sparkling wines which have received awards for excellence.

Although the place where cricket was first played is in some doubt, Hambledon claims to be the 'Cradle of Cricket'. In the late 18th century a team of Hambledon gentlemen beat an All England team, and it was said that the team 'raised the game from a sport to an art'. Most games are now played at Ridge Meadow, but the original field at Broadhalfpenny Down is still occasionally used.

It may seem that the busy days of markets, several inns, blacksmith's forge and brewery are long gone, and the village is a quiet backwater with little to disturb its quiet lanes. Not so. The market may have gone but there is an excellent shop, and a tea room which is much loved by many walkers and the cyclists who rest their lycra'd bottoms there. There is still a 16th-century pub, the Vine, and the village hall, opened in 1982, is in constant use. Apart from the societies and general use the hall is used as a doctors' surgery on three mornings a week, and medicines can also be collected here. Beneath its peaceful exterior Hambledon is a ferment of industry, talent, learning and community spirit, with a delicate seasoning of gossip.

Occasionally trouble visits the village, but the villagers have always remained undaunted. The terrible floods which occurred in 2000 and again

The Bat & Ball inn, Hambledon

in 2014 saw stalwart folk wading through the fast flowing inundation to help pump out cellars and keep houses dry, even at 2am. Volunteers were kept going by a constant supply of sandwiches, cakes and hot drinks and many helpers were seen paddling through to the village hall with baskets of supplies. Then came 'The Year of the Pipe' (more like two years actually) when an enormous pipe, designed to take the water and prevent further flooding was put through the village. Roads were closed for months, and villagers almost got used to having to use the single track lanes round the village, and became adept at reversing round blind corners when faced with a large lorry coming the other way. At least some did. It seems that all is completed now. At least we hope so.

The youth of the village are not neglected. There is an excellent pre-school and an outstanding primary school. Clubs for the various age groups are held in the village hall and youth hut and there are many after school activities, including Beavers. The seniors are given lunch once a month and there always seems to be a celebration requiring many bottles of wine. The Horticultural Society organises an annual Spring Flower Show, and one in August which is followed by a torchlight procession and barn dance. There are also carols in the High Street, fireworks in November, an Art Exhibition and Poetry in the Garden, music in March and a very popular Christmas evening of music, poetry and drama.

Hannington

Set in an Area of Outstanding Natural Beauty, the pretty village of Hannington has the advantage of being approached in any direction by single track roads that intrigue visitors and yet keep juggernauts at bay. Any visitor making the journey will be rewarded by the unfolding scene of an unspoiled and well laid out village clustered around a picture-postcard village green with a tiled well head. This once provided villagers with drinking water from an artesian well on nearby Hannington Farm. Before this welcome modern innovation, water came from two ponds on the green – the deeper of the two was for villagers and the shallow one was for animals and steam engines. One can't help but admire the constitutions of the hardy folk back in those days.

The backdrop to the village green is the ancient brick and flint All Saints' church, parts of which have Saxon origins and date back more than 1,000 years. A rare Anglo-Saxon sundial set in the south wall, was discovered

Bertha Cottage, Hannington

as recently as 1970. Inside are two fine window engravings by artist Laurence Whistler.

Hannington sits on one of the highest parts of the Hampshire Downs at 660 ft above sea level. It is close to the Portway which was an ancient Roman road, and the countryside is much enjoyed by horse riders, walkers and cyclists, who are enticed by its outstanding views. The playing field, known as Michael's Field, shares those fine views. It was given in memory of Captain Michael Mosley MC, son of the Bishop of Southwell whose home was in Hannington during the Second World War, when Michael fell on the last day of the Battle of El Alamein in 1942.

There is a thriving pub with attractive gardens called the Vine, previously known as the Wellington Arms, as the village once formed part of the Duke of Wellington's estate. The village had its own Methodist chapel and its legacy today is the much admired and highly acclaimed Hannington Silver Band. Modernity intrudes in the form of the transmitting station erected on nearby Cottington Hill, broadcasting digital TV and radio signals. Its lofty mast can be seen from miles around but curiously, and perhaps thankfully, not from the village itself. Back in history, Cottington Hill was the site of one of King John's hunting lodges and he was a regular visitor there in the 13th century. The hamlets of Ibworth, White Lane and North Oakley are also part of the parish.

A particularly pretty thatched cottage is known as Bertha's Cottage after a lady of that name who lived there in the 1940s. A village eccentric, she was never seen without her hat, and a tale is told of how, on her death, her hair had been found to grow through and into it!

Hannington was once considered so remote that naughty children in surrounding villages were told they would be dumped there if they didn't behave. A visit from the local doctor in Kingsclere would see him arriving on horseback. If he issued a prescription, some poor child would then have to run the three miles back down the hill to the chemist to collect the medication. The village, once bustling with the movement of farm workers and their machinery, supported a shop, a blacksmith's and an excellent primary school, which sadly closed in 1984. The community fought hard for its survival but eventually lost the battle once the last headmistress retired. It had successfully educated generations of village children but the powers that be considered it to be too small to expand the horizons of more modern youngsters.

Village life continues to evolve and Hannington has a good mix of 'old originals' and more recent incomers, many of whom commute or work from home. Together, they organise and support celebrations and community events, the most notable being the biennial Country Fair and Barbecue held in June. Members of Hannington WI play a pivotal part in the success of the Country Fair, serving cream teas and home-made cakes in abundance.

Hartley Wintney

Hartley Wintney is a pretty village sitting astride the A30, once a stage coach route.

The afternoon coach, the Telegraph, ran from the Phoenix Inn to London every day at 1 pm and the Defiance left each morning at 8.30. Highwaymen were also known to use the same road holding passengers to ransom for their money and valuables.

Along the road is Hatten's Pond, named for Robert Hatten, landlord of the nearby Waggon and Horses pub from 1875 until his death in 1903. In the centre of this pond is a duck-house with a thatched roof, courtesy of the inhabitants of the village, and at Christmastime it is decorated with fairy lights to match the rest of the illuminations.

Trafalgar oaks stretch across the common, planted long ago to provide wood for shipbuilding, and cricket has been played on the green since 1770. The old field names tell their own story: Sheep Down and Hog Moor were grazing lands beyond tilled soil; Flax-field was where flax, with its lovely pale-blue flowers, was grown, and the stems, soaked and combed, provided the fibres for linen to make the villagers' clothes. Furzy Moor was where teazels were employed to tease the cloth and White Field where the spun and woven cloth was laid to bleach in the sun.

At West Green House once lived Lieutenant-General Henry Hawley, a prominent soldier during the Jacobite Rebellion of 1745. After Culloden when he rivalled Judge Jeffreys for cruelty, he returned to Hartley Wintney, where it's said that on the night of 16th April each year, the anniversary of the battle, the skirl of the pipes and war cries of the Highland clans can be heard in the garden!

Hatch Warren

Hatch Warren is a district and ward of Basingstoke in Hampshire, situated on the west side of the town centre. Before Hatch Warren was built the area was almost entirely farmland, part of the estate of the Earls of Portsmouth. The current Hatchwarren Lane and Beggarwood Lane run on the original country lanes which crossed the Basingstoke and Alton Light Railway where Viables roundabout is today. A section of the track lies on the roundabout as a permanent reminder of the railway.

Some 35 years ago the masterplan for Hatch Warren began. Plans for extensive areas of green space, newly planted woodland, and the infrastructure for more than 2,000 homes, retail and community facilities, were put into place. But before all this could take place there was the archaeological excavation!

Beneath the green fields of the proposed Hatch Warren site lay the hidden secrets of human habitation over many centuries, from the Iron Age to the medieval period. Excavation of those parts of the settlements which were to be destroyed by the housing development was undertaken by Wessex Archaeology, worked in stages between 1984 and 1987, and a leaflet was produced on behalf of J. Sainsbury plc, HCC and Basingstoke & Deane District Council, from where some of these facts have been taken.

In the Iron Age (3rd-1st centuries BC) a small settlement was established. First found was an enclosure which may have been used for keeping livestock and to the east of this enclosure there were areas in which pits had been used for the dumping of household rubbish. Some of the pits contained various seeds and grains which indicated that cultivated fields also lay nearby. At this stage no buildings were found, if there were any houses these must have been situated outside the area excavated.

In the 1st century BC a number of ditched enclosures contained the remains of buildings and pits grouped together in different areas. Most of the buildings were small and rectangular with just four upright posts, one at each corner, these were thought to have been for storing grain. Again no actual houses were found but they must have been close by as broken cooking pots, tools and small personal items were found, along with evidence that beef cattle, sheep and pigs were being raised, as well as dogs and horses. Loom weights and spindle whorls made from fired clay or bone, and bone needles were found, telling us that weaving, spinning and sewing were being done. This little farming community seems to have continued to thrive here until sometime late in the 1st century AD, after the Roman Conquest of AD 43, when for unknown reasons this site was abandoned.

Then came the remains of a medieval settlement – possibly those of 'the lost village of Hatch' – which included a small church built in the 11th to 12th centuries. It was surrounded by a wooden fence and at least six timber, square and rectangular, houses stood nearby. In the 12th-14th centuries the graveyard was surrounded by two enclosure ditches. At least 240 graves were found in the graveyard with several more burials inside the church. One of these graves contained a pewter chalice and paten, religious items which indicated that this was the burial of a priest. The small village, served by the church and graveyard, grew gradually between the 11th and 14th centuries. It included timber houses with tiled roofs, some surrounded by fences, with pits and probably hearths, and at least one well and a bread oven.

This apparently peaceful little village seems to have prospered in the 14th century but by the 15th century the area covered by the settlement seems to have been reduced. Some houses were pulled down and the church had been demolished and extensive areas of building rubble were spread across the graveyard. The village was abandoned, and its name and position were lost until the excavations of 1980s.

The plague remained endemic during the 15th century. Could this have been the demise of Hatch?

The present day Hatch Warren is a thriving community with ultra modern schools, community centre, sports facilities, retail outlets and a traditionally designed thatched public house and lots of green spaces, some of which protect our underground history.

🍁 HEADLEY

The history of Headley, which lies in the east of the county, dates back to Saxon times and it is mentioned in the Domesday Book, when it was called Hallege. The church in the village centre has existed since the 12th century, although the first Headley church in Saxon times was completely made of wood. In 1900 Sir Robert Wright gave the church clock in memory of his son, who died at the age of six. On each corner of the clock are the initials of Sir Robert and his wife, their son and the year. In 1935 a peal of six bells was given in memory of Mr and Mrs Charles McAndrew. They also gave the village hall to the Women's Institute. The lychgate was erected to commemorate the Queen's Coronation in 1953. The work was carried out entirely by Headley men under the supervision of Mr Johnson-Burt.

In 1601 Queen Elizabeth I granted a charter for a fair to be held annually on the village green. In 1795 the parishes of Headley, Bramshott and Kingsley combined to build a House of Industry, which is now called the Grange. The terrible conditions in the workhouse led to riots and arson. Some of the culprits were transported to Australia and some were hanged. The Grange later became a private house. A flourishing chestnut tree is a well-known local landmark in the centre of the village. It was planted by the rector, Rev Laverty. A sovereign coin was buried at its roots.

Headley is an ever-growing and flourishing village. Tennis, cricket, football and bowls are all enjoyed in the recreation grounds. Headley Mill, a famous beauty spot, is still a working mill and its surrounding pond, with the swans and wildfowl, is well worth a visit. Some of the timber in the mill is from the 16th century.

🍁 HEDGE END

The earliest evidence of the history of this area is that the Roman road from Clausentum (now part of Southampton) to Porchester and Chichester probably passed through here to cross the river Itchen at Mansbridge and the river Hamble at Botley. Some of the land was owned by the kings of England and used for hunting. Farming is recorded at Shamblehurst Manor in 1219 and, at that time, the region was called Botley Common. From 1250, an Englishman could build a home on common land as long as he could raise the roof and light a fire before sunset. As there was an abundance of freshwater springs, a market at Botley, and mills at Botley and Bursledon as well as the frequent travellers, it was an attractive place to make a living.

The origin of the name Hedge End is uncertain but it was in use in the 18th century. The Enclosure Acts 1863 -1865 ended open farming on common land but enabled a number of small farms to establish themselves. Botley Common was divided into plots. Some of these were assigned to the lord of the manor of Botley, William Warner. He gave two acres to be used as allotments by the villagers and three acres for use as a recreation ground... all that now remains of Botley Common.

1863 saw the building of St John's school, also funded by William Warner. St John's church was consecrated in 1874 and a sub-post office opened; a Victorian postbox still exists. Strawberry growing was the main source of income and families borrowed against the future harvest. If it was not a productive season, many families suffered severe hardship. The school playground was funded by the community in celebration of Queen Victoria's Golden Jubilee.

In the 19th century, two toll roads were built, encouraging more people to visit Hedge End. Since the construction of the M27, the size of the 'village' has escalated and the community spirit reduced.

Shamblehurst Manor died out in the 16th century but the manor house remains and is now a family home, retaining some of its historic construction. The estate was broken up and sold over the centuries. Botleigh Grange was built on some of this land in the 17th century and Oliver Cromwell, a frequent visitor, possibly helped with its design. Its estate gradually grew in size with arable land, pasture and woodland. However, it went through hard times and in 1868, Mr Foord bought it and added the present tower and established a herd of 200 deer. There were two lakes, fountains and a cascade in the grounds; some are still there today. He added oak panelled walls and a magnificent ornate ceiling which can still be admired. Carvings on the walls and mantlepiece depict acorns, a reminder that Mr Foord's family business was carried out at Acorn Wharf, Rochester, a key location for the building of warships between 1791 and 1814.

In the First World War Botleigh Grange was leased out to the Americans coming into Southampton. It was used as a base camp and as a minor injuries unit. Some of the land was used by the British Army as a surplus equipment dump.

Botleigh Grange has its own ghost stories. The tower is believed to be haunted by the daughter of one of the owners. Her father locked her up in one of the main bedrooms because she had a rumoured affair with a knight. In her desperation to escape, she clawed the door with her fingernails. The scratches could still be seen until recently. Her attempts were futile and she died of starvation. Her spirit is said to walk the landings at the hour of midnight. A haunted oak tree grew at the spot where her father stood to witness her confinement and revel in her suffering. A monument stands in the garden with no inscription but is thought to mark the position at which another owner's daughter fell from her horse and was killed.

In 1927, Charles Lindberg made the first transatlantic flight in his monoplane, the *Spirit of St Louis* from Long Island to Paris. He was mobbed there and his plane damaged. It was brought back to Gosport, dismantled by the RAF and shipped back to America from Southampton. It is said that Charles Lindberg stayed at Botleigh Grange. In 1932, Mrs Plumpton bought the Grange and turned it into a private hotel.

During the Second World War many thought Hedge End was a safe haven and migrated to sleep there overnight, away from the bombings of Southampton. However, one night a stick of bombs was dropped and there were fatalities, one boy lost his parents and only survived because he was using the outside privy. A military camp, called Cricket Camp, close to Hedge End also suffered bomb damage.

In 1949, the hotel was sold again and the name Botleigh Grange Hotel established. Sometime after the war it suffered a major fire but was reconstructed exactly to the original design. The hotel has been sold several times and now there are several large, modern office blocks built on its land.

Hedge End is no longer a village but designated as a town. The characters of the village who used to contribute so much to its welfare are no more. The open fields are covered by huge housing estates. There are several large superstores and links to the motorway. However, there is a swimming pool, a library, a post office, several banks, many local societies, a print shop, solicitors, many schools, a good rail link to London and other parts, doctors, dentists and opticians so there are some advantages. Needless to say, Hedge End WI is successful with more than a hundred members. It tries to encourage as much friendship and participation in local activities as possible.

HIGHCLERE

Highclere lies in the northern part of Hampshire. There is real beauty surrounding the place – a fine view from Chericot of Sidown and Beacon hills and a view from 'Heaven's Gate' on Sidown hill looking down on to Highclere Castle, the home for years of the Herbert family, the Earls of Carnarvon and lords of the manor. The 5th Earl was the great Egyptologist who discovered the tomb of Tutankhamun. Sir Charles Barry, the architect of the Houses of Parliament, and the 3rd Earl of Carnarvon together converted the mansion, which for 800 years had been a home of the Bishops of Winchester, into the present day castle.

In 2010 Highclere Castle became internationally famous when it was used as the filming location for the popular TV series *Downton Abbey* created by Julian Fellowes. Fans of the series now flock to the castle to go on behind-the-scenes tours and to explore the beautiful gardens.

One of the old Highclere industries was brickmaking. The deep excavations can still be seen where Pyke's brickfields and kilns were situated, from the north-east end of Tubbs Lane to Old Kiln Cottage, The Mount. Mr Pyke lived at Pyke's House, on the corner at the junction of The Mount and Andover Road. He supplied bricks for the construction of Highclere Castle.

Highclere Street, now a small hamlet, is about one mile from the centre of the present village. It is evident from the centrally placed ancient inn and several medieval and hall-type houses around it, one of which has a 15th-century moulded plaster royal coat of arms on it, that this is the original village. The lane to the original church leads from here. The present Highclere has a 19th-century church and most of the houses are of the same date. It has virtually no older or ancient buildings.

HINTON AMPNER

Hinton Ampner is now within the same parish as Bramdean and is largely an estate village tied to the National Trust's Hinton Ampner House.

Hinton Ampner House has an interesting history and not-so-distant past. The original house on the site was built in Tudor times but in 1793 that house was pulled down and a replacement built on the current site due to an alleged haunting by a poltergeist which was so severe that it was said to make the house uninhabitable. The present house was remodelled several times over the centuries to suit the fashions of the day. Most recently in the 1930s Ralph

Dutton, later Lord Sherborne, returned it to be in keeping with its original design as a Georgian country house. He also masterminded the now famous gardens. Sadly the house was badly damaged in a fire in 1960 and had to be restored once again. On Lord Sherborne's death, as he had no heirs, the house was left to the National Trust who have continued to keep the gardens in tip-top condition as well as using the house as imaginatively as possible with exceptional decorating at Christmas and music events in the summer.

The house was also behind an interesting rags-to-riches story which now benefits the local community. Local legend has it that in the 18th century William Blake who was a stable boy at Hinton Ampner House eloped with the daughter of the house. As was usual in those days his new wife was disowned by her family who were not to know that their erstwhile stable boy was to become very rich as a coal merchant in Winchester. When he died William Blake resolved that no other poor child should be discriminated against and so he left provision in his will for a school to be set up for the children of the parish. This school operated into the mid 1980s when the buildings were sold and the children integrated into Cheriton primary school. The old school and schoolmaster's house can still be identified on the main road. The monies raised from the sale of the buildings are now managed by Blake's Trust which accepts applications from any child within the parish for financial assistance with education. It is rather pleasing to think that an 18th-century romance lives on to benefit youngsters in the 21st century.

Hook

Neolithic flints, Bronze Age artefacts, Roman pottery, tiles and coins found around Hook show that there has been occupation in the vicinity since Stone Age times. In the late 1700s, Hook was a tiny hamlet with several public houses, a number of ponds and few cottages – the oldest of which is probably the 14th-century 'Forge'.

One of these public houses was the White Hart Hotel. It was a staging post at the crossroads of the London to Exeter and Reading to Gosport turnpikes and therefore it attracted a lot of trade to the area. Nearby was a road-wagon station which repaired stagecoaches.

1883 was an important year for Hook because it won its long campaign for a railway station – village life was never quite the same again. The village school, built in 1843 to serve Hook and Newnham, had to be enlarged for the second time in 1896. In 1902 the goods station was added and what had been principally a farming community started to change. Industry arrived in the form of a cornmill, a sawmill and a coal yard. The new railway sidings at Hook also meant that livestock was able to be transported to and from market more easily and Gowers iron foundry was able to move larger items of machinery.

By 1938, Hook needed a new church to serve its growing community and to replace the tin church which had been built in 1886.

The 1960s saw the start of the building of private housing estates. Growth, which had been gradual, increased considerably with the village doubling in size during the 1980s. Hook, which falls in the Hart District, has tried to keep pace with its dramatic increase in population by investing in a new surgery, a larger primary school and a new community hall.

HORDLE

The original church stood two miles distant from the village, on the cliff, 'in sound of the sea'. In 1830, in response to a petition from the parishioners, the church was dismantled and re-erected on Hordle common. Sad to say, this had again to be rebuilt 40 years later, owing, perhaps, to faulty construction. The third church, an example of mid-Victorian architecture, was consecrated in 1872. Stones from the ancient church can still be found scattered around the parish.

The church of All Saints has always been the hub of village life. This is still evident today. Together with the newly formed Community Association, great efforts are being made to combine the old and the new in the social life of the community.

One or two thatched cottages remain in the village. Building development increased rapidly in the 1960s. Agricultural land was sold and country houses were demolished to make way for housing. The pattern of the village inevitably changed. Early census returns give the population numbers in the region of 400. The latest figure is nearly 5,000.

Past inhabitants of Hordle worked mainly on the land. Some do so today as there are still a few farms and some fine horticultural nurseries.

A well known benefactor of the village was John Collett (1798 – 1856). Known as the poacher's friend, he was opposed to the Game Laws and frequently paid fines imposed on poachers. A large grey monolith erected to his memory, stands in the churchyard.

Mrs Mary Ann Girling was a strange religious figure who claimed to be immortal. She was foundress of the sect 'The Children of God', nicknamed

'The Shakers' from the manner of showing their religious fervour. Mrs Girling (her followers called her 'Mother') arrived with her disciples at New Forest Lodge, Hordle in 1872, and completely changed the lives of about 170 people, it is claimed, by hypnotism. The group suffered much hardship in the 14 years of existence. Due, in large measure, to their peculiar beliefs, the Shakers were evicted for failure to pay monies in connection with the property they had occupied. Mrs Girling died in 1886. The few remaining followers kept a dawn vigil at her grave awaiting her resurrection. Three said they saw her spirit rise from the grave.

Smugglers once used Hordle Cliff to watch for danger, for it commands an extensive view of the ocean. The treacherous route along the cliff became a nightmare for a Customs Officer one dark night, when his horse mistook the path and hurtled him down 70 feet toward the sea. Lovey Warne passed this way with her contraband silks and lace bound about her person beneath her crinoline.

Horndean

The village of Horndean is located in the south-east corner of Hampshire, on the edge of the South Downs some ten miles from Portsmouth, and lies directly on the main A3, which links Portsmouth to London. Today it is a growing community within easy access of good road, rail and air links, and it has become a largely commuter area.

The earliest record of the village of Horndean is a mention in the 14th century when a charter stated that the men of the Manor of Charlton had the right to pasture their animals in the Forest of Bere from 'Rolokscastle to Dene' (Rowlands Castle to Horndean). On a map dated 1611, it is shown located in the Hundred of Finchdean and then spelt as 'Harneden', but the map shows no roads or buildings so determining its size is impossible; none the less we know that as a community it has existed for over 600 years. By 1751, though then smaller than the two closest communities of Blendworth and Catherington, Horndean showed evidence of growth, its name now having become 'Horn Dean' as two distinct words. It was still in reality a small hamlet of a few houses, a blacksmith's forge and a public house.

It is said that Horndean began as a place where travellers who wanted a shortcut to Portsmouth through the densely wooded area of the Forest of Bere, could find a guide. The main road then went through Rowlands Castle and along the coast, but by the beginning of the 19th century the route of the current

A3 had been set and Horndean was then an established community within a wooded and agricultural area. The word dean or dene comes from the Saxon 'den' meaning a hollow or dell, which describes Horndean's position exactly. It is also a local tale, that the horn prefix was added as the horn of travelling coaches was sounded as they descended the hill into the village. But the name was firmly set at Horndean by the early 19th century.

Some of the features of Horndean were then evident, including Merchistoun Hall, the Hazelton Estate and the Red Lion public house and through the 19th century others emerged. Perhaps most famously the Gales Brewery was established in 1847 right in the heart of the village, to remain there for over 150 years before it was sold to Fuller's of London and closed down. Gales Ales are still available, especially *HSB* – Horndean Special Bitter, but sadly it is no longer brewed in the heart of the village. The brewery has been redeveloped with modern housing and apartments though the brewery tower and features of the frontage have been retained.

By the end of the 19th century the centre of Horndean had taken on the shape and layout that still remains today, with the crossroads and small square outside the Red Lion. The village school had been built in 1860, though then it was just for boys, and Merchistoun Hall, the home of the Napier family was built by Admiral Sir Charles Napier in the Georgian era and remained in the family until the 1950s. The old school remains today as the village library and the Hall is the local community centre offering a wide range of activities and events for all ages.

It was the opening of the Horndean Light Railway in 1903, however, that brought about the most significant changes and began the real growth of Horndean. The tram route ran from Cosham to Horndean some six miles along the route of the A3 and it brought people from the city of Portsmouth and area out into the countryside. It was described in *Williams Guide* as a chance for all those who seek 'fresh woods and pastures new', the countryside around Horndean being 'full of ever changing beauties'. It was also advocated as a popular holiday resort and a locality where invalids and those seeking restoration to health should reside and which was noted for 'its extremely bracing and restoring effects'.

Horndean at this time was 'simply crowded at holiday times'. To meet the needs of visitors, there were many cafés and tea gardens as well as a number of hostelries within the village. The Red Lion, the Ship and Bell, the Blue Anchor, the Brewers Arms and the Good Intent were all thriving businesses, though today only the first two remain. And with easy transport came those who decided to buy land and build summer cottages, which later were developed into permanent homes. By the mid 20th century Horndean had outgrown the other local villages. Today as then, it is the good transport links that continue to allow the village to grow.

As with all villages of some age there are the inevitable tales, from the earliest inhabitants who were also said to be outlaws who robbed the hapless travellers through the Forest of Bere, to the ghost stories with both Merchistoun Hall and the Red Lion reputed to have a female ghost. Though the lady at the Hall seems the more friendly (she is simply reputed to walk the house); the ghost at the Red Lion was said to have tried to push a guest out of an upstairs window, but more usually if you were standing in the bar you would feel a tap on your shoulder and turn around to find no one there.

And in all of this beauty and serene locality who would expect to find a nodding donkey? Modern day Horndean sits on an oil field and has been producing oil since the 1980s. From tiny hamlet to modern commuter settlement, Horndean still retains its charm with a strong community offering opportunities to all.

Houghton

In 1934, the *Hampshire Advertiser* noted that even the arrival of bus services, telephones, electric light and a village hall could not mar the 'great charm and rare beauty' of Houghton, or dent 'its atmosphere of peace'.

Archetypically Saxon, both in its ribbon development along the banks and water meadows of the Test, and in its name, which suggests village by the hill – the chalk uplands and wooded slopes of Houghton Down rise to the west – Houghton's essentially timeless nature has much to do with the possibilities the landscape has always offered for agriculture, animal husbandry and fishing, all of which continue today.

History might tell of tumuli, Celtic field systems, buried Roman artefacts, traces of a villa or the Black Death. No fewer than four rectors had their names inscribed in commemoration on a church pillar in the nave at the height of the plague in 1348, whilst the legend that the mound outside the church porch covers a plague pit lingers on. The church is the oldest building in the village; rebuilt in stone in the 12th century to replace an earlier wooden church, it is listed in the Domesday Book. During the First World War, troops preparing for battle were held in the meadow near Bossington House, just as they had been, on the same spot, before Agincourt. In the Second World War, Sheep Bridge shallows was used to test waterproofing on vehicles by both British and

American troops. The concrete ramps they built can still be seen.

The single, unnamed road that runs through the villages broadly follows the course of the river Test from north to south. If you approach from the north, the road runs past Houghton Lodge, the gardens of which offer access to riverside lawns looking out across the water meadows, peaceful woodland walks, a cob and chalk walled garden where seasonal flowers, herbs, wild flowers and fruit trees fill the senses. Further along the road, the Boot Inn has gardens reaching down to the Test's crystal clear waters, and further along again, it is almost impossible to cross the river at Sheep Bridge without pausing to reflect on the serenity of its setting. Generations of local children have dangled their bare legs here and waded through the shallows in search of crayfish, tadpoles and minnows. The route across the lovely spreading footbridge, so very popular with two and four legged walkers alike, forms part of the Clarendon/Monarch's Way and links to the Test Way and beyond Houghton. Leaving Houghton to the south, the river splits into three streams and is joined by the Wallop Brook. Nine road bridges are crossed between Bossington Mill (formerly Houghton Mill) and Horsebridge.

A dilemma for the villagers of Houghton today is how much change to accept in the name of progress. A glance at the school logbook between 1869 and 1871 tells us that excuses for absence ranged from 'minding the bees' to 'at Weyhill Fair', at Stockbridge Races', or hay-making'. This rural way of life lives on in the names given to cottages and houses: Cobblers, Forge Cottage, Orchard Cottage, The Wheelwrights, Dairy House, the Old Post Office, the Old School House. The Old Rectory and Chapelside Cottages tell their own story. Homefield prompts memories of the Land Girls who were billeted in Houghton. Farmhouses, manor houses and mills are now private residences. Houghton has over 50 listed buildings and structures and lies within a conservation area.

Hurstbourne Tarrant

Hurstbourne Tarrant which embraces the hamlet of Ibthorpe, originated as a Saxon settlement. Most of the higher ground around the village was at one time forested. These were once part of the extensive King's Forest and in 1226 this crown property was granted to the Cistercian nunnery of Tarrant in Dorset – hence the present name of Hurstbourne Tarrant.

St Peter's church was built at the end of the 12th century. The font dates from the 13th century, and 14th-century wall paintings still survive faintly on the north wall. One depicts the 'Morality of the three living and the three dead'; and other 'The Seven Deadly Sins'. In the 14th century the vicar and many of his parishioners died of the plague.

We learn much about conditions in the early 19th century from William Cobbett, who often stayed in the village with Farmer Blount at Rookery Farm while gathering material for his *Rural Rides*. 'In no part of England', he wrote 'have I seen the labouring people so badly off as they are here'. Cheap corn was coming in from the colonies and local farmers could not compete. Two other industries allied to farming helped to sustain the villagers' malting and forestry.

The malthouses not only supplied Andover breweries but became brewhouses in their own right supplying the village inns, of which there were six. The Five Alls stood by the toll gate at the top of Hurstbourne Hill. At the other end of the village, on the Newbury Road, stood the King's Arms. The Coopers' Arms in the centre of the village was destroyed by fire in 1904. Close by was the Plough and, at Ibthorpe, the White Hart, now both private residences. The only remaining inn is the George and Dragon, at one time a posting house with stabling.

Hythe

Hythe Ferry goes back to 1575 but Hythe (the meaning of the name is 'landing place') has been on the map since 1293 and maybe before that, when a wherryman would row you over to Southampton from the hard in Hythe. Then a quiet fishing village and landing place, where fishermen hung their catch of the day on the quay for the local housewives to come and buy, it is a very different place today.

But let's look at some history first. The pier was built in 1870; this allowed passengers to board and land without getting their feet wet. Previously passengers had to board from the shore; lots of wet hemlines! From the early 1900s there were yachting regattas, rowing races and swimming galas (weather permitting) and these took place at the end of the pier. This gave the local villagers a viewing platform and meant the community became more involved.

1922 saw the arrival of the little narrow-gauge rail train that transports passengers up and down the pier. This is famous as the oldest working pier train in the world today. Hythe Pier has had a chequered history. During the First World War soldiers marched down the pier and distorted the planks because they didn't break step. At other times it has been rammed by shipping

Hythe Pier train

and needed repair work, leaving disruption for passengers and commuters.

Hythe was very busy during the Second World War, when the British Power Boat Company was based in Hythe and they built the famous torpedo boats. The famous flying boats provided a service from the same yard and slipway in Shore Road and the 'Big Shed' is still in use today, now housing businesses that are connected to little boats and watercrafts. The Pier train carried royalty when King George VI came to Hythe to inspect the troops for the D-Day landings in 1944, and for many years there was a little plaque to show the seat that the king had used.

From 1953 to 1963 the Royal Navy had a base, HMS *Diligence*, in Shore Road. In such a small village with a base full of sailors I bet there was fun. At that time Hythe boasted a little cinema, a converted wartime building with a tin roof. This meant that when it rained the projectionist had to turn up the sound – 'happy days'.

Sometimes the Forest came into the village when the forest ponies would wander into the High Street and mingle with shoppers and traffic but cattle grids put an end to that. At other times on very high tides, the High Street would flood and local boatmen could be seen rowing through to help out the shopkeepers.

As a little village we have had a wealth of history. During the 1940s and 1950s Sir Bernard and Lady Docker of the Daimler car company, were frequent visitors, mooring their luxury yacht at one end of the pier and parking their Daimler at the other. Sir Christopher Cockerel, inventor of the hovercraft lived in Hythe. He designed and developed this technology using the testing tanks that once were in the grounds of the Grove. The Grove was formerly a large, grand house in the centre of Hythe that is now council offices. T.E. Lawrence, Lawrence of Arabia, once lived in Hythe; a blue plaque can be seen on his former home in Shore Road.

Hythe is fortunate enough to have benefited from pioneering changes in the NHS, when in 1964/65 the local medical centre was built, being the first of its kind in the country. The High Street has changed little with many original buildings, for example the oldest pub, the Lord Nelson, just off the pier. This is said to have been visited by Lord Nelson himself. Hythe attracts visitors all the year round, with many coming to see where land meets sea and the past meets the present, as many still use the pier in their daily commute, or just to watch the new queens of the sea as these majestic ships sail past with their passengers of the world.

The modern Hythe is a much busier place with a much bigger population, new houses and homes all around and the Hythe Marina, with its smart boats and yachts moored in the basin, have brought a different style of seafarer. No more fish hang on the quay, but jet skis and power boats rush out into Southampton Water. Our village has moved on with the times and technology but still kept some of the original feel of village life with its three churches, one pub (there used to be five), a post office and one supermarket – not bad for a dot on the map.

ITCHEN ABBAS

Three miles from Alresford, Itchen Abbas lies in the lovely Itchen valley. It is a small rural village with church, primary school, police house and a country pub – the Plough Inn.

The church of St John the Baptist is of Norman design, rebuilt in 1863 on the site of the original church dated 1092. Some of the original stones and part of the chancel arch were used in the rebuilding. In the churchyard a magnificent and stately yew tree, which was possibly a sapling when the first church was built, shades the grave of the gypsy John Hughes, the last man hanged in Winchester in 1825 for horse stealing. He was buried in consecrated ground due to the Christian spirit of the rector, Rev Robert Wright.

There are several old houses in the village. Bignall's Cottage at the top of the hill was the home long ago of Peter Bignall, the village carpenter and wheelwright. He is reputed to have seen the village ghost, a white lady who walked up and down on moonlit nights without her head.

Charles Kingsley often visited Itchen Abbas. He stayed at the old Plough Inn, the predecessor of the present Plough, and immortalised the village in *The Water Babies*. On his visits here he used to fish what he described as 'the loveliest of vale rivers' and in *Hereward the Wake* he described the waters of the Itchen, so clear 'that none could see where water ended and where air began'. Robert Browning also loved Itchen Abbas and wrote his well-known verse *The year's at the spring* as part of his poetic drama *Pippa Passes*.

ITCHEN STOKE

The village of Itchen Stoke lies east of Itchen Abbas, on the B3047 road to the nearby town of Alresford. There are delightful thatched cottages and later ones built of flint and brick. The old school and schoolhouse built of undressed flint is now a private house and lies at the top of ancient Water Lane, which leads downhill to a once very important ford over the river Itchen. A footpath along the riverbank is much used by people walking to the village of Ovington about a mile away.

On the opposite side of the road is the church of St Mary the Virgin, which lies in the centre of the village. The present church was built in 1866, the design based on that of La Sainte-Chapelle in Paris. There is an ancient font of stone, standing on four pillars which was found in pieces in the present churchyard hedge and reassembled by a recent vicar, and the rose windows are beautiful. The pulpit is unusual and can be entered only from the vestry. Although no longer used for regular worship it remains consecrated and is now in the care of the Churches Conservation Trust.

KEMPSHOTT

Today Kempshott would be considered a district of Basingstoke, but it was not always so. There is a long history here, back to several Bronze Age round barrows, mostly now built on. Pack Lane was an Iron Age tinners' trading route from the south west.

The Roman road between Silchester and Winchester is now a footpath along the edge of what the Domesday Book called Campesette. By the 1700s it was known as Basingstoke Down. Sheep and cheese fairs were held since the 1400s and for 200 years from the 1700s, it served as Basingstoke's racecourse. In 1787 it was enclosed as part of a wider movement in Basingstoke district. Lord Bolton compiled maps of the area in the 1760s and by this time the Ship Inn existed (it's now the Stag and Hounds). The Prince of Wales rented Kempshott House in 1788-9 and the medieval Kempshott Park was rebuilt in 1795.

Now Down Grange is Basingstoke's sports complex – rugby, hockey, athletics and local events from 'Race for Life' to fairs, bought by the Council in 1965. In 1800, Down Grange was an estate and we can trace the various owners through records like land tax returns and censuses. The 1851 census has Kempshott's population as 75. This figure increased but not uniformly – in 1861 it was 113, 107 in 1871, back up to 139 in 1881, then down a little to 134. By 1911, the last census publicly available, it was 205. In this time, cottages and a new farmhouse had been built on Down Grange but also Homesteads Ltd had proposed development of farmland; the first poultry farm was established at Old Down. The Tin Tabernacle, the forerunner of the Methodist church was built in 1912. In the 1920s, Kempshott Park estate was auctioned and part became Basingstoke Golf Club. The house was used as a petroleum warfare research establishment during the Second World War and was later demolished.

Pack Lane shops were built in the 1930s as was the Pied Piper restaurant, which later briefly hosted the Beatles on one of their tours. In the 1950s, house building increased, and the poultry farms experienced fowl pest. The Berg Estate of bungalows was built in 1958 and further Kempshott estates in the 1960s – now known as the Birds, Flowers and Lakes estates after the road names chosen. The primary schools were built in the early 1970s; there is now the parish church of St Mark which is at the top of Homesteads Road, named after the earlier poultry farms.

You can see from this that even places which now look distinctly un-villagelike have a long and distinguished history behind them. Modern Kempshott is a pleasant place to live, tucked to one side of the A30 and M3, with a vibrant village hall and great open spaces in Down Grange and Stratton Park.

Alverstoke village

Barton Stacey knights

St John the Baptist church, Boldre

New Forest Airfields Memorial at Thorney Hill

Godshill Pond

Hatch Warren

St Mary's church, Kingsclere

The Watch House, Lepe

River Meon at Meonstoke

New Forest ponies

Odiham Castle

St Mary's church, Old Basing

Overton sheep fair

Sunset over Petersfield

South Parade Pier, Portsmouth

Stokes Bay to Osborne House

Wallington

🍁 KINGSCLERE

Kingsclere was once a Saxon royal manor. The 'clere' bit harks back further to the Celtic sub-tribe who had lived there. That said, there have been other changes of 'ownership' or 'control' during the centuries, involving royals, the Church and a series of invaders. All left their mark. King William I split up the royal manor to reward his supporters, granting part to the monks of Hyde Abbey in exchange for land in Winchester to build his palace. Abbey monks then constructed the Norman church at their new (Kingsclere) territory.

Situated midway between Newbury and Basingstoke and seven miles equidistant from each, this village is currently recognisable as a rather attractive little town with village atmosphere and commuter advantages. But it has a good heart and shows concern for its residents (such as volunteer lift-clubs to assist persons with reduced mobility to go shopping or keep medical appointments). There have been other, ever-so-discreet good deeds such as those that come about during snowbound conditions. More than 100 people have been recognised by Kingsclere's 'Volunteer of the Year' scheme since its Millennium inception.

The village is also fiercely intent on the preservation of its history. The Kingsclere Heritage Association (KHA) and its subsidiary, the Village Archives, see to that, publishing a set of four historic periodicals individually named *Kingsclere Bedbug Recorder*. No 'typo' that; 'bedbug' it is and to find out why you might have to check out the relevant issue.

Seismic change came about both at home and abroad during the last 100 years – political, social, industrial and agricultural – all affected by *de*-population (eg men 'lost' during the Great War) and later by *re*-population via sporadic bursts of immigration and urban growth. As an isolated community once reliant on its own resources Kingsclere had thriving industries. Against a background of substantial agricultural activity there were four mills, a tannery, a brewery, two forges and a wheelwright, and five maltings that supplied 400 London breweries! Additionally, there was brick-making (eg the 'Newbury Blue'), bread-making, rope-making, canvas products, saddlery, water and drainage and a gasworks. Trades-directory-listed too were inns and pubs, more than a dozen further trades and small businesses and the already famous horse racing industry.

In 2018, the centenary year of both the Hampshire Women's Institutes and the end of the First World War, trades and business are considerably less visible. A discreet business park, two or three shops, a small draper's business, hair salon, butcher, estate agent, pharmacy, coffee shop, local Health Centre, an art gallery, Italian restaurant, funeral services, only three mid-village inns (one of great age) together with the famous and durable horse-racing industry (first established at Cannon Heath, then re-built as Park House Stables) and a much-reduced agricultural profile but a rather nice golf course and club.

The geographical heart of Kingsclere today is as quaint as one would expect of any ancient British village. Coming from the north brings one over a meandering trout stream past an erstwhile brewery now a rather charming nest of residences. Close to is the Golden Falcon – a pub now re-dubbed Falcon House and oddly modern in appearance compared to its slightly younger hip-to-hip attachment which had at some time been an attendant barn – a place of crooked charm, half-timbered and now safely stabilised into permanent eccentricity. Though watered down into respectability as private living quarters like so many other old pubs, it still manages to hog the limelight by flaunting its drunken stance as a clue to its origins. These and other 'golden oldies' stand in the shadow of the Norman church, St Mary's, still a sanctified place of worship and cosy meeting place for elderly residents at regular coffee mornings and venue for other events as in summer when the grounds lay out the green carpet for fetes and fundraisers. Diagonally opposite is Kingsclere's Methodist church.

Other old buildings still in good standing order include Kingsclere House along Fox's Lane which, among other connections, was turned into a military hospital during the First World War, and a fine medieval Great House situated in Swan Street. And then there are the hidden gems; anonymous cottages that

On the gallops in Kingsclere

keep their secrets of indoor wells, traces of medieval murals and mysterious tunnels, pretty much to themselves.

As for sports and leisure facilities, the modern village scores way above the ripest imaginings of its older self although there is recorded proof that the late great Dr W.G. Grace played cricket here (not just once but twice). The structure now known as Kingsclere Village Club (KVC) was bequeathed to the people of Kingsclere prior to 1880 by attorney William Holding, DLL. The KVC was run as a coffee and reading room when Victorian temperance held sway and it still gives a respectful nod to old club rules. It now incorporates the public library and both are independently run by trustees. The club is offered for hire in part, to suit most social- and crafts-and-hobby needs, and accommodates the parish council offices and the local police 'beat' office. KVC was also the site of the very first local Women's Institute launched in 1918. On a rise above the village there is Fieldgate Centre with its indoor and outdoor sports, drama and social club facilities.

A slight detour but of real interest is nearby Tidgrove Warren Farm, whose name reflects an unusual legacy. Roman invaders brought rabbits to this country as a ready food source, even preparing warrens for them. Incredibly, some of these are still used by their furry descendants! The farm was the site of a nine-year archaeological project overseen by Southampton University/Wessex Archaeology, supported by the Kingsclere Heritage Association. Technologies brought in such as resistivity and magnetometry confirmed Romano-British occupation in the area and also the 'footprint' of the royal hunting lodge built in 1172 for King Henry II. This was his 'halfway-house' en route to the coast and territories 'over the water'.

Literary connections include James Seward, born in the workhouse and later to be apprenticed in Kingsclere as a little chimney sweep, who inspired author Charles Kingsley to include Tom in *The Water Babies* to write about the awful use of children in that trade. Kingsley drew upon Seward's early life when hard work had helped him break through the 'glass ceiling' of natural-born privilege of the time to attain the status of Alderman. Surprisingly, it was not only Charles Hamilton writing under the name 'Frank Richards' who wrote the 'Billy Bunter' stories published in the *Magnet* but also George Samways of Kingsclere, a particularly prolific contributor. More recently, *Watership Down* by Richard Adams became an international 'best seller'. In telling of rabbits' lives in the wild, has Adams created a fitting eulogy for Tidgrove's Rabbits of Rome and their descendants? Those of us who live in Kingsclere just below the real place that is Watership Down might fancy thinking so.

Cruck Cottage, Kings Somborne

KINGS SOMBORNE

The Sombornes lie in the low hills on the edge of the beautiful Test valley. Up Somborne is a ribbon of houses some three miles from the main village, and Little Somborne is scattered around an enchanting small chapel of Saxon origin.

Kings Somborne, known to walkers as it lies on the intersection of the Test and Clarendon Ways, has probably never been so pretty, as affluence and paint have brightened its buildings. Barely 40 years ago the impression was tumbledown and shabby. The shortsighted policy then was to destroy unfit buildings rather than repair them, so some character has gone from the village. There is still one pub and a few shops, and the ecclesiastical parish is unusual in that it is joined only with nearby Ashley. The church of St Peter and St Paul, basically Norman, was regrettably rebuilt in 1885. It and the pub stand pleasantly on a mini-green, complete with war memorial.

The 'Kings' of the village name were Saxon. Somborne was a royal manor before the Norman Conquest, then, in medieval times, it was the centre of its Hundred and Deanery. It remained a royal possession until sold by Charles II.

The boundary of John of Gaunt's deer park is still marked in places by a bank and yew trees.

The village achieved fame in the midst of the agricultural depression that beset rural Hampshire in the mid 19th century. In 1837 Richard Dawes, blocked by his liberal views from an academic career, was appointed to the living of Kings Somborne. He found a parish run down and demoralised, so in the belief that education would improve social and moral conditions he organised a school, which opened in October 1842. He believed that the school should be self-supporting and that teaching should be practical and interesting and of evident benefit to everyone – views much ahead of his time. By 1847, the school was one of the best-known in the country, and it was visited by the Prime Minister, Matthew Arnold and Florence Nightingale. Dawes became Dean of Hereford in 1850. The school continues in the same building today.

Langley & Lepe

When Hugh St Quentin of Normandy was surveying his land for the agent of the king in 1086, he could little have imagined how the two hides of land credited to him in the Domesday Book would change over the next thousand years. Could he have peered across the centuries, he would no doubt have recognised the fighting spirit of another old soldier, that of T.E. Lawrence (of Arabia) who lodged on the same land almost 100 decades later.

Between those notable ages of history others have made their mark on the little Hampshire village of Langley, on the edge of the New Forest, sandwiched between Blackfield to the north and Lepe to the south. Once an area of unenclosed common land, with a road running through it down to the beach at Lepe, it was described in 1626 as twelve acres of bad meadow, 30 acres of arable pasture and 30 acres of bad pasture. This bad land obviously did not deter the estate holder and the farm continued to grow until the land was fenced in the early 19th century when a new model farm was built by the Cadland Estate.

On the other side of the road from the farm was a field of heavy clay which, although useless for farming, was very suitable for brick-making and so the Langley Brickworks was formed, which produced the distinctive yellowish Cadland bricks used for buildings throughout the area until the First World War.

Brick-making was thirsty work, and refreshments were on offer at the nearby Langley Tavern, first shown on the Ordnance Survey map of 1868. That building was eventually demolished, but the tavern still exists in the centre of the village.

The need for refreshment was not exclusive to farmers and brick-makers. Down at the beach at Lepe in Nelson's time, shipwrights worked fitting out the Navy ships that were built at Buckler's Hard and floated down the Beaulieu River. The coastal habitats along the Beaulieu river estuary these days form the North Solent National Nature Reserve. It makes up part of the New Forest National Park, and is a fine example of the Hampshire coast, with heaths, valley mires, and the ancient oak woodlands that built Nelson's naval fleet.

The maritime activities at Lepe were not all so legitimate. Built in the 1820s when the Coastguard Service was formed, there is still the Boat (or Watch) House perched upon the rise overlooking the Solent, where a fast cutter was kept to catch and deter the smugglers that were rife in the area. The slate-hung Coastguard Cottages behind the Watch House were built at the same time to house the coastguard officers and men.

Keeping watch across the Solent is an activity that is still very much in evidence today. Still under the control of HM Coastguard, the watchers are more likely to encounter a kite-surfer or a full-bellied sailing yacht circumnavigating the Isle of Wight during Cowes Week. Although the stretch of water between Lepe and Gurnard on the island looks temptingly narrow enough to swim, the currents here are treacherous and would sweep away the unwary. Legend has it there once was a causeway with a gap in the middle which it was possible for a man to 'leap', hence the name.

No boats are built at Lepe these days, but the special significance of its position came into its own again in the Second World War when troops and tanks, landing craft and Mulberry Harbours were gathered together in preparation for the D-Day landings. British and Allied forces waited in trepidation for the signal to start the invasion which would change the course of history. And so, across a span of one thousand years, our little village had come full circle, with a soldier about to embark for the beaches of Normandy.

Lasham

The tiny village of Lasham adjoins Herriard, and for about 200 years was part of the Herriard Park estate. We know from the records of Herriard and other villages how the name has changed over the centuries. In Lasham it is happening in our lifetime, not so much in the spelling, but in the pronunciation. Until about 20 years ago it was called 'Lassum', but more and more it is called 'Lash-am'. No doubt in another 20 years 'Lassum' will have passed into the history books.

During the First World War, Mrs Beatrice Jervoise managed Church Farm at Lasham. She was so concerned by the shortage of water that she brought in a dowser. His findings were so successful that Major and Mrs Jervoise were able to found the Herriard and Lasham Water Company, with reservoirs in Lasham Wood. This enabled water to be piped to Lasham, Herriard, Shalden, Bentworth, Wield, Tunworth, Weston Corbett, Ellisfield, Medstead, Bradley and Preston Candover. This remarkable feat is recorded on Mrs Jervoise' tomb in Herriard churchyard.

Although a small village, Lasham is known throughout the country for its gliding club, the National Gliding Championships often being held at Lasham Airfield. The airfield was built during the Second World War, when the beautiful beech avenue planted by George Jervoise in 1809 was sacrificed to make way for it. The old road between Herriard and Lasham was closed, and gangs of Irish labourers and Italian prisoners of war were brought in to make the 'concrete road' which is now part of the A339.

The village is justly proud of its pretty pond, which is fed from local springs. It is regularly cleaned out, and is the home of mallard and moorhens, as well as large numbers of goldfish.

LAVERSTOKE & FREEFOLK

The parish of Laverstoke and Freefolk was united in 1872, when, on the closure of St Mary's in Laverstoke Park, the tiny 13th-century church of St Nicholas became the parish church. St Mary's in the Park then became the vaults of the Portal family. In 1896 a new church named St Mary the Virgin was built, dominating the village of Freefolk.

Portal's Mills originated in 1712, when Henri de Portal, a French refugee, landed with others at Southampton. He was eventually offered an apprenticeship at Stoneham, and on completion he became naturalised. He then acquired the lease of Bere Mill, where he perfected papermaking. As he progressed he needed to expand, so he applied for Laverstoke Mill, and built a new mill on the site in 1718. In 1724 the Bank of England requested him to submit samples for use as banknote paper. It was approved and the contract still exists, amid strict security.

Laverstoke Mill

The production takes place at Overton Mill, two miles to the east, which one of Henri's successors, Sir William Portal, built in 1922. A great deal of its success is derived from the river Test, which rises at Ashe a mile upstream. After use and recycling the water then flows on through Laverstoke, Freefolk and on to Southampton Water.

Lord Portal, who died in 1949, was Head of the Olympic Games when it was held in Germany in 1936, and as a mark of respect for his services to the Games, Hitler awarded him the Iron Cross. In 1948 the Olympic Committee honoured Lord Portal by allowing the Olympic Flame to be carried by a runner through the Park.

Lord Portal had 18 thatched cottages built in memory of his father Sir William Portal, for the use of employees in Freefolk. A white house in Laverstoke bears a plaque indicating that it was the residence of the Bank Officer, 1785, built by Joseph Portal.

🍁 Lee-on-the-Solent

Lee-on-the-Solent is a small seaside town, about four miles west of Portsmouth. The area is located on the coast of the Solent, opposite Cowes on the Isle of Wight.

In 1884 Mr C.E. Newton Robinson persuaded his father, a wealthy Dorset landowner, to purchase land in the area. They spent the next 25 years investing in Lee-on-the-Solent and developing a seaside holiday resort. The late Victorian era saw its expansion with the building of grand houses, the pier and a branch railway.

Marine Parade was laid out stretching for over one mile. The pier was opened in 1888. It had shelters and a pavilion, where it is said that Noël Coward played. When the pier first opened, it provided a stopping point for paddle steamers which ran between Southampton, Lee Pier, Stokes Bay, Portsmouth, Ryde and Cowes. Unfortunately, in 1932, the pier was badly damaged by fire and never regained its former glory. It was sectioned in 1940 for defence, and was demolished in 1958.

Lee-on-the-Solent had a train line which was opened in 1894. It ran for three miles alongside the beach and the Lee terminal was a very convenient stop for the beach…imagine a train arriving at Lee, puffing away with the happy trippers coming to spend the day on the beach! It was also used for freight and transporting service personnel. It closed in 1931.

In 1935 the Lee Tower, an Art Deco complex, was built on the seafront next to the pier and railway station. It had a cinema, which proved to be very popular. The big film on opening night was *In Town Tonight* featuring Stanley Holloway and the seat prices started at one shilling. It also had a ballroom, which hosted many functions, a restaurant and a 120 ft tower with a viewing platform. The foreign holiday boom of the 1960s and 1970s saw a gradual decline in the town's fortunes, and the tower was demolished in 1971. Its land is now used for the promenade, the War Memorial and Remembrance Gardens which are in a sunken area sheltered from the wind.

During the First World War, the area was identified as an excellent location for a naval aviation base. In 1917, the station which would later become HMS *Daedalus*, opened as the HM Naval Seaplane Training School. Hangars, workshops, accommodation and a double slipway into the sea were constructed. During the Second World War it housed Swordfish torpedo bombers and seaplanes. During the Battle of Britain in 1940 the airfield was bombed, killing 14, wounding five and destroying three hangars and 42 aircraft. The area around Lee-on-the-Solent was used extensively for the D-

Day Normandy landings. Pier House, which was then the Pier Hotel, was used by the Canadian forces as their headquarters. In 2010 an elderly gentleman wanted to take a photograph of the grassed area and hedge that is to the east of Lee Press the printers. When asked why, his reply was, 'I want it to show my family in Canada where I slept the night before D-Day!'

Early in 2006, 20 unexploded Canadian pipe mines were found whilst undertaking runway repairs. They were packed with a total of 2,400 lb of gelignite, planted in the Second World War to make the airfield unusable in the event of enemy invasion. The subsequent removal is thought to have been the largest of its kind in peacetime Britain.

In the 1970s, the Naval Hovercraft Trials Unit made extensive use of *Daedalus*. You can now visit a Hovercraft Museum on this site, open to visitors at the weekends. The Royal Naval Air Station HMS *Daedalus* closed in 1996. The airfield remains a civil airfield. Over 100 aircraft, helicopters, gliders, microlight, operate from there.

A lot of the historical buildings have gone, but if Charles and John Robinson could see Lee-on-the-Solent now, they would be pleased to find that it remains a thriving small seaside town. Housing developments have been built for families as well as retirement homes and flats, along the Marine Parades. The fine coastline with the promenade and cliffs typify the character of a 1930s seaside resort. The views across the Solent to the Isle of Wight and the New Forest shoreline are impressive and full of interest.

In the heyday of sea travel many of the great passenger ships navigated the waters of the Solent, passing Lee-on-the-Solent before turning right off Seaview on the Isle of Wight and proceeding into the English Channel – some names from the past include the *Queen Mary* and *Queen Elizabeth*, not forgetting the *Titanic*. Fifty years ago, many of the ships were carrying migrants to Australia, and other locations.

Lee is a very popular venue for families. They come to visit and walk along the long promenade. There is an amusement arcade which was once the booking hall for the Lee railway station and is all that remains of the station and railway line. As you continue along the Promenade you will see a children's play area. This used to be the site of Lee-on-the-Solent's Lido. It was said to be the only open-air heated seawater bathing pool in England when it was constructed in the 1930s.

The sheltered coastal waters make it ideal for sea anglers and water sports enthusiasts. You can enjoy water sports of all kinds, sailing, windsurfing, jet-skiing and pleasure boating. Perhaps you would prefer to sit and watch the ever-changing scene, see container ships and cruise Liners travel to and from

Southampton, the home port for both Cunard and P&O, enjoy an ice cream or other refreshments offered by the restaurants, wine bars, and tea-rooms, not forgetting the two fish and chip shops!

🍁 LIPHOOK

Six roads converge on the Square in the centre of Liphook and in the early days of the 20th century there were hardly any houses along them. Now there are blocks of flats tucked into every conceivable corner.

On the northern boundary the river Wey winds through water meadows, which in olden days were flooded regularly in order to provide a second cereal crop. This area has now been restored to parkland, which serves as a much needed recreational facility for the residents of the village.

The village carnival, which takes place in October each year, started life as an 'Old Boys' Bonfire Club', which celebrated the anniversary of the Gunpowder Plot.

In the beginning it was simply a bonfire made from wood, cut and collected by 'the boys' of the community, but it evolved into pranks being played upon other residents and gradually the Carnival came into being. When a chimney sweep by the name of Stacy entered a float depicting a model of his cottage, which sported an advertisement and had a brush sticking out of the chimney, the character of the procession changed. Today the event attracts floats from all sections of the community.

The square, which is dominated by the Royal Anchor Hotel, is a designated conservation area and some of the old houses and shops are still there, even if the smithy is not. People who need to have their horses shod rely on travelling blacksmiths, who set up their equipment wherever it is required, usually in the open fields.

Liphook boasts of having Flora Thompson, the author of *Lark Rise to Candleford*, as one of its celebrities. She used to be the local post-mistress. The post office was once housed in a building completely on its own. It is now only a counter in a local supermarket. What would Flora have said?

🍁 LONG SUTTON

The village lies on the Harrow Way, one of the main routes between Winchester and Canterbury and was probably a stopping place for pilgrims. It is likely that the 13th-century church replaced an earlier timber building. Marks on the church door arch are believed to have been made by knights returning from the crusades and the 14th-century South Chapel contains a medieval oak vestment chest. Yew trees in the churchyard are estimated to be between 1,500 and 3,000 years old.

Lying in a fertile valley, the land has been farmed for many centuries. Today there are arable fields and pasture for cattle and sheep. The village pond, once used for watering horses, is now home to ducks and moorhens.

Cottages, impressive timber-framed houses and modern homes offer a wide variety of architecture and interest. There is no longer a village shop, but the Four Horseshoes pub offers B&B accommodation, real ale and home cooked food. The Chequers in the nearby village of Well is a picturesque pub with an award-winning restaurant. The 1970 village hall now has excellent facilities and is the venue for the varied village activities. Tennis, cricket and football clubs are active, and the church fete is a lively annual event.

Primary school children are educated in the village and move on to secondary school three miles away in Odiham. Impressive gates designed by Sir Reginald Blomfield, an eminent architect, mark the entrance to Lord Wandsworth College. Set up in the 1920s, it was a model farm established for children of farm workers who had lost one or both parents. The boys spent most of their time working on the college farm, the girls were educated elsewhere. The college is now co-educational with a wide curriculum and students no longer work on the farm. Bursaries are awarded for ability and need due to challenging home situations. The college is the largest employer in the village. Farms and nearby business parks also provide local employment and with easy access to the M3 and mainline railway, many residents commute.

LONGPARISH

Towards the end of the 10th century the area known as Longparish was in fact the manor of Middleton (or Middletune). The manor was in the possession of the Benedictine nunnery of Wherwell, which was founded in AD 986 by Elfrida, widow of King Edgar, who was indirectly responsible for the murder of her step-son King Edward at Corfe. Lower Mill House was originally a cloth mill known as 'Middletune Mill' and belonged to the abbess of Wherwell. Middletune Mill is mentioned in the Domesday Book.

The name Longparish first appears in the middle of the 16th century, at about the time of the Dissolution of the Monasteries, when it was said to consist of East Aston, Longparish, Middleton and Forton and the greater part of Harewood Forest.

In Harewood Forest there is a monument known as Dead Man's Plack. In the year AD 963, King Edgar, called the Peaceable, sent for the Earl Athelwold to meet him in the forest to hunt. Athelwold had betrayed Edgar and had married his intended bride, Elfrida, daughter of the Earl of Devonshire. So Edgar slew Athelwold with his own hand.

Cricket at Longparish has a long and chequered history, stretching from the first memorable match in 1878. In 1980 Longparish reached the final of the Whitbread Village Cricket Championship, and on 24th August they went to play their opponents Marchwiel from North Wales on the hallowed ground of Lords, but sadly they lost. However, on Monday 31st August 1987 Longparish played in the final again, against Treeton Welfare from Yorkshire. Longparish won by 76 runs and returned home with the cup to the celebrations of the village.

Longstock, Leckford & Stockbridge

Longstock, Leckford and Stockbridge are three villages in the centre of the valley of the river Test, closely linked but of very different characters.

Stockbridge is an ancient town built on a chalk causeway over the valley, with a long history of sheep droving, horse racing and breeding, and still has world-renowned dry fly trout fishing in the Test chalk stream. A lord of the manor and ancient manorial courts oversee the management of the common lands of Stockbridge Down and Marsh.

In recent years it has become a meeting point with many good places to eat or drink, and many independent shops, as well as a Co-op with post office which is open from early morning till late at night. There are no shops in Longstock, but Leckford still has a village shop. Stockbridge has an annual food fair, and a Christmas late night shopping event with a celebrity switching on the festive lighting, as well as a summer fête. The thriving town hall hosts many clubs and activities.

Longstock remains a rural community, with a pub and a family-run organic mixed farm, while the Leckford Estate extends also to Longstock, and has many enterprises including a dairy and milk bottling plant, mushrooms, vines and orchards, a café and nursery garden centre. It markets many of its crops under the Leckford label, such as champagne, apple juice, rapeseed oil and flour. The water garden, created by John Spedan Lewis, attracts garden lovers

The Peat Spade inn, Longstock

from all over the world and is open for charity during summer weekends.

Many of the estate houses, which used to house employees, have been sold, bringing new families to the villages, some of whom run their business from home. Several houses have become second homes, but the cost of village houses has been inexorably rising, so putting them out of reach of so many who grew up here; the search for suitable sites for a few 'affordable' homes has been going on for at least 20 years, but never coincides with funding or planners' approval.

In Longstock the village hall is run by volunteers and provides a focal point for the village. The annual village fête is a key event on the recreation ground in late summer, with funds raised for the church and other village groups.

There is a thriving NeighbourCare scheme for the villages, as well as a community bus, started by a WI member over 20 years ago, which runs three days a week to Andover through different villages; both schemes are run by volunteers.

Each of the three villages has its own church and together they form a single benefice, but discussions are under way to amalgamate with other villages with a single stipendiary vicar. The bells of Stockbridge church have recently been recast, so now are once again rung before services. Each church organises events for the community, both to create community cohesion and to raise much-needed funds for the upkeep and costs of the churches.

Life in villages like ours has been greatly changed by the advent of the internet, which has been accompanied by a serious decline in public transport to rural areas. People can order groceries, clothes and anything they want online, without journeying to local towns where parking can be a problem, and there are frequent visits from online delivery vans or cars, which can record by GPS exactly where and when they leave each package. There is also now the possibility of working from home, with internet connection all over the world, so more working-age people can live in the country and still run their businesses with infrequent trips to London or to clients.

Lyndhurst

The village of Lyndhurst is known as the capital of the New Forest. Written as Linhest in 1086, its name is derived from the linden or lime tree, 'hurst' being a wooded hillock.

Of the few really old buildings still extant in Lyndhurst, the best known is the Queen's House. This handsome brick building is now occupied by the Forestry Commission. Attached to the Queen's House is the Verderers' Court with a history going back hundreds of years. The present court, as now constituted, dates from 1949, but it still has the power to deny Lyndhurst its urgently needed bypass. The heavy commercial and commuter traffic passing through the High Street is the only blight to the village.

The offices of the New Forest District Council are situated in Lyndhurst. At Foxlease the Girlguiding training and activity centre entertains Guides from all over the world. The Hampshire Police Force are represented by a large modern police station.

Churches supply the need of three denominations. The largest, St Michael's, an imposing brick building, contains a famous fresco by Lord Leighton and windows by Burne-Jones and William Morris. In the churchyard is the grave of Alice Hargreaves, for whom, when a little girl, *Alice's Adventures in Wonderland* was written.

There is a golf course and a very old cricket ground. The beautiful little mound known as 'Boltons Bench' hill, makes a perfect grandstand for cricket spectators and attracts skiers and tobogganists in winter. The opposite end of the village to Boltons Bench is Swan Green, world famous for its picturesque thatched cottages, often depicted on postcards.

🍁 Martin & Damerham

Martin and Damerham are on the very edge of Hampshire, with Dorset and Wiltshire surrounding them on three sides. Until 1895 both villages were in Wiltshire but they still remain in the Salisbury Diocese. Martin is included in the Cranborne Chase Area of Outstanding Natural Beauty.

Both villages have thriving communities, Martin has a community shop held in the village hall, run by volunteers and selling locally reared pork and chickens as well as eggs from Futurefarms and a wide variety of vegetables and groceries. Although there is not a pub in the village, a working men's club fills the need.

All Saints' church is set in the centre of the village and dates back to the 12th century. The village, known as Mertone in the 10th century, has some fine thatched cottages and was the 'Winterbourne Bishop' of W.H. Hudson's book *A Shepherd's Life*, the story of a Victorian countryman.

Martin is steeped in ancient history, with many burial mounds, Roman remains, ancient earthworks and the famous Bockerley Ditch, built about 1,600 years ago. Not too sure what the Romans would have thought of an episode of BBC's *Doctor Who* being filmed there in the 1980s.

Legend has it that between the two world wars, at a bridge halfway between Martin and Damerham, the young men used to fight each other to keep their village girls for themselves. This does not happen now!

Damerham is set on the Allen river, which rises above Martin. After many turns and twists it flow into the Avon at Fordingbridge, which then flows into the sea alongside the river Stour at Christchurch. The trout farm on the outskirts of the village was one of the first trout farms in the early 1960s. Georgie Fame, the blues singer, lived in the village for a time, and a frequent visitor to his home was John Lennon. We do not know if they fished together.

The village shop closed several years ago but the village thrives with a village hall, the money raised by fundraising by enthusiastic people with some help from the National Lottery Fund. Every year on Easter Saturday a Duck Race is held when over 1,800 yellow plastic ducks 'swim' down the river. It attracts hundreds of people who watch the spectacle and enjoy tea and cakes afterwards. This is the major fundraiser for the village hall.

For the millennium a beacon was built near to St George's church which stands on a hill overlooking the village. It is lit on special national occasions, usually as part of a chain of beacons throughout the country. The church is one of four churches of the Western Downland Benefice, the other three being Martin, Rockbourne and Whitsbury. The rector of the four villages lives in the rectory in Damerham.

Snowdrop Weekend is a big part of St George's year. Held in February, a carpet of snowdrops growing in the ancient Norman churchyard entices lots of visitors from a wide area to visit and enjoy the interior of the church where various stalls sell their wares. Refreshments are served in china cups and saucers with homemade cakes to the delight of visitors who love the old-fashioned atmosphere.

Damerham still has a pub where beer used to be brewed. Even though that has stopped, the pub attracts locals and visitors to the area.

There used to be a blacksmith's, now it is a thriving family garage business, unfortunately no longer selling petrol.

The village school thrives, it is one half of one of the first Federated Schools in Hampshire, the other half is in Rockbourne two miles away and the children at both sites meet together regularly. The village shop closed a few years ago and now people travel to Fordingbridge or Salisbury for shopping, many using a weekly bus which goes from village to village eventually arriving in Salisbury.

There are several farms surrounding the village; one of the biggest rears outdoor pigs and provides employment for over 20 people. There are also several office-based businesses but a lot of people commute to the surrounding areas. House prices are expensive, attracting retired people and there is always a demand for social housing and affordable homes but due to strict planning rules it is rare for them to be built.

Both Damerham and Martin are off the beaten track but, once found, people tend to stay and so the community spirit goes on.

Medstead

Medstead is situated in East Hampshire just north of the A31 road and is one of the highest villages in the county having an average elevation of approximately 600 ft above sea level. The nearest town is Alton which is about four and a half miles away. The earliest evidence of occupation in Medstead comes from two tumuli burial grounds which are thought to date back to 1000 BC. Roman coins and pottery have been found in the village. One theory for the name of the village is that 'Mid-stead' signified a halfway point on the road between Farnham and Winchester. Medstead is now quite a large village with a lot of house building being developed to the south of the main village.

St Andrew's church dates back to 1160 having been built on the site of a previous chapel which was mentioned in the Domesday survey of

1086. Medstead Manor dates from the 14th century and the Manor is currently the Convent of St Lucy. There is also a small United Reformed chapel known affectionately to locals as the Tin Tabernacle! The village has six Grade II listed buildings including St Andrew's church and its war memorial.

Medstead railway station was opened in 1868 and was renamed Medstead & Four Marks station in 1937 as it lies between the two villages. The line closed in 1973 but was reopened in 1983 as part of the popular Watercress steam railway line which runs from Alton to Alresford. Because of the high ground the railway line traverses, it is often known as 'Going over the Alps'.

The village has excellent facilities including a primary school with associated pre-school and nursery, a doctors' surgery, dentist, handy stores with post office, a hardware store, butchers and greengrocers. A modern village hall and the church hall, (formerly the school), provide space for a large variety of organisations to use and the village green is used for sports activities. The village has a caring and friendly atmosphere aided by the Medstead Voluntary Care Group who assist with transport to medical appointments, shopping etc and also run a monthly lunch for the over 70s which is very popular. The afternoon Medstead WI celebrated its centenary in 2018 – a copper beech tree and time capsule has been planted on the village green to mark the occasion.

The village offers an excellent range of footpaths where walks can be enjoyed in woodland and open countryside, some with views across to Winchester. Then where better to end a walk than with a drink and food in the village pub, the Castle of Comfort, tucked away behind the church?

The Castle of Comfort, Medstead

Meonstoke, Exton & Corhampton

When the Danes invaded southern England they came up the now much smaller river Meon in their longboats, and a battle against the local farming Saxons took place in Meonstoke. Some Danes subsequently settled in Meonstoke and there was friction for hundreds of years with the farmers across the river in Exton and Corhampton.

Corhampton church was built in about 1020 and is one of the very few small Saxon churches which has always functioned as an active church. Its dedication is unknown but part of the frescoes remaining in the chancel depict St Swithun restoring the dropped eggs to the widow's basket. In the churchyard, a 1,000 year old yew tree still stands, protecting some unusual vaulted brick graves and shadowing the old sundial on the church wall, which is divided into eight tides, not twelve hours.

As the people 'across the water' did not speak to each other, each village had its own footpath to Bishop's Waltham. The bridge into Exton was not built until 1805. Where the present pub, the Shoe, now stands, was the wheelwright's workshop. The old Shoe was a tiny pub in the garden opposite next to the river, which sometimes flooded in spite of the sluice and mill 50 yards upstream. Corhampton and Meonstoke also had their mills, as each village had to be quite self-contained.

The north outlet from Exton onto the A32 is known as The Grinch, but whether the word has any bearing on the fact that a gibbet was sited there is not known.

Very close by a Roman villa was recently excavated; and in the same field Saxon bones were found. In one lucky dig a complete warrior lying straight was found with his sword by his side and his circular shield boss on his chest.

The South Downs Way long-distance footpath comes through Exton and the Wayfarer's Walk comes through Droxford and the back of Corhampton and Exton on its way from Emsworth to Inkpen Beacon. There are several other footpaths and pleasant walks around the villages up to Beacon Hill to the west and Old Winchester Hill, an Iron Age fort, to the east, both commanding extensive views.

Micheldever

Motorists from Popham, driving along the A30, feel that they have some knowledge of Micheldever, a mere scattering of buildings, whilst those on the

A33 from the same point are under the same impression. Travellers by train stopping at Micheldever station are even more deceived, especially as they are aware of the oil terminal and can see a pleasant early Victorian building on one of the platforms, while an elegant Georgian building stands outside the station yard. It is therefore a revelation to some who venture a few miles on these routes to discover the lovely and interesting village of Micheldever itself. Over half the dwellings are over a hundred years old, many of them thatched, while the newer ones, with well-kept gardens, fit snugly into the overall pattern of well-loved homes.

The village, together with East Stratton, has been fortunate with its benefactors. Lady Rachel Russell, who lived at East Stratton House, presented the church of St Mary the Virgin with a silver chalice in 1703. Later benefactors have been the Barings, and more recently, Lord Rank, who farmed in this area and resided at Sutton Scotney.

There are several farms in the vicinity, so some people work on the land and with animals, some at the watercress beds and others commute to Winchester, Basingstoke and London. In late summer, the village is alive with tractors pulling loaded wagons of grain to and from the dryer.

Refreshment is obtainable in Micheldever at the Half Moon and Spread Eagle, a fine Georgian building standing on a piece of rising ground on Gin Hill. East Stratton boasts the Plough, attractively rural and used gratefully by walkers among others. The Dove at the station is popular for its cuisine and is quite well known outside the village.

Milford on Sea

Milford on Sea, with a population of approximately 5,000, is a Hampshire village straggling the south coast, situated three miles from Lymington and within striking distance of the New Forest.

The main village, just a short walk from the sea, is attractively set round a village green and it is easy to see why so many famous people chose to live here in years gone by. The road names are testament to the input of many naval connections such as Cornwallis, de la Warr, Whitby and West and during the 19th and early 20th centuries the mansions dotted along the cliff top were homes to such illustrious people. Although those mansions have now been replaced with modern flats, Westover Hall still remains (now a hotel and restaurant renamed the Beach House). This magnificent home echoes the previous clifftop dwellings in its splendour, built in 1896 by Alexander

Hurst Point Lighthouse, Milford on Sea

Siemens, the world famous electrical engineer, and later occupied by Viscount Nuffield, better known for Morris cars.

Another famous dwelling still in existence is Newlands Manor, a fine Gothic building with an interesting history. This was built in the very early 19th century and has links to the Cornwallis, Whitby and West families. It was the home of Patsy Cornwallis-West who, it is said, had a longstanding affair with Edward VII, proving that this village is not without some scandal.

Late in the 19th century a member of the same family, William Cornwallis-West tested his entrepreneurial skills by purchasing a good deal of land in and around Milford and planned to turn the area into a large seaside resort to rival Eastbourne. A railway link from Brockenhurst, a golf course and many tourist attractions were part of this plan but all failed due to lack of investment. He did however succeed in renaming the village by adding 'on sea'.

There's no doubt that present day Milford is a welcoming and satisfying environment in which to reside. It seems that the combined churches set an example every February by holding a free supper for all newcomers. Everyone who has moved into the area in the previous year is invited along and this gives the new residents an opportunity to meet representatives from local organisations. Perhaps this unique occasion is the reason why so many people in the community become volunteers.

The community centre is not the only meeting place as the various church halls also play host to several associations, including those established many years ago. The thriving WI celebrated their centenary in 2018, with the local historical society a close runner up.

Anyone visiting the village is bound to be impressed by its self-sufficiency, still boasting a butcher, fishmonger, greengrocer and so much more. Arriving in the spring or summer months, the village green will be playing host to various exhibitions. An annual food festival gives local eating establishments the opportunity to further their reputation and the very traditional May Fayre brings people from surrounding villages to enjoy the maypole dancing and crowning of the May Queen. In late July the biggest event is held when marquees and a stage are set for the Music Festival lasting several days, with music to suit all tastes culminating in performances from local choirs and a village sing song. This is a particularly popular event and once again an opportunity for local tradespeople to benefit. Just prior to Christmas local choirs and groups set the mood for the season with an outdoor carol service and an opportunity to taste local fare, al fresco.

Those who prefer peace and quiet can visit the historic All Saints' parish church and take a walk round the graveyard where so many famous and infamous have been laid to rest. A walk along the cliff path towards Barton-on-Sea gives a chance to drink in the magnificent view of the Isle of Wight Needles, and to the west, the Christchurch area with the Purbecks as a backdrop. Alternatively walk in an easterly direction to Keyhaven, famous for yachting and its bird sanctuary, or along the shingle bank to Hurst Castle commissioned by Henry VIII.

So, having given a taste of what this Hampshire village has to offer let's conclude that a deviation down the A3058 to enjoy the interesting and vibrant village of Milford on Sea will surely be well worth while.

New Alresford

New Alresford is an attractive market town in the heart of Hampshire, which draws thousands of visitors each year. There are three main streets, Broad Street, East Street and West Street and they are laid out very much as they were when plans were made by Bishop Godfrey de Lucy in about 1200. It takes its name from the river Arle which flows between Old and New Alresford. Near the parish boundary the Arle is joined by the Candover and Tichborne streams, the three forming the river Itchen which flows on to Winchester.

Broad Street is justly famous as one of the most beautiful streets in Hampshire, and is planted with lime trees and with lighting from old-style lamps which have been refurbished. Mary Russell Mitford, the authoress of *Our Village*, lived in Broad Street when she was a child and another house bears a plaque proclaiming that the 47th Infantry Regiment of the United States Army made their headquarters there during the Second World War in the run up to D-Day.

The Watercress Steam Railway draws thousands of visitors each year, eager to travel on the line from Alresford through Ropley and Medstead to Alton. A favourite walk is along the river which goes past the charming old Fulling Mill. Another popular walk is out past Town Mill and the watercress beds to Old Alresford, walking along the Little Weir and returning along the Great Weir alongside Alresford Pond.

There are many old tombstones in the churchyard of St John's, but four in particular are worthy of note. They are the graves of French prisoners of war.

From 1808 to 1814, during the Napoleonic Wars, there were something like 200 prisoners on parole in Alresford. Some died here and were buried in the churchyard, and their gravestones are still cared for.

North Baddesley

The original name of 'Bedeslei' is thought to be a derivation of Baeddes Leah, 'Baeddi's Wood' or clearing. There are signs of Roman and Saxon settlements within the area. In medieval times, the centre of the village was the parish church of St John the Baptist (still its most cherished possession), and the manor house, which was a Preceptory for the Knights Hospitallers of St John of Jerusalem from around 1167.

There are two gravestones in the churchyard both bearing the same name. In 1822 Robert Snelgrove, an assistant keeper on the Broadlands estate belonging to Lord Palmerston, found two men poaching at Toot-hill. One of the men, Charles Smith, fired when the keeper was close at hand and wounded him seriously in the thigh. Both men got away but many months later Smith was caught and condemned to death at Winchester Assizes. Palmerston did his utmost to get the sentence reduced to one of imprisonment but failed and Smith was duly hanged. The first gravestone was erected by William Cobbett, writer and social reformer of the time, who felt that Smith had been a victim of oppression.

The second gravestone appeared many years after Lord Palmerston's death and was erected by his grandson, Evelyn Ashley, in an attempt to absolve the family from any blame.

Street names in the village have generally been adopted from the families who owned the manor of Baddesley: Seymour Parade after the famous Tudor family; Mortimer Drive commemorates the Earls of March who held the manor in the reign of Richard II; Chamberlayne Court after the last recent owners; and Tottehale Close and Launcelyn Close are taken from the Preceptors of the Knights Hospitallers.

North Waltham

The village of North Waltham has existed for many years. Wealtham, meaning 'clearing in the wood', is an early Anglo-Saxon name and old maps also record that the village was called Cold Waltham. The population of North Waltham in 1801 was 338 and the current number is about 900. Even the Plague in 1665-1666 which devastated nearby Basingstoke did not have a huge impact on North Waltham. Only one burial is recorded for that year and no cause of death was recorded. There are two reasons given for why North Waltham escaped this epidemic – it's a very self-contained village, off the beaten track for travellers who may have had the disease, and there were also 40 wells in the village which assured a plentiful supply of clean water all year round.

Until the Second World War the majority of the villagers were either directly employed in agriculture or provided essential services required by the farming community. One such was the North Waltham carrier service started in 1897 and continued until the end of 1965 when it was the last carrier business in Hampshire to close. The carrier was an important link between the village and the wider community and would carry goods and people to and from Basingstoke.

In 1919, a 'gang of mummers' was set up in the village, who toured the district each Christmas. Mummer means player and the Mummers' play was looked upon as a grand form of entertainment and 'helped to bring amusement and entertainment to liven up the festive season'. In 1947 the North Waltham Mummers were filmed at Denham Studios for a brief appearance in the film *Uncle Silas*.

There are accounts that in the late 1930s a small fair came to North Waltham in the summer. A 'donkey man' also came every year and would set up his tent on the green – he put on a show with the rats, mice and budgies he had, as well as giving donkey rides up and down the street. Another memory is that the radio comedian Kenneth Horne and his partner Richard Murdoch came to the village to provide entertainment at the Harvest Supper, Mr Horne's sister being secretary to local farmer Mr William Rathbone. This was such an event that it was talked about in villages all around the area.

Pond View Cottages, North Waltham

When Mr Rathbone retired in the 1950s he donated a meadow for recreational use in the centre of the village under the auspices of the North Waltham Village Trust. In the 1980s the Rathbone Pavilion was built. It has rooms for hire and a daily pre-school moved here from Dummer in the 1990s. A youth club was restarted in 2012. The WI is still active. There is an annual church fete/big lunch when residents, family and friends come together on the meadow for a picnic or barbecue. St Michael's church also holds social events during the year, together with a service each Sunday.

There are currently three pubs – the Wheatsheaf Hotel, once a coaching inn, and the Sun Inn are both on the A30, while the Fox was built in 1836 on the edge of the village. Up until 1897 there was another pub called the Flowerpots (now residential houses) from where there was a tunnel to the Wheatsheaf – legend says that smuggling of contraband goods took place and that the Flowerpots was a house of ill repute.

The first school in the village, now a residential building, was built in 1833. In 1836 an entry in the school logbook gives details of life in the school when Mary Hardy, Thomas's sister, arrived to find her 66 pupils ill-disciplined and 'behind in every subject'. Education in North Waltham improved under the new rector, Reverend Blackley, 'through whose untiring zeal and energy the school has been built', referring to the current school which opened in 1873. The school has continued to grow and at the Village of the Year competition in 2017 the headmaster and an ex-pupil won awards for Inspirational People.

In 2017 at the Hampshire Village of the Year Competition, North Waltham received nine awards including Best Small Village, Champion of Champions and runner up for Community Engagement. The village shop was fully refurbished during 2017 and won an award for Inspirational Place. The Fox has received several awards at the Village of the Year competition over the years, the latest being Highly Commended in 2017 as a community hub.

Although working life and leisure time has changed over the years, North Waltham has always had a sense of community, perfectly summed up by the following comment: 'we live in a lovely village, with great community spirit shown by many people'.

NORTHINGTON & SWARRATON

Divided only by the beautiful Candover stream as it meanders through the water meadows to the river Itchen, Swarraton and Northington have long been a united community, being closely linked to the families living at the Grange. The Victorian church standing high on Northington Hill has a commanding view across the valley to the village hall in Swarraton. The flow of the Candover stream is more constant these days, thanks to the action of the Parish Council who had to rescue the fish in buckets during a dry season and lobbied the water authorities to add a supplementary source at Totford.

Lawyers, bankers, a king and the military have inhabited the Grange with its stunning Greek-style temple portico, sweeping parkland and lakes. Among its illustrious owners were Robert Henley (lawyer), created 1st Earl of Northington in 1764, who was appointed Attorney General and Lord Keeper of the Great Seal, and Alexander Baring (banker) who in 1803 negotiated the sale of Louisiana between France and the US. During his long residence at the Grange Alexander Baring greatly changed the landscape to create an extensive stretch of water meadows. With his American wife he hosted many eminent transatlantic guests as well as artists and writers of the day.

The 2nd Lord Ashburton, William Bingham Baring (1799-1864), was passionate about country life and education. He was responsible for the building of the school and a church. He and his wife, Lady Henrietta hosted many literary celebrities including Thackeray and Charles Kingsley.

During the time of Alexander Hugh Baring, the 4th Lord Ashburton (1835-1899), improvements were made to the house, park, villages and farms. A Clerk of Works was appointed and cottages were restored or replaced and the population, largely agricultural, grew rapidly. A carpenter's shop, woodyard and forges were installed. This was a period of lavish wealth and development in the area and the population was at its peak. Times and fortunes change and in 1924 some of the properties were sold. The sale of the Grange in 1934 led to a period of stagnation and decay. The great portico was even used for storing hay bales.

The 47th US infantry arrived in the winter of 1943. Winston Churchill and General Dwight D. Eisenhower met at the Grange on 24th March 1944 to discuss plans for D-Day.

In 1964 the 7th Lord Ashburton, John Baring, bought back the Grange. After much debate it was saved from demolition and is now managed by English Heritage. It has been vibrantly re-invented, initially as Grange Park Opera and now as the venue for the Grange Festival. In the summer months it is once again a place for music, dance, fine dining and picnics in the park.

Charity and friendship have long been core values in the village. In times past the Clothing Club provided for poor families. On Christmas day the schoolchildren were given smocks and plaited straw hats. More recently the WI took part in a friendship scheme to 'Adopt a Granny'.

The George Harding Trust emerged from an incident during agricultural riots of the 1830s, when a mob arrived at Northington Down Farm to destroy agricultural machinery. Henry Cook, 19, attacked William Bingham Baring with a sledgehammer and George Harding warded off the blow and saved the victim from serious injury. William Bingham Baring made strenuous efforts to vouch for his attacker but Henry Cook was executed for his part in the riots. George Harding was financially rewarded and given a job for life at the Grange. At his death in 1875, his will bequeathed £200 to be held in trust for the provision of bread for the poor but in later years the fund was put to the general relief of poverty. In 2011, no calls having been made on the charity for many years, it was wound up and funds were distributed to the school in Preston Candover and Northington church.

In 1991 the WI members of Swarraton and Northington hatched 'Operation Fruit Cake' to support troops fighting in the Gulf War. Their idea took Hampshire Women's Institutes by storm. Mixing bowls and ovens ready, 123 WIs joined in and baked 1,090 cakes, which were handed over to the Army at Winchester Guildhall; ironically in view of the statue of King Alfred of burnt cake fame.

As the County Chairman said, 'Even more than the cakes themselves was the goodwill and the expression of fellowship they embodied.' This is just one of many projects undertaken by the WI.

Parish records provide fascinating glimpses of life in bygone eras. Rural remedies as recorded by the Rev William L.W. Eyre in 1890 include a 'cure' for bronchitis or whooping cough –'catch a spider, place it in a muslin bag and hang from the centre of the cottage ceiling. If the spider dies, the child may die. If the spider continues to live, the child will recover.' Perhaps more successful could be the remedy for a bee sting – 'bruised honeysuckle leaves to be applied to the wound.'

The language of the villagers is also recorded by the Rev William Eyre. Severals, a livery stables in the village, takes its name from the ancient practice of strip farming. Other local words include *chopper* – not a tool or a bike but a dried pig's face. To *hacker* was to stammer and a *meush* is a hole in a hedge made by a rabbit. Children playing chase in the playground still shout '*scribs*' when hoping to evade capture.

The fortunes of the village may have fluctuated with those of the Grange but the village hall and the WI remain the hub of this friendly Hampshire community.

OAKLEY

Oakley is a village four and a half miles west of the town of Basingstoke. In the census of 2001 it had a population of over 5,000.

In AD 851 one of the great battles between the Saxons and Danes was at Aclea or Acleah, which is believed to be the present village of Oakley. The Danes, who had gone from the neighbourhood of London south across the Thames to Surrey, were severely defeated by Ethelwulf. This could have been the origin of the area and farm still named Battledown between Oakley and Basingstoke.

Oakley is mentioned in the Domesday Book of 1086 with the name Aclei. It had a church, which was probably on the same site on which St Leonard's church stands today. This area became known as Church Oakley and to the east of it was East Oakley.

William Warham of Malshanger Park was a favourite of Henry VII and became Archbishop of Canterbury in 1503. He was a diplomat and lawyer and friend of the great intellectual Erasmus. During the latter half of the 19th century, Malshanger Park was owned by Wyndham Spencer Portal, whose family was noted for the Portals Limited banknote manufacturing company in Laverstoke, a few miles west of Oakley. He was created Baron Portal of Malshanger in 1901, and was Chairman of the London and South Western Railway Company, a local benefactor and very active in the affairs of the county. On his death in 1905 his son William sold the property to Mr Godfrey Walter, whose wife Edith Elizabeth Walter was the founding president of the local WI in 1918.

Malshanger is now owned by Sir Michael Colman, of the mustard family. When he retired from the family business he started a mint-growing business at Malshanger in addition to the other crops grown there. The mint is used to make several products including chocolate peppermint creams and mint tea.

Sir Harold Gillies, the plastic surgeon (1882-1960), lived in Oakley for a while at Yewbank, Rectory Road, when he worked at Rooksdown House, part of the Park Prewett Hospital in Basingstoke. Dr Dukinfield Henry Scott FRS and his wife Henderina, both notable botanists lived in East Oakley House. He died in 1934 and was responsible for planting the garden with many exotic plants.

Oakley Hall is just outside the village to the west and is now a hotel with

Forge Cottage, Oakley

a nursing home in the same grounds. The present building was built in 1795, but there has been a hall there since 1299. It was privately owned for many years and was visited by Jane Austen who would walk there for tea with her neighbours, the Bramston family. Jane lived in the neighbouring village of Steventon. In 1940 Hilsea College re-located to Oakley Hall from the Portsmouth area to escape the wartime bombing of the city. The school only closed in 1992.

Another historic building is Oakley Manor, a large detached 18th-century Grade II listed building, located in the Church Oakley Conservation Area. Oakley has over a dozen other buildings of interest mostly built in the 1800s or early 1900s. They are on a local list of buildings of architectural or historic interest.

The village has two sports fields, one at Newfound and another in Church Oakley which is called Peter Houseman Field. This is named after Peter Houseman (1945-1977) who played for Chelsea Football Club and founded the Oakley Football Club.

Oakley has three public houses, the Beach Arms on the B3400 to the west of Oakley, which was called the Red Lion until 1927, the Fox also on the B3400 in Newfound, and the Barley Mow near the schools and the main pond.

Odiham

Odiham has had its glory days. The Romans built a villa by the river Whitewater; Saxon kings created a royal deer park for recreational hunting and as a living larder; as a royal manor it is the first entry for Hampshire in the Domesday Book; King John stayed at his castle by a bend in the river on his way to face the barons at Runnymede; Queen Elizabeth I held a Privy Council at Odiham Place or Palace, long-since disappeared but commemorated in the housing development called Palace Gate; and the second Queen Elizabeth reviewed her Air Force at RAF Odiham in her coronation year. A national institution, the Royal Veterinary College, grew partly from a local 18th-century initiative for farm animal welfare, the Odiham Agricultural Society, which held its meetings in the George Inn (currently 'Bel & the Dragon').

In between times Odiham with its semi-detached neighbour down the hill, North Warnborough, lapsed into a quiet rural slumber, making its living as a small market town serving an agricultural community. North Warnborough made use of the little streams bubbling out of the chalk for tanneries, enhancing neither the atmosphere immediately around nor the waters downstream, while another minor industry produced coarse woollen cloth from Hampshire sheep. Greater prosperity and social status could be seen up the hill in Odiham High Street, where by the 18th century elegant brick fronts were being built on to the houses whose timber structure can still be seen in the less visible side and back walls. From the High Street narrow alleys lead to the Bury and All Saints church, much restored but dating in parts from the 13th century. Behind the church a picturesque quadrangle of 17th-century almshouses has been augmented over the last century with modern dwellings.

In the early 20th century Hilda and Ida Chamberlain, daughters of the Birmingham industrialist Joseph Chamberlain and sisters of prime minister Neville Chamberlain, settled in Odiham. Active in public life, they were quick to see the potential of the new Women's Institute movement and established WIs in both Odiham and North Warnborough (now combined as Odiham WI). Between the wars the RAF came to Odiham, where they have remained active contributors to community life, their helicopters a familiar presence in our skies.

The pace of life here speeded up with the opening in the early seventies of the M3 nearby. At a time when employment in agriculture and its ancillary trades was declining locally a new commuter population was attracted by better communications combined with Odiham's historic interest and countryside setting. The population has increased steadily over the last half century with the development of sheltered housing complexes on the one hand and estates of family homes on the other. Contrarily, at the same time some local amenities have disappeared. Both banks have recently gone and the half dozen food shops of a few decades ago are now reduced to a single Co-op store. There is an hourly bus service to Basingstoke and Alton, supplemented by the essential door to door service provided by the voluntary care group.

The secondary school in Odiham, Robert May's School, is a comprehensive school serving Hook and Hartley Wintney and the surrounding villages as well as Odiham, and is directly descended from the grammar school founded by local benefactor Robert May in 1694. Most of its pupils go on to sixth form colleges in Alton, Basingstoke or Farnborough, and many thence to university, but few can afford to return to Odiham to live. The need for affordable housing for local young people is very much a live issue here.

For all ages and interests there are clubs and societies as well as community activities that have become traditions: the church fete in the summer, for example, always with a helicopter on display, or the Odiham Extravaganza as the start of the Christmas season.

Is Odiham a 'town' or 'village'? To older inhabitants who have lived here all their lives it has always been a town. Ironically, as it has grown in size newer residents more often speak of it as a village and it is true that it has lost some of the amenities of a town even as the population has increased. In either case, if you want to start a lively debate in Odiham, ask a random group of residents whether it's a town or a village...

Old Alresford

The village of Old Alresford, on the ancient route from Winchester to London, is just north of Alresford. A great fire in 1160 destroyed the original village. This was rebuilt by Bishop De Lucy who also made the causeway connecting it with his new town of New Market, now known as New Alresford. This causeway, commonly known as the Great Weir, is the greatest medieval construction in England still serving its original purpose as both road and a dam.

Nearby at Abbotstone are the visible remains of a deserted village. The community was affected by the Black Death in 1349 to 1350, but it started to finally decline in the 18th century when large numbers of agricultural workers deserted the countryside for the towns.

Old Alresford Place, now a Diocesan Retreat Centre, was occupied at the time of the Civil War by the rector, Dr Heylyn, a fervent Royalist. He was driven from his rectory by his neighbour, the Cromwellian Colonel Norton.

Alresford House, Old Alresford

Oliver Cromwell often stayed with Colonel Norton, whose local knowledge was an important factor in the victory over the Royalists, fighting over unknown territory, in the decisive battle of Cheriton.

In St Mary's church is a memorial to Mary Sumner, who founded the Mothers' Union in 1875, now a world-wide organisation. The original meetings were held in the drawing room of the then rectory, now Old Alresford Place.

The watercress industry plays a major part in the local economy due to the clear running Hampshire chalk streams and the constant water temperature. The attractive village green is now registered as common land. A generous resident bought the land for the village and with other volunteer residents built drainage chambers from which the spring water is piped into the brook.

Old Basing

Old Basing is a village located east of Basingstoke, and the name is thought to date from Saxon times; basa (meaning 'Saxon chief') and ing (meaning 'place of'). The village is mentioned in the Domesday Book of 1086.

It can be reached via Swing Swang Lane. 'Swang' is Saxon for a marsh or swamp. Indeed at one end is Basing Fen and the roundabout at the other end floods every time it rains. The Swing is probably a corruption of the name of whichever Saxon owned the land at the time.

The village is situated on the south-east side of the valley of the river Loddon, which is a tributary of the Thames, and in the past was a clear chalk river important for fish and the watercress industry. Baskets, for transporting the cress to market, were made in the village. The Basingstoke Canal, which was completed in 1794, passed round the ruins of Basing House and through the village.

Basing House was one of the greatest private houses in Tudor England. The stand against the Parliamentarians during the Civil War has made it one of the most historic sites in Hampshire. When it fell in 1645, Cromwell ordered it to be 'totally slighted and demolished' and after the siege people freely carted from the ruins the building materials, which are still seen today in the older red brick parts of the village. The siege of Basing House was the longest of the war, lasting over two years. Although of course this was not continuous – armies didn't fight in the winter and men went home for the harvest! At the fall Inigo Jones, the famous architect, was marched out wearing only a blanket. All his clothes had been stolen.

Ghost watchers might be interested to know that a cavalier can allegedly be seen guarding the Garrison Gate in The Street. A lady dressed in a long blue dress and dark cloak is supposed to be seen drifting across the recreation grounds towards the Loddon river.

At one time there were three working mills, known as Upper, Lower and Barton's. Alongside the mills, there were two blacksmiths, and there was still a forge opposite the church in The Street in the 1930s, run by Richard Hall and partner Mr Wiggins. Four farm complexes – Grange Farm, Parker's Farm, Brown's Farm and Mill Farm supplied the village and surrounding towns with much needed produce.

St Mary's church, which is where Old Basing WI meet each month, dates back as far as 1089, although what we see today is mainly 16th-century. It was used as stabling in the Civil War when it was greatly damaged and plundered.

The landscape was dramatically altered when the village was bisected by the London to Southampton railway line built in the 1830s. Today, the Mill Field nature reserve is home to several types of orchid, over 20 species of butterfly, 400 species of moth and over 100 kinds of birds. There are also dormice. Barton's Mill is now a pub and restaurant, a popular destination for visitors and local people, and every summer sees the annual village carnival and flower show.

Edward Lear wrote in his *Book of Nonsense*:
>There was an old person of Basing,
>Whose presence of mind was amazing.
>He purchased a steed,
>Which he rode at full speed,
>And escaped from the people of Basing.

OVERTON

Overton is a large village in the north of Hampshire situated on the famous river Test and surrounded by beautiful countryside. The source of the river Test is only a mile away and this clear chalk stream offers residents the chance to see plenty of wildlife including herons and kingfishers, and children regularly feed a large number of local ducks. There is evidence of habitation since the Stone and Bronze Ages and Overton is mentioned in the Domesday Book.

There is a history of banknote paper manufacture here starting in the 18th century. Henry Portal founded Portals Paper Mill at Bere Mill, on the river Test between Overton and Whitchurch, in 1712, adding Laverstoke Mill to his enterprise seven years later which allowed him to win the contract to make banknote paper for the Bank of England in 1724. Portals significantly expanded in the 20th century with the development of a new Overton Mill near Quidhampton in 1922 and the Bank of England relocated a significant number of employees to the area during the Second World War.

Papermaking is still undertaken within the village at the Overton Mill, however the Portals business is no more as in 1995 the firm was sold to De La Rue. Overton Mill now produces high-security paper for over 150 national currencies. The Portals Laverstoke Mill is now used by Bombay Sapphire gin, with a visitors' centre.

The village was on a major stagecoach route, hence the number of pubs, and now has a railway station with quick links to London. It has a population of over 4,000 and growing, with a thriving centre including several shops, pubs, coffee shops and a library in the community centre. There is an outstanding primary school. St Mary's church, dating from Norman times, looks out over the recreation grounds busy with football, athletics and cricket. An outdoor swimming pool, run by a dedicated band of volunteers, encourages the local children to learn to swim.

There is a great community spirit which shines through at the sheep fair held every four years. This commemorates the farmers leading sheep through the village for fairs recorded as early as 1245. A scarecrow festival is held every other year plus a wheelbarrow race through the village, providing plenty of entertainment. Overton Mummers perform in the village every Boxing Day continuing a long tradition. The Children in Need fundraising event, Carfest South, is held near Overton during August Bank Holiday. Literary connections include Jane Austen who lived nearby at Steventon and who would have walked to the village for provisions. There is also a connection with Richard Adams' *Watership Down* set on the nearby North Wessex Downs.

Pamber Heath

The village of Pamber Heath is situated in north Hampshire close to the Berkshire border. It is six miles from Basingstoke and, with Pamber End and Pamber Green, is part of the parish of Pamber. St Luke's church forms the centre of the village along with a large village hall, opened in the late 1970s and paid for by fund raising from the local people.

The name Pamber, originally spelled Pambeare, goes back to Norman times, the addition of 'Heath' coming in later centuries.

Henry de Port founded Pamber Priory in the 12th century, and its remains stand today as a reminder of the time when this was one of the most important monastic establishments in Hampshire.

The three Pambers are surrounded by open lands: Silchester Common, Tadley Common and the extensive Pamber Forest, an ancient woodland. Pamber Forest is a nature reserve of some 478 acres and designated a Site of Special Scientific Interest. Hazel, chestnut and oak have been coppiced for many years, and the structure of the woodland varies from dry open heathland through to dense hazel, to streams lined with alders and willows. The forest is home to many species of butterfly, some 30 species have been recorded. Bat boxes can be seen high up on some trees, to provide a home for the bats that choose to live in the forest. Flora, insects, small mammals and birds all make the forest their home, as do roe deer and fallow deer. Snakes, especially adders, are in abundance and can often be seen basking in the warm sunshine.

PENNINGTON

Pennington is situated on the south coast of Hampshire, stretching from the salt marshes on the Solent through to fields and the boundary stream of Yaldhurst, and was in the past held in undivided thirds by three different lords of the manor. Today it is still divided by name into three parts – Lower Pennington, Middle Common and Upper Common. It is considered to be an annexe of Lymington which is a mile away but in its own right it is a separate community though developments have encroached on the fields between the two and now the boundary is marked only by Yaldhurst stream.

The name Pennington was first recorded in 1272, the derivation from 'penny farm' or a farm for which a penny geld was payable. Today it is more affectionately known as 'Donkey Town' from when donkeys were grazed on the common. The village itself is the centre of day-to-day life having St Mark's church, shops, a pub, schools, WI hall and a busy post office, but the Middle Common is the 'playground' where various activities have taken place over many, many years. In the spring the common blooms with bright yellow gorse, blackthorn bushes covered in a froth of white, then bluebells, pink pyramid orchids, and as summer is ending many little delicate harebells. Deer can be seen grazing at certain times of the day and wildlife finds sanctuary in the dense bushes.

During the threatened invasion of the Napoleonic Wars bands of militia were encamped there, and in 1814 a duel was fought between Captain Souper and Lieutenant Dietrich due to a refusal to retract an insult. Dietrich was killed and Souper found guilty of murder. He was sentenced to be hanged but there was a public outcry and Souper was given a free pardon.

More recently an article in the *Independent Magazine* featured cameo photos of local people who used the common for recreation from walking their dogs to horse riding. A photographer, Nick Dawe, lived next to the common and found inspiration from people's activities, the text noting that 'this piece of land means different things to different people'. There were fears that the land could be lost but it has now been included in the New Forest National Park. For years it has been visited by a circus and funfair and in the 1970s there was a parade of elephants, camels and horses as the performers made their way through the streets of Lymington and Pennington to the big top on the common. It has been home to the football and cricket club before land was purchased specifically for a sports ground and social club.

Magdalen Chapel existed in Pennington in the 13th century and was used for divine service down to the early part of the reign of Elizabeth I, but where it stood is not known even though efforts have been made to trace it. In 1839 the first church, St Mark's, was built but was replaced with a larger building in 1859 which is now a Grade II listed building. The chancel has elaborate wall paintings carried out in two phases in the 20th century by Nathaniel Westlake and William Aikman, which recently had to be restored as they were in a sad state of repair.

The Rev William Lambert who was the vicar in the Victorian era, was appalled to find that most of the residents of Pennington were illiterate and undertook to see that a school was built; money was raised and in 1852 the school was opened. The main change however came to Pennington when after the Second World War prefabricated houses started to be put up for rehoming people and the population began to grow. Then the school became too small and new ones were built.

An injection of life was brought to the village in 2014 when the then landlord of the Musketeer public house started a Christmas Fayre. It is held in the Square during an evening in December when the streets are decorated with fairy lights and a band plays Christmas music; several children's fairground rides are in great demand. The atmosphere buzzes with vibrancy.

Gradually development has taken place like a pincer movement so that the population has grown from a few hundred residents in 1800 to over 9,000 in recent years. Then, most of the population worked on the land, now there is a great diversity of trades and professions supporting local needs.

It is perhaps fitting to end this brief account by mentioning Mrs Joan Stephens who died at the age of 105 years. She was born in Pennington in 1912, her family having lived in the village for several generations; she was very interested in local history and wrote two vivid accounts of Pennington thereby preserving stories that could have been lost. She concluded *Pennington Remembered* with the following: 'Time marches on – yet in the sweet memory of a bygone day there is a charm time cannot take away'.

PETERSFIELD

Situated an hour away from London by fast train and half an hour north of Portsmouth on the old coaching route (a day's journey in those days), Petersfield was originally founded by William, Earl of Gloucester as a market town in the 12th century. The market square is at the centre of the town in front of St Peter's church, which is originally from the 11th century and has a Norman arcaded chancel arch. The town grew up around the church and market on high ground between two streams. These still maintain a head of trout – why not have a close look at the stream running alongside the central car park?

The name Petersfield was derived from St Peter's Feld, where a 'feld' was an open area without trees. The town's flag features a background of rolling green hills representing the nearby South Downs, overlaid by the crossed keys of St Peter. The Square is dominated by a large equestrian statue of William of Orange on a tall stone plinth. This was first erected by Sir William Joliffe in 1757 as part of the grand entry to his residence and later moved to its current site. William of Orange had no connection with the town and despite being something of a town icon, his statue does restrict the usefulness of the Square for community events. On Wednesdays and Saturdays it is surrounded by the stallholders of the regular market and on the first Sunday of the month by the farmers market. Local watercolour and pastel artist Flora Twort, who lived from 1893 to 1985, painted several iconic scenes of the Square on market days, showing the livestock market, which finally closed in 1962. Her pictures can be seen at the town's museum.

During good weather, the cafés around the Square have tables and chairs out on the pavements and this, together with several beautiful silver maple trees, gives the Square a 'continental' feel. In 1726 Daniel Defoe described Petersfield as 'a town eminent for little but being full of good inns' and in his diary in 1661 Samuel Pepys describes staying at an inn in Petersfield in the room where the king, Charles II, had stayed the previous week. Today there are still plenty of pubs, restaurants and cafés to suit every taste. Petersfield has the usual major retailers found nationally, many of which are situated in Ram's Walk, a shopping arcade off the Square. It also has many interesting small independent shops to be found down several alleyways, notably Bakery Lane, Pages Court and the Folly Market.

Off the north side of the High Street, the Physic Garden, established in 1988, is a quiet oasis in the town, popular with office and shop workers as somewhere to eat their packed lunch. Bounded by brick and flint walls, this very pleasant garden has been set out in authentic 17th-century design with a knot garden, topiary walk, informal orchard, rose arch and beds of medicinal herbs in a geometric design. Its style would have been very familiar to John Goodyer, the distinguished botanist who lived in Petersfield in the 17th century.

Take a five minute walk east from the town centre and one arrives at the Heath. This, as its name suggests, is a large expanse of open heath and grassland, owned by the town council and surrounding a 22-acre pond known as the Heath Lake, home to many waterfowl. During the summer there are boats for hire, lots of space for picnickers and a surfaced path to circumnavigate the pond. These features together with a refreshment kiosk and children's playground are a big draw for visitors and residents alike – Petersfield's 'jewel in the crown'.

Swimming is not recommended in the Lake which is very shallow anyway, but Petersfield is fortunate in having the Taro Leisure Centre which has a 25m indoor swimming pool, a teaching pool and a toddler pool. There is also a lovely open-air swimming pool behind the Festival Hall, which is one of very few public outdoor pools left in Hampshire. It is run as a charity by local volunteers, has a friendly relaxed atmosphere, and is maintained to the highest standards. It is another very popular place to go in the summer, opening from April through to mid-September.

Petersfield has much of historical interest, ancient and modern. The 21 barrows on the Heath, for instance, the subject of international research are probably the largest Bronze Age cemetery in Britain. Politically, the Joliffe family ran the town as a 'rotten borough' until the reform act of 1832. Events and people are commemorated by 17 blue plaques on buildings in the town. The history of the town is very well-documented at the town's museum which has recently expanded to occupy the old police station as well as the former magistrates' courthouse next door. It also houses the Bedales Historic Dress collection, and the Edward Thomas Study Centre.

Petersfield is a gateway to the South Downs National Park and very much connected to the surrounding countryside. A network of footpaths and cycle routes lead into the Park. It was the first town in the SDNP to agree its own Neighbourhood Plan to ensure that development reflecting the aspirations of the population will enhance the built and natural environments to the benefit of both residents and visitors alike.

🍁 PORTSMOUTH

Once a collection of villages, the development of Portsmouth started around 1180 in the south-west corner of Portsea Island. A merchant, Jean de Gisors, owned a fleet of ships and some land around a small inlet called the Camber and with a thriving import/export trade the area became known as Spice Island. In 1194 King Richard I granted Portsmouth a charter.

Developments continued apace with fortifications constructed to protect the city starting with a round tower at the harbour entrance and in 1494 King Henry VII added a square tower which was used to store ammunition. He also built a single dry dock in what would become the dockyard. King Henry VIII enlarged the dockyard and built Southsea Castle from where, in 1545, he watched as his ship, the *Mary Rose* (named after his sister) sank in the Solent. The *Mary Rose* was raised from the seabed in 1982 and after extensive preservation over many years is a main tourist attraction in the Historic Dockyard. Visitors can see history brought to life with artefacts and interactive displays illustrating what life would have been like on board.

Near the Square Tower in 1212 the Domus Dei was built as a hospice for pilgrims; this later became a church and it was here in 1662 that King Charles II married Catherine of Braganza.

In the late 17th century the dockyard and surrounding area continued to grow and expand northwards into what were fields and small villages. Houses were built in a new area called Portsea and then Landport which encroached onto the villages of Buckland and Stamshaw.

The 1800s saw further expansion eastwards with a new suburb Southsea. It was here that Thomas Ellis Owen, an architect and builder shaped the development of Southsea with magnificent terraces and parades. He also designed and built Highland Road Cemetery in which are buried several holders of the Victoria Cross, as well as people associated with Charles Dickens, including his mistresses. Charles Dickens' birthplace now houses a museum.

Another character with a connection to the city was John Pounds (1766-1839). Injured in an accident in the dockyard, he became a cobbler and was the founder of the ragged schools which provided free education to poorer children.

Arthur Conan Doyle practised as a doctor in the city whilst writing the Sherlock Holmes novels and another author – Nevil Shute – moved to Portsmouth in 1934 working in the aircraft industry.

Clarence Esplanade was built in 1848 by convict labour and Clarence Pier (now a funfair) opened in 1861. Continuing eastwards the villages of Milton and Eastney were developed. The promenade stretches for three miles from Clarence Pier, past South Parade Pier and on to Eastney and the entrance to Langstone Harbour.

By the early 1900s the city had engulfed Copnor and spread northwards to North End, Hilsea, Cosham (which is just beyond Portsmouth Island) and north east to Drayton and Farlington.

During the early 20th century the main employer was the dockyard with a workforce of over 8,000 in 1900. Other industries were brewing and corset making. As these industries declined electrical and electronic engineering became the major employers as well as the tourist industry.

In the Historic Dockyard, along with the *Mary Rose*, visitors can see Admiral Lord Nelson's flagship HMS *Victory* and HMS *Warrior*, the first ironclad warship built by Isambard Kingdom Brunel (who was also born in Portsmouth). Other very interesting museums are the D-Day Museum which houses the Overlord Embroidery and the Royal Marines Museum with the figure of the 'yomping' marine depicting their engagement in the Falklands War of 1982.

Apart from historical places of interest another tourist attraction is the 560ft Spinnaker Tower, resembling a spinnaker sail, which was opened in 2005 and from the viewing platform gives panoramic views across the Solent to the Isle of Wight, along the coast and north to the South Downs. A major retail park surrounds the Spinnaker Tower with many outlet shops and a wide variety of restaurants.

And turning full circle back to the city's maritime heritage, the largest ship ever built for the Royal Navy, the aircraft carrier HMS *Queen Elizabeth*, will be based in the dockyard. And down at the Camber, first developed in 1180, is the headquarters of Ben Ainslie Racing, the United Kingdom's contestant for the America's Cup.

Originally made up of a collection of small villages, Portsmouth and the surrounding area has developed into a conurbation with a population of over 205,000 and is now the most densely populated city in the UK.

Purbrook

A Roman road from Chichester to Clausentum (Southampton) went through the site of Purbrook.

Until the 19th century a great forest stretched across South East Hampshire (the Forest of Bere) and although a track led through the forest from Portsmouth to Horndean it was only usable in summer. In winter coaches had to make a detour to Havant. In 1711 a much better road was built from London to Portsmouth which went from Horndean to Cosham, through Purbrook, which is now the London Road.

On the southern fringe of the forest was a stream called Purbrook. Its name is a corruption of the Saxon word Pucanbroc, which means 'brook of the water spirit'. A settlement at Purbrook grew up in the 18th century.

Purbrook Park House was built in 1770 and rebuilt in 1837 by John Deverell, it being part of the large estate owned by him. He was born on 29th March 1800 and died in Purbrook on 6th November 1880. He was a convinced evangelical and a major benefactor for the community. In 1868 in spite of some local opposition and through the efforts of John Deverell, who donated the school premises and 18 acres of land, the Purbrook Industrial School for Boys was opened. Here vagrant boys would learn trades such as tailoring, shoemaking etc. In 1871 38 boys were in residence and by July 1977 there were 67 inmates and the school facilities included a mast and rigging to provide nautical instructions for boys inclined to the sea. Places were found for the boys leaving on licence and discharge, frequently in gentlemen's houses or gardens. In 1933 the institution became an approved school, one of the new institutions introduced by the 1933 Children and Young Persons Act to replace the existing system of reformatories and industrial schools.

John Deverell was lord of the manor of Farlington. In 1826 a meeting with the landowners of Purbrook was convened by the Rector of Farlington (where the residents of Purbrook were expected to attend church) to raise money and land to build a church in Purbrook. Deverell offered his support and agreed he would give a great deal towards the construction costs once he completed his house. At a sermon preached in the church at Farlington specific reference was made to those who were more concerned with building their own houses than providing for, and supporting, the House of God! John Deverell withdrew his support until he received an apology. Finally he agreed to support the new chapel of ease and St John the Baptist church was built, completed in 1858. John Deverell attended the consecration and become one of the first churchwardens.

In 1860 the War Department compulsorily purchased Portsdown Hill for military purposes. Included within this was 190 acres of John Deverell's estate. The building of Fort Purbrook was completed in 1870 and forms part of the line of five forts overlooking Portsmouth to protect the harbour from an invasion force attacking from the north or east by land. Fort Purbrook had 21 guns and a complement of 220 men. Deverell expressed concern over the lack of spiritual welfare for the troops based in the new forts and the Secretary of State for War granted a one acre site for the building of a church. In return for providing the endowment he was granted patronage of the church, to be known as Christ Church. In return for giving the land the army was given rights to hold services in the church and the churchyard was to be used for military burials as required. Records of baptism in the church began in 1871.

Today Purbrook Park is a co-ed comprehensive school, the main building of which was the home of the Deverell family until 1919. Fort Purbrook is an activity centre. St John the Baptist church and Christ Church are still serving the community. The community hall was built in 1920 and named Deverell Hall and continues to serve the residents and many local organisations, including Purbrook Women's Institute.

QUARLEY

Quarley lies north of Grateley, and is a neighbouring parish. Whereas Grateley derives its name from the 'great lea', Quarley derives its name from a quarter of the lea. It has a manor house and a church which are mentioned in the Domesday Book. A feature of St Michael's is that three church bells are housed in a frame, with a roof over it, in the churchyard.

The village hall was built and opened in 1987, due mainly to fund-raising efforts by the villagers. The school, which was built in 1817 for 36 pupils, is now a private house and the children of the village go to Amport school.

The village used to have a public house, but this was destroyed by fire in the late 1920s. The Marquis of Winchester, who then owned virtually the whole village, gave the villagers a choice of a new pub or a water supply for the village. The villagers chose the water supply, and an artesian well was dug, with a water tower. Hence the villagers who wanted something stronger walked across the fields to the Plough Inn at Grateley.

Quarley is still a small village, although a few new houses have been built over the last few years, but it remains fairly quiet and unspoiled, with a great community spirit.

Quarley church bells

🍁 ROMSEY

Romsey began as a Saxon village, but has now grown to a town. The name Romsey is probably a corruption of 'Rum's eg', which means Rum's area of dry land surrounded by marsh. The river Test and its associated waterways run through Romsey.

Romsey Abbey was founded in AD 907 and after Henry VIII closed the abbey in 1539, it was bought back by the townspeople for £100. La Sagesse convent was the home of the nuns known as the 'Daughters of Wisdom'. They arrived in June 1891, lived in the Abbey House and had an altar made of packing cases. They taught French lessons, took in boarders and ran an orphanage for up to 100 boys. They now run a wisdom centre and a care home. Many of their signs were painted by Barry Hobbs, a local artist and signwriter, responsible for many beautiful pub and shop signs in the town.

Romsey was fought over in the Civil War and there are several ghost stories from that time, including one about a soldier who was hanged from the sign that is on the wall of the Conservative Club in the square. Those who worked in the town's brewery, corn and paper mills, as well as the jam factory, all had ghost encounter stories to tell. The local theatre, the Plaza does spooky ghost walks in the darker months! There is reportedly a ghost that haunts the White Horse Hotel, wearing a white dress and drifting through the Mummers Gallery, and a young boy haunts the waterways of the town where he drowned, trying to catch eels.

Broadlands Manor was initially owned by Romsey Abbey. It was architecturally transformed in 1767 and is now owned by the Mountbatten family. Its retaining wall around the estate was made of soft local bricks, and those building it put in clay pipes to strengthen the structure. One such was there for years until a convoy of American vehicles knocked down a big portion of the wall during the Second World War.

Local signwriter Barry Hobbs did two huge murals of Prince Charles and Lady Diana, which were displayed on the roof of the Bishop Blaize pub when they drove through Romsey to honeymoon at Broadlands in 1981. Barry Hobbs recounts that his friend was butler at Broadlands and lived in the garage cottage at the back of Broadlands House. One evening Barry visited him and did a wheelspin on the gravel drive. Lord Mountbatten's valet ran out and said, 'His Lordship requests you to drive away in a more dignified manner.'

Broadlands was a source of employment for many local people who also worked as forestrymen and farm workers on the estate. Romsey boys often went beating for Mr Grass, the gamekeeper at Broadlands. They would tell stories of when the royal family came down. Prince Philip was known for his colourful language when talking to the hunting dogs!

Another famous owner of Broadlands was Lord Palmerston (1784-1865), the Prime Minister, who was born and lived there. A statue of Lord Palmerston was erected in 1867 in the town square. In the early 1960s there were subterranean toilets at the front of the town hall. One day a lad from Romsey thought it would be funny to paint footprints from Lord Palmerston's statue, down the stairs and into the toilets!

The railway arrived in Romsey in 1847. It was a departure point for soldiers going to fight in both world wars and horses arrived there to be taken up to the Romsey Remount Depot at Pauncefoot Hill, a vast military village where they were trained and prepared to support the fighting and war effort.

Then, in 1864, a corn exchange where grain could be bought and sold was built and in 1866 a new town hall was built, with signwriter Barry Hobbs more recently painting the gold leaf mayor board.

In 1858 Thomas Strong purchased a brewery in Romsey and renamed it Strong; in 1886 David Faber brought two more breweries under the Strong and Co. name. For nearly a century Strong's brewery was a major employer in Romsey but it closed in 1981; local men and boys for generations worked for the company. Strong's lorries would load with beer and would stop at the transport café that is now the Water Margin restaurant.

The waterways of Romsey are ancient and have developed from streams connecting to and from the river Test, creating almost an island of Romsey. The waterways had several purposes – the streams were needed to drive the mills and it is said that Cromwell developed the Middlebridge stream to provide water for his soldiers, fighting during the Civil War. The waterways also served to provide water and drainage for the Abbey Fishlake, today an important nature reserve. Reggie Edmunds used to live along the Fishlake footpath by the railway tunnel; he kept animals and the locals took leftovers to feed his pigs. He gave the children chocolate in return. The river was a great place for fishing. It was full of roach, pike and eels. In the 1880s, storm water drains were dug in Romsey but there were no sewers in the town until the 1930s.

SELBORNE

The name Selborne originates from the Old English pre-7th-century words 'sealh', meaning sallow and 'burna', a stream, the place name first being recorded in AD 903.

Most noted for being the birthplace of Gilbert White, the famous naturalist, and where he lived and wrote his famous book, *The Natural History and Antiquities of Selborne* (never out of print since its first publication in 1789 and a first edition commanding a price of around £3,000), visitors come from miles around to see the museum and to venture up the zig zag walk, cut out by hand from the steep side of Selborne hangar by Gilbert and his brother in 1753.

Selborne Common at the top of the hangar is a good site for high summer butterflies, notably silver washed fritillaries, and nearby Noar Hill (a medieval chalk workings site, now a nature reserve managed by the Hampshire and IOW Wildlife Trust) is a thriving habitat for the brown hairstreak and Duke of Burgundy as well as the pretty holly blue. More particularly, it is home to the only British species of the curious fairy shrimp which survives in puddles on the tracks. It is carpeted with cowslips in spring and as well as being home to many chalk loving flora species, its chief pride are the eleven species of beautiful, delicate orchids, which paint the hill with purpling colour in early summer. The colony of musk orchids of about 10,000 is of national importance.

Alongside the Gilbert White exhibition in the Wakes museum is the equally fascinating exhibition dedicated to Captain Lawrence Oates, who was part of the tragically fatal *Terra Nova* expedition led by Captain Scott to the Antarctic from 1910-1912. This moving display charts his intriguing life and the fated course of the expedition with original artefacts from it and remarkable film footage taken by the expedition cameraman, Herbert Ponting. It is a distinctive and worthwhile exhibition.

The village church was founded in Saxon times but the present building with its Norman tower and nave dates back to 1180. Its famous 1,400 year old yew (with the greatest recorded girth), blown down in the storms of 1990, is reborn in a sapling sited opposite the porch, due to a judicious cutting. The church is home to a beautiful stained-glass window installed in 1920 as a memorial to Gilbert White, showing St Francis with aspects of the village in the background, preaching to all the local birds referred to in White's book.

Back in the village hall is another crowning glory; the Celebration Window. This astonishing and beautiful piece of glass art work, created by Lorraine Smith, was a project started in 2003 and finished in 2005 and represents a huge and varied cross section of village life. It is designed to depict Selborne's past, present and future. The artist held workshops and involved people in the village

Gilbert White Museum, Selborne

to realise visions of life in and around the village. These were translated into a glass collage of images representing local buildings, societies, associations, institutions, activities, people, nature and places of interest. It is a stunning and inspirational piece of art of which the village may be justly proud.

SHALDEN

The heading for a newspaper article from 1970 about Shalden was: 'Shalden – the Sleeping Beauty village has its own magic'. Shalden had obviously not changed as much as many villages have during the past 50 years and this is because of one important fact: no main road passes through the village proper.

It is however divided into two parts, the old original village and the much more modern part that follows the Old Odiham Road. This joins onto the new Odiham Road and heads north to Odiham – the junction being marked by a famous pub called the Golden Pot (one of the tales about the Golden Pot is that when Charles II was there, he needed a lavatory and was given a golden pot to use!).

The original part of Shalden is just over three miles north of Alton, the road climbing all the time to one of the highest parts of Hampshire. The centre of the village is positioned in a shallow valley, hence the name – the shallow dene or shallow valley.

At the southern end of Shalden lies the church, which replaced the Saxon building in 1865, financed by the generosity of the squire. It is small and seats about 150 persons. The old font has been retained together with silver chalice and paten cover that date from 1628. The nephew of Gilbert White, the naturalist who was the incumbent at Selborne, was one of the clerics and a close connection was kept between the two families.

Jane Austen mentioned Shalden in a letter to her sister Cassandra in 1883. Her brother Edward Knight sold the manor of Shalden to John Wood in 1840.

The earliest remains of this area, field banks called lynchets, date from the Iron Age and have been found at Shalden Park and Gregory's Wood. To the west of the present village there was a Roman settlement which is mentioned in the Domesday Book.

There are several notable buildings in the village. In the south is the Lodge where Joachim von Ribbentrop (1893-1946), German diplomat and foreign minister of Nazi Germany), stayed with the Wingfield family. This family were Blackshirts who were sympathetic to the Nazis and eventually a policeman called Inspector Case arrested them and they were deported to South Africa. All the guns were thrown down a well. Mr Cass later retired to Shalden.

Opposite the Lodge is the Manor House where Charles II is said to have stayed the night. He also held a manorial court in the field next to the present village hall, which is now positioned on the other main village street. The house that now stands there is called Court.

On the western side of the village street, north of the manor is a glorious tithe barn that dates from about the 15th century. Adjoining this building is the site of a hop field. At the T-junction is a most picturesque house called the Old Forge, with a long green lawn in front of it that used to be the village green.

One of the most historic and oldest houses in the village is the Old Cottage which is situated adjacent to the church. It was constructed over 400 years ago and contains many remarkable stout timbers and oak beams. It probably stands on the site of an even more ancient habitation, for a large stone plaque of indeterminate date, and hardly legible, records the wording of an original Domesday Book entry which noted that Shalden was held by four freemen of King Edward; they paid a geld of five hides, there were six ploughs in the demise and its inhabitants included eleven villeins and eight serfs.

Close to the centre of the village is the sports field, donated by Charlie Bury, where cricket and football were played. Heading east up Southwood Road is the Old School House, now a private dwelling, and further along the Old Post Office. Of course with modern transport, these buildings are no longer used for their original function and are private dwellings. In fact, it is most noticeable that almost every house in this charming village has been extended, which keeps village life vibrant. In the 1930s the other part of Shalden was added – the golf course and some of the houses in the Old Odiham Road.

At the beginning of the 20th century, the railway was built from Alton to Basingstoke, which passed close to Shalden but is now sadly defunct.

Two families have been responsible for much of the village life, the Harts and Trapauds. Reggie Hart organised the building of the village hall and his wife started the WI, which is still going today. Their son John continued to be a notable villager, being a member of the Inner Magic Circle. Another villager who added much to the life of the village was the late Mike Trapaud.

John Hart said that to have been born an Englishman is to have won first prize in the lottery of life, but to be a true winner it is necessary to live in Shalden.

Shedfield

Shedfield parish is made up of three villages – Shedfield, Shirrell Heath and Waltham Chase. However for much of their history, this was an area of scattered farms and smallholdings and it was only in Georgian and Victorian times that the formal elements of a village such as a church or school were first built. One of the great factors in its growth over the last 200 years was the quality of the soil, influencing the growth of market gardening and serving the growing conurbations of Portsmouth and Southampton.

Evidence of early settlement comes from a large find of Mesolithic flints and axes (8000 BC) in Sandy Lane. There is also Bronze Age evidence (2000 BC) of settlement when burnt mounds were excavated also in Sandy Lane as part of the extension of the Meon Valley golf course in the late 1980s. Also in fields near to Sandy Lane, one of the largest Roman kiln sites in southern England was excavated in 1989 with 27 kilns revealed. The site of the kilns is not far from the important Roman road which ran from Portchester to Winchester via Wickham. Evidence of it can still be seen clearly as it crosses the golf course.

The name of the village, Shedfield, comes from the Anglo Saxon, 'scida' meaning a split piece of wood or board and 'felda' meaning open fields. This may relate to a wooden footbridge on the Roman road crossing the streams in the parish. The village used to be known as Shidfield but Victorian sensibilities changed it to its present name.

The only Tudor house in the parish is Spencer Place in Sandy Lane which was built in 1492 and retains a timber frame, some of the original window frames and wattle and daub walls.

Shedfield House and the surrounding land appears in the records of the Bishop of Winchester from the early 13th century but only some features from the 16th century survive and most of the house is a mix of Georgian, Victorian and Edwardian additions. From 1866 until recent years it was home to the Phillimore family who also owned the surrounding estate. Much of the land is now part of the Meon Valley Hotel and Country Club.

It was in the same period, that some of the elements of a formal village began to be created. The original village centre, including the first post office (18th century), was along the Botley Road between the entrances to Sandy Lane and St Anne's Lane, as Old Shidfeld Lane is now called.

Important in the early development of the village was James George Crabbe who in 1832 retired from the East India naval service and married. He had been given Shidfield Lodge as a wedding present in 1834. He gave the village its first school for boys in Church Copse. When in 1861 plans were made for a mixed school his wife gave the land on which Shedfield school was built. This church school was taken over by the county and in 1990 the school moved to a new building in Solomon's Lane, Waltham Chase.

Shedfield Lodge in St Anne's Lane remains and is now a large care home. During the Second World War, it was requisitioned as were a number of large houses in the village and in the run-up to D-Day was the Brigade Headquarters of the 9th Canadian Brigade.

A redbrick chapel of ease was built on common land in 1829 and was generally welcomed by the community though it became redundant after 51 years because it was considered inadequate for the health and comfort of parishioners. The remains of this are in the churchyard and after a major renovation programme in the 1990s it is now a listed building called the Old Tower. It was opened by Chris Packham in 1999 and is home to a colony of bats.

In 1875, a new church began construction with a major financial contribution of £1,000 from Frederick Townsend of Shedfield Lodge – as long as the walls were not plastered. The architect was John Coulson whose family lived at Hall Court and the design is considered to be one of his best. The foundation stone of 1875 is to be found under the east window. He had planned a spire but there was insufficient money and eventually this was given by Mrs Franklyn in 1887. The original six bells were given by Mrs Franklyn and the first peal was on 30 November 1891. Two more bells were added in 1941 and their first peal in 1942 celebrated the Battle of El Alamein. The organ, installed in 1885, is in regular use. The latest addition to the church, dedicated by the Bishop of Portsmouth in September 2003, is the Study Centre which was the lifelong ambition of the Rev Geoffrey Morrell, vicar of this parish for 25 years. To mark the Millennium the Parish Embroidery was stitched by ladies of the parish and is displayed on the north wall beside what is thought to be one of the oldest Mothers' Union banners.

A famous villager was Mrs Mary Townsend who founded the Girls Friendly Society on 1 January 1875 – by 1880 it had 40,000 members. The focus was on protection and girls away from home in service or factory work were given accommodation and mentors to take them under their wing.

New Place was built in 1906, designed by E.L. Lutyens, and includes plastering and woodwork from J. Langtons in Bristol. Gertrude Jekyll designed the garden and in 1908 Mrs Franklyn gave the house to her son as a wedding present. It was sold in 1956 and became a school and in 1978 a conference centre. At least 13 market gardeners rented from the estate before it was sold.

An important facility which attracts Scouts and young people from across the south of England is Lyons Copse in Sandy Lane, home to an activity centre run by the Scout Association. It has gone from strength to strength with the original twelve acres now 38! A smaller, but also, active centre for Guides is nearby. Both were acquired with the help of Richard Phillimore.

SHEET

The village of Sheet in Hampshire is situated within the boundary of the South Downs National Park, its nearest neighbour the town of Petersfield a mile away. Sheet was originally a small village with traditional houses surrounding the village green, but a steady development of housing during the last 30 years has transformed the area around the village.

The heart of the village is the triangular green, the centrepiece being the magnificent chestnut tree that was planted in 1897 to commemorate Queen Victoria's diamond jubilee. The village consists of the church, two public houses, the village hall, a primary school and a pre-school for the under-fives.

The church of St Mary Magdalen stands at the top end of the village, and celebrated its 150th birthday in 2018. The primary school was founded in 1888 in the centre of the village but moved to the present position ten years later in School Lane.

The village hall is run by the parish council and is the centre of many activities. There is also a film club held regularly and Scouts, Guides and Cub associations. Although a small village, there is a thriving community which makes it a very pleasant place to live in and to visit, with many beautiful walks around the surrounding villages.

SHERBORNE ST JOHN

The name Sherborne probably means 'clear stream' and certainly there is a stream running through, and no fewer than three duckponds. There has been a settlement here for a very long time and Roman remains have been found in many places.

It must have been larger too, as at one time there were seven alehouses. Now there is only one, the Swan, which is over 500 years old and is still thatched. Just round the corner from the Swan stands the Haye. This has one of Lutyens' earliest extensions and it is said that you can tell it is Lutyens' work because you can't see out of the windows! It was once a Quaker meeting house and some of their graves have been found not only in the garden and under the kitchen floor but in the grounds of the school next door.

At Numbers 6 and 8 West End is a rare example of a Wealden house, of the kind which is usually found in Kent and Sussex. It is thought to be unique in Hampshire and dates back to 1450. Next door to this is Cleeves, which used to be the village brewhouse but which is now a pleasant home. Legend has it that hidden in a well in the garden is the treasure of Vasco da Gama, though what he could have been doing here is difficult to imagine!

The beautiful village church of St Andrew dates back in part to 1150. After the siege of Basing House, Cromwell is supposed to have given two of Basing's bells to Sherborne St John. Whether this is true or not is unknown, but it is a fact that Sherborne has two pre-Reformation bells and Basing has none. There is also a chained *Foxe's Book of Martyrs* which is rare in a village church. A most entertaining stone stands by the church porch and is to the memory of George Hickson who:-

> '… had lived above 20 years in the service of William Chute Esq. as whipper in and huntsman and continued after he died in the family as coachman …'

He may not really have been a phantom coachman but there is a ghostly coach and horses which was last seen on the Kingsclere road in 1944. This

The summerhouse at The Vyne, Sherborne St John

is Smith Grindle who returns from time to time to search for his treasure in Smith's Green, not to mention the exorcism which was performed in 1923 to stop the rattling of chains in Church Path.

SHERFIELD-ON-LODDON

Sherfield-on-Loddon lies in the north of Hampshire, just off the A33. A very pretty village built around the village green, it is growing quicker than some villagers like because of government building regulations.

One of the historic buildings in the village is Longbridge Mill. In its day it was the largest corn mill in Hampshire. It was built in the 15th century and ceased working in 1977 and became derelict. The mill was restored by Mill House Inns in 1996 in return for the authorities' acceptance that it would become a restaurant with modern additions to the mill building that did not affect the milling machinery. When visitors arrive for the first time there is often surprise when they realise it is still a working mill with demonstrations of milling once a month.

For the Millennium, Sherfield-on-Loddon Women's Institute and other women from the village completed a wonderful cross stitch wall hanging depicting the main buildings and features of the village – the Four Horseshoes, White Hart, Breach Barn, the garage, shop, village hall, horse pond, Longbridge Mill, the post office, Breach Lane chapel and St Leonard's church and lychgate. These pieces of work formed the border, and, in the centre, there was a map of the village itself. This work now hangs in the village hall. It won a national WI award.

In 2016 the Village Allotment Society decided to build eight raised beds for the use of less able people who loved gardening but for whom bending was difficult. In April 2017 seeds for vegetables and wild flowers for the bees were sown. A barbecue brought everyone together and great satisfaction was enjoyed in growing and eating their own produce.

After much fund raising, St Leonard's church was extended to include a meeting room, kitchen and facilities. This is very much appreciated as the church is quite a distance from the village itself. In 2017 St Leonard's celebrated its 900th anniversary and, once again, stitchers from the village created a wonderful piece of work – an embroidery covering different aspects of services and events in the church, where it now hangs.

With commemorations taking place to remember the end of the First World War, the village is proud to acknowledge the residents who made the supreme sacrifice, in particular, Captain John Aidan Liddell who was awarded the Victoria Cross. In his memory, a service was held in 2017 (100 years after his death), attended by uniformed young airmen from the local RAF station, RAF Odiham, and a memorial stone was placed on the green opposite the post office.

Shipton Bellinger

Surrounded on three sides by Wiltshire and bordering on Salisbury Plain, Shipton Bellinger is in the Bourne Valley. The Bourne is a winterbourne and rarely sees water but when it does, Shipton Bellinger WI organise a Duck Race. On rare occasions it sees too much water and the village is flooded.

Shipton Bellinger is at the centre of a network of footpaths, bridleways and drove roads and it is on one of these footpaths that the site of the rare Brown Hairstreak butterfly can be found. These paths provide great walking, cycling, horse riding and dog walking opportunities and the forager with a plethora of blackberries, sloes, crab apples, wild apples, sweet chestnuts, mushrooms and even walnuts.

Originally a Saxon settlement called Sceaptone or Sceaptune, it gained Berringer from one of the first Norman owners. Over time this has become Shipton Bellinger. A parish of poor soil only fitted for sceap, or as we say, sheep. It remained this rural backwater, with no one lord of the manor but many tenant farmers until the Army bought Tedworth Manor and Salisbury Plain as a training area in 1892 when the storm clouds were gathering for the First World War. People poured into Shipton from all over the country to help build the barracks at Tidworth and to provide services for the Army. The village grew and grew until by 1911 there were 18 shops, a restaurant, a pub, a mineral water factory, a men's club and a laundry which washed the blankets of the soldiers. The fields around the village became the drying fields for the laundry with miles and miles of washing lines, a wonderful playground for the village children. Shipton was surrounded by tented camps used by the soldiers about to go to France and even today the landscape bears the scars of the practice trenches that they dug before they went to battle.

Shipton is now a shadow of its former self. New houses cover the old laundry site and because of its easy access to the A303 it has become a sought-after place to live. There is still a shop, a school, a pub, a church, a mobile post office and a thriving village centre. History has made its villagers independent; the parish council was formed as early as 1894. Shipton always has and still does welcome newcomers. To mark the Millennium a village book was made showing where people had started their lives. As in the past, most had been born in various parts of the country, but all seemed happy to have finally settled in Shipton Bellinger.

Shirrell Heath

Shirrell Heath derives from two features – the hill now known as Gravel Hill, which used to be called Sheer Hill, and the heath. The heath stretched as far as Biddenfield Lane and included Shirrell Fields, Shedfield common and the cemetery. Described in 1846 as 'a wild heath with here and there a few wretched huts', most of the land was later cleared and used for market gardening or sand pits.

A living was hard to make particularly in the 19th century and in November 1830 *The Times* newspaper carried an account of how 300 men met on Shedfield common 'armed with implements of husbandry' and walked towards Wickham. News travelled fast for they were soon met by two gentlemen, probably magistrates, with a detachment of military. The report says that at this point some of them became violent, whereupon three of the ringleaders were arrested and taken to Wickham to stand trial. The rest separated but made their way to Wickham in groups and then reassembled. A certain Major Campbell addressed them and asked what complaints they had. They explained very rationally that it was the lowness of their wages, upon which it was impossible to live. On being assured that the matter would be looked into, they dispersed quietly.

By the 20th century cherry and strawberry growing had become important and the cherry blossom made the village very pretty in spring. Often the cherries were taken to Portsmouth to be sold and the strawberries were taken to Wycombe station from where many went to London hotels. At this time there was a train line, sadly closed but now a popular walking route.

James George Crabbe was given Shidfield (later Shedfield) Lodge in 1834 as a wedding present.

In 1867 his daughter Elizabeth founded a cottage hospital at Hill House, Shirrell Heath. This proved so successful that the number of beds was doubled and it was agreed that a new hospital should be built as soon as the money was available. A new hospital was founded in Hospital Road but this was demolished in the 1970s and replaced by houses in Hearne Gardens named after Matron Hearne.

The 1850s were also notable for the first meetings of Methodists in Shirrell Heath which led to the building of a Primitive Methodist chapel in 1864 in Shirrell Heath. This was extended in 1917 and then pulled down and a new much larger chapel built in 1976. A similar story of development can be seen in Waltham Chase. The first Primitive Methodist chapel in Waltham Chase was built in 1869 and in 1997 a much larger chapel and study centre was built. Both chapels form part of the Meon Valley Methodist circuit which is very strong in this area.

In the late 1920s a Mr Clarke from Swanmore ran a bus through Shirrell Heath to Fareham for 10d return. On Mondays passengers travelling to Fareham market were allowed to have a crate of rabbits or chickens transported on the roof. Sometimes people stopped the bus and asked the driver if he would do some shopping for them in Fareham, such as buying a tin of paint or a matching roll of wallpaper. He waited in Fareham for about ten minutes or long enough to do any errands which had been requested. The Anzac bus was eventually taken over by the Hants and Dorset Bus Co, but for service it has never been equalled.

Quite the opposite, as in the 2010s the bus service ceased to run. Sadly the village has no services with the demise of the shop and pub. However, there are several small housing developments and the area remains a very popular rural area to live in.

South Hayling

The oldest building in South Hayling is the parish church of St Mary the Virgin. Building began in 1225 and the fabric remains today almost as the original builders left it.

One of Hayling's profitable trades in the olden days was smuggling. They used to start out on a dark night from the ferry in a four-oared gig and row over to France, and it is said they had specially made canvas bags for brandy which would be hung from ladies' crinolines and so be transported to their destination.

The number of 'real tennis' courts in the British Isles is small. The one on Hayling opened in 1912, built by Mr R. F. Marshall. There is also a tennis war memorial, now in the gallery of the clubhouse.

A large East Coast oyster company constructed oyster beds at Salterns

Creek at the end of the 19th century. The oysters were dredged up from the large beds in the Solent, brought into the creek and preserved there for the winter. A terrible winter in 1901 froze them all and the local industry died out soon after.

After the First World War Commander David Joel and his wife started a business building wooden houses. They were the pioneers of Empire Wood near Hayling station. After many appearances at the Ideal Home exhibitions they left Hayling to open a factory near London.

The golf club was founded in 1883. The Royal Hotel served as the clubhouse until the club was able to build its own. The Hayling Island golf club can boast of having the first lady captain in England. This was Mrs Howard Fairhough, who captained the ladies' golf team in about 1885. She was also the first woman to win a ladies' golf competition in England.

South Warnborough

This pretty village is situated three miles south of Odiham and six miles north of Alton. It is home to about 700 people, some of whom commute to local towns and to London as there are good railway connections at nearby Hook and access to the motorway network is within easy reach. Local work is available on the farms and other small businesses which surround the village and the beautiful and peaceful countryside also attracts retired residents.

The village was mentioned in the Domesday Book under the ancient name of Wergeborne, which had the horrific meaning, 'stream where felons were drowned' – thankfully we don't treat felons like that now!

The 11th-century church of St Andrew given by William the Conqueror to Hugh Fitzbaldric, has an unusual 14th-century wooden bell turret and many other interesting features. Recently the church has been sensitively updated to enable its use by schools, other groups and for concerts as well as worship.

The Ridley Hall is in the centre of the village and is the venue for social occasions, exercise and dancing classes as well as the parish council meetings. Every month there is a screening of one of the latest films. Children are not forgotten as there is a splendid playground and a large all-weather surface area where tennis and other sports can be played. The village fete is held annually and is well attended by locals and visitors.

There is a thriving village shop which serves food as well as being the focus of some afternoon tea clubs. The Poacher Inn offers bed and breakfast accommodation as well as serving food and hosting many evening events.

The Alton-Odiham road brings passing as well as local trade to these amenities.

The quiet country lanes attract walkers and cyclists keen to enjoy the beautiful North Hampshire scenery.

South Wonston & Worthy Down

South Wonston is not a traditional Hampshire village. Originally used as farmland, it was such poor quality that Stavedown Road is derived from 'Starve Down'. A New Stone Age barrow 97 metres long, part of an ancient burial ground, is located in Long Barrow Close. In 1892 W. Young sold the land on which the village now stands to Henry Brake, who offered 199 one acre plots for sale. These were located along the two main tracks in the village, now Downs Road and Westhill Road. Sales were slow and the electoral register of 1914 shows fewer than 30 residents in the village. Some of the early residents lived in old railway carriages on these plots until they could afford to build houses. Prominent local families, the Groves and the Wrights, have streets named after them, and the Groves family burial ground is still located in the village.

The tin tabernacle church was built in 1909 at a cost of £89 10s with the foundations costing £13. It was used until 2006 and was then transferred to the Weald and Downland Open Air Museum, opening as an exhibit in 2011. The first village hall was built in 1922 and Cloudbank stables in 1935. Even in the early 1970s there was no mains gas, most houses were not connected to the main sewers, and there was no doctor's surgery, recreation ground or bus service into the village. A village school was built in 1968, and in 1996 a church facility was built attached to the school to be used by St Margaret's and the school jointly.

South Wonston had close links with Worthy Down, although today mainly through the primary school. A two mile racetrack was built at Worthy Down, probably in the reign of Charles I, and although racing was banned under Cromwell, the racecourse flourished again under Charles II. Queen Anne was also recorded as visiting the races in 1705. Stabling for the horses was provided in Lower Road in South Wonston. Formal racing had ceased by 1896 and in 1917 the land was put to military use. In 1885 the Didcot, Newbury & Southampton railway opened and the route took it from Sutton Scotney, past Worthy Down to Winchester. Trains carrying horses would stop at Worthy Down for the racecourse, although the actual platform (which still exists today) was not built until 1917.

In 1940 the Luftwaffe bombed Worthy Down which was being used for development and test flying operations for the Spitfire after the Southampton factory was bombed. Worthy Down was considered critically important during the war and was heavily defended with a ring of 32 pillboxes in the area, several of which are still in situ in South Wonston today including some underground. Sir Ralph Richardson and Sir Laurence Olivier both served at Worthy Down, with Olivier putting on an impromptu show.

Southwick

Southwick is a very small, very old village. In 1988 the owner of the village and estate of Southwick, Mrs Eva Borthwick-Norton, died in her nineties and left it complete to a nephew, Mr R. Thistlethwaite.

The first mention of Southwick was in 1150 when the Augustinian friars found that the priory they had built at Portchester in 1129 was too small. Southwick priory itself was never very large but it was extremely influential at times, indeed the church which now is incorporated in Portsmouth Cathedral was in the priory's possession. The village church is known as 'St James without the Priory Gates', which indicates it belonged to Southwick rather than the priory.

At the Dissolution of the Monasteries, the priory and its possessions were given to a John White and the estate has passed down more or less intact since then. By the beginning of the 20th century everything in the village – school, churches, shops, pubs, as well as all the houses, belonged to 'The Squire' and so it has remained. Only the 'Big House' and the Park have gone – to the government.

A major event of the 20th century was the planning of *Operation Overlord*, D-Day, in 1944 at Southwick House. Southwick House was acquired by the Ministry of Defence and remains as HMS *Dryad*. HMS *Dryad* is very much part of Southwick, and the Navy and the village work amicably together.

The village is most attractive. Because of its single ownership all the woodwork of the cottages and smaller houses is painted the same colour. A stroll down West Street (one of the two streets) takes in five centuries of architecture – from a wattle and daub thatched cottage to Victorian flint houses. Most noticeable are the houses by the green – Tudor cottages mainly, and the 'Terrace', which runs from the Old Post Office to the Red Lion. The two pubs are both 'Lions', the Red and the Golden.

🍁 Sparsholt & Lainston

Through the centuries the histories of Sparsholt and Lainston have always been interwoven but there is one past inhabitant and benefactor who had quite a considerable bearing on the day-to-day lives of the villagers.

It was a Mr Samuel Bostock, a barrister formerly of Lainston House, who finally managed to organise a reliable water supply for the area. Before this, the villagers obtained their water from a variety of wells in and around the parishes of Sparsholt and Lainston. The chief supply came from the village well, which relied upon one or two people walking a treadmill for an arduous 20 minutes or so, to draw water from 247 ft below ground. As if this were not problem enough, long hot summers could cause the well to dry up, and villagers were known to cart barrels into Winchester in order to draw water from the river Itchen.

In 1897, to mark Queen Victoria's Jubilee, a new well house was built which disposed of the old well house and the treadmill within. In its place a brick building was erected to house a wind-assisted pump. However, over the years this still did not prove very satisfactory. Fires were frequent and several thatched cottages burned down because the water pressure was not strong enough for fire-fighting. So in 1908, Mr Bostock arranged for a piped supply from Crabwood Reservoir to service Sparsholt and Lainston, as well as the neighbouring village of Littleton. The well house can still be seen today opposite the church.

The site of the village hall is again due to the generous benevolence of Samuel Bostock, and the land for the village cricket ground was donated in the same way, with the only interruption for its use coming during the war years when it was converted to a bowling green. This was presumably due to the fact that most of the men from the village were away fighting for King and Country. Today, Sparsholt Cricket Club still plays on the same ground in Locks Lane.

🍁 St Cross

St Cross is situated about three miles from the City of Winchester. The Chapel of St Cross was founded around 1135 by Henry of Blois, Bishop of Winchester and brother of King Stephen 'for the provision of thirteen poor men who are so feeble and lacking in strength that they can scarcely look after themselves without the help of others'.

Prior to Henry of Blois it was a small hamlet known as Sparkford and there are numerous references around the area, with various places having that name. However, when St Cross was established the name of Sparkford was no longer given to the hamlet.

The Hospital was placed under the care of the Knights of St John and the 13 Brothers of this foundation still wear black gowns and a badge depicting the Jerusalem Cross.

The Chapel was started in the 1160s and retains much of its Norman purity. In the 15th century Cardinal Beaufort provided the second order of almsmen known as the Noble Order of Poverty and these brothers wear magenta gowns. The Hundred Menne's Hall is where 100 poor men received their daily sustenance and was in existence in the late 14th century. The Wayfarer's dole, consisting of a small pot of ale and piece of bread, is still handed out by the porter on request during opening hours.

In 2008 a group of mothers in St Cross, whose children had moved on to secondary school, decided they missed the camaraderie at the local primary school gates and thought they might set up a WI. Another factor coming into play was to honour the memory of Caroline Benton, a much loved local mother who had died in tragic circumstances after a fire in France. After a couple of false starts for a venue they were fortunate enough to end up in the Hundred Menne's Hall – with its thick whitewashed walls and uneven floor the hall is very atmospheric. After the Christmas event, Songs and Reflections, in the chapel they make their way from the church across to the Hall and have mulled wine and mince pies for the final meeting before Christmas. During the summer they have a party and use the Master's Garden to wander round if the weather is good. The borders are very colourful during the summer months with shades particularly sensitive to the historic location and grey garden walls. There is a large deep rectangular pond in the garden covered with lilies in the summer. St Cross is frequently used as a film location and attracts historians and archaeologists.

St Mary Bourne

St Mary Bourne is in the Hampshire Highlands, the highest points of the southern range of the South Downs running a little distance away to the north of the parallel Bourne valley. The Bourne, from which three villages on its bank take their name, is an intermittent chalk stream. The volume of water has undoubtedly lessened over the centuries. Some are inclined to attribute this to springs tapped for the nearby watercress beds.

The original church of St Peter was probably a Norman building without aisles. Of this, the only parts now remaining are the chancel arch and the responds of the tower, which are of the late Norman period. The church contains several items of considerable historic interest, including what is undoubtedly one of Hampshire's greatest antique treasures – a massive font, carved eight centuries ago from black Tournai marble. An ancient part of the church has a recumbent effigy in stone of an armoured knight, whose crossed legs indicate that he had been a Crusader.

In the centre of the village is the Summerhaugh, used for festivities such as May Day, when it was decorated with hawthorn in flower, and dances took place round a maypole. The name Summerhaugh probably comes from a place by the stream where the cattle were brought down from the hill slopes in summer into an enclosure surrounded by a hedge, 'haga'.

One of the oldest houses in the Bourne valley is Butlers, a mellow brick and beam building in Gangbridge Lane. In alterations made there recently a beam dated 1590 was discovered. Another thatched cottage of interest is Mundays, which used to be the home of a rope maker. There are certainly other houses in the village dating from the early 17th century.

STEVENTON

Steventon is a small village between Winchester and Basingstoke, reached along narrow, winding country lanes, within the rolling hills of the north Hampshire countryside. It is a chalkland settlement situated near the source of the river Test, surrounded by farmland and wooded areas. It is almost totally untouched by modern development. With outlying farms and cottages, the village comprises some 80 dwellings, with a population of about 190.

The route of the London to Southampton railway runs close by the centre of the village but Steventon has never had its own station, the nearest being Micheldever, or Overton on the Salisbury line. Two routes into the village pass through low tunnels under the railway line making access a problem for large vehicles.

Steventon was mentioned in the Domesday Book, but its history goes back further, with traces of a Bronze Age settlement and several barrows in the south of the parish and small finds of Iron Age and Roman remains in the fields. The shaft of a Saxon cross stands in the Norman church, which is pre-dated by the huge yew tree standing outside.

The church, dedicated to St Nicholas, lies to the east of the village. It has hardly changed in 900 years. A spire was added to the tower in Victorian times and early 19th century murals decorate the chancel arch. Services are held on alternate Sundays and church breakfasts are held in the village hall. The Jane Austen Society of North America (JASNA) has strong connections with the village and has helped to fund various renovation projects in the church.

Jane Austen was born in Steventon in 1775 while her father was rector of the parish. Her fame attracts visitors from all over the world. She lived in Steventon until she was 25 years of age and the first versions of three of her books, *Pride and Prejudice*, *Sense and Sensibility* and *Northanger Abbey* were written during that period. Much of the inspiration for her writing must have come from her life in and around Steventon. The old rectory no longer exists, it was pulled down in the 19th century, but on the site is a large lime tree planted by her brother and the remains of the pump. There is a timeless quality about the village, little has changed since Jane's time. There are a few more houses, some smaller cottages have been joined and renovated as one, yet there are fewer people. There is no longer a village shop or tradesmen and still no main drainage or street lighting.

Jane would certainly not recognize the manor house. It has undergone three dramatic changes, the property now standing on the site near the church being a renovation of a small part of the old Victorian manor house.

In earlier years Steventon was self-sufficient with many people working in agriculture or employed locally. Today many commute to London or to other nearby towns. There are small commercial and light engineering business units at Stoken Farm and in these days of modern technology some people work from home.

There are three farms within the parish. For the most part farming is arable but Bassetts Farm has a Holstein-Friesian herd, supplying milk to Müller Dairies. Stoken Farm is arable, while Warren Farm is mixed with some beef cattle. Sheep still graze on pastures, as they did in days gone by. There are many wooded areas and shelter belts where pheasant and partridge are reared by the gamekeeper for winter shoots.

Popham airfield, in the south of the parish, is a private facility used by owners of light aircraft and microlights. It was formerly the home of the Spitfire Flying Club.

Steventon has few amenities. There has never been a public house, the nearest shop and primary school are now two miles away in North Waltham, and older children attend a variety of schools in the surrounding area. There is a bus service to Basingstoke, but only once a day on Monday, Wednesday and Friday. The old red telephone box is a Jane Austen Information Centre.

However, Steventon is fortunate to have its own parish council with five members working to resolve local issues such as planning, roads and conservation. In recent years they have built a brick and flint bus shelter, a seat around the tree on the Triangle, and have improved footpaths with gates, steps and handrails where needed. These footpaths are used by many individuals and groups walking around and through the village.

This small community comes together regularly for church, summer fetes, harvest celebrations, and most recently, in 2017, the festival to remember the 200th anniversary of the death of its most famous resident, Jane Austen. The village hall, built in 1932, is central to village life with many activities taking place there. Also meeting in the hall are the Steventon Singers, a community choir who meet and perform regularly, and the Steventon Players who perform pantomimes or other entertainment for the whole village. Steventon Strummers are an enthusiastic band of ukulele players who play for pleasure and at various village events.

Although there are very few facilities Steventon has a strong sense of community – people do not move away without good reason. As in Jane Austen's day, life is still made up of friends and neighbours joining together to celebrate happy events and giving help in difficult times.

🍁 STROUD

Once part of the parish of East Meon and Langrish, then of Petersfield Urban District, Stroud gained autonomy in 1994, with its own parish council. Prior to that at least one farmhouse was divided down the middle between the two areas and received not only two sets of utility bills but two sets of voting papers. The land, which is heavy clay and tends to be wet, was once part of two local estates, the Legge Estate and Basing Park, and subsequently some tenant farmers were able to buy their farms, and the families are still there. In the past the farms were mostly dairy, but now they have diversified into sheep, arable and beef.

The very heavy clay was ideal for making bricks and a thriving brickyard was on the site of the present garage and the houses behind. The bricks were used to build many of the village houses and were stamped with the company's logo, a cat's paw.

The First World War tin hut, which served as the village hall for many years, and housed both WIs, has been demolished. It was commandeered during the last war for use as a mess hall for the POW camp behind, housing mainly Italian and Austrian prisoners who worked on the local farms. One of the Austrians returned after the war and cycled along the A272 until he recognized the farm where he had worked. He bought a derelict barn and turned it into a very successful art gallery. After his death this was turned into a private house.

Stroud had its own policeman for many years, as well as a post office which is now a private house. A speed limit through the village is very welcome with the increase in traffic. The Seven Stars now caters for more passing trade as well as the locals, and the WI bench and tree which were in the forecourt have been moved to the very popular recreation ground behind the school, which was moved to the village from Langrish in the early 1900s and is flourishing, bucking the trend for rural schools.

Being part of East Meon parish, Stroud had no church until one was built to commemorate Queen Victoria's Golden Jubilee, although there was a Primitive Methodist chapel which later became a hen house and is now converted into a human habitation.

The site of the Roman buildings has been excavated over the years and what was assumed to be a small Roman villa is now thought to be a much larger complex. The excavations are still on-going.

Stroud is a happy, busy village with a flourishing play group and an old people's home and many events throughout the year. New housing is planned, and with a new hall the village will have a central meeting place again.

Sway

Estate agents describe Sway as a village in the heart of the New Forest. In fact it sprawls untidily on the southern edge of the forest.

For centuries a poor living was scraped from smallholding, farming and seasonal forest work. Smuggling and poaching were rife and in about 1777 the vicar of Boldre, whose parish then included Sway, described his parishioners as 'little better than bandits'.

The opening of the Brockenhurst to Christchurch section of the London & South Western Railway in 1888 changed the village in more ways than one.

Prosperity was increased as businessmen moved in. They built houses, providing more local employment for labourers, craftsmen and domestic servants. Also two local roads were renamed Manchester Road and Brighton Road as a reminder of the railway gangs from those towns.

Sway has grown round the church, railway station and school and has not expanded so much as filled in. It is fortunately limited on two sides by the boundaries of the forest. There are no ancient buildings in the village, though there are a few cob cottages. A local landmark is Peterson's Tower, designed by Andrew Peterson on his retirement from India. It is 218 ft high and built of mass concrete by unskilled labourers who were paid five shillings a day. It was finished in 1885 and still stands straight and true.

Local myths associate Sway with docks and treacle mines! Ironic references to these among the older generation can be heard today. The origin of these myths is not known. However, it is interesting to note that there is a house called 'Switchells' built on the site of Switchells coppice and according to *The Chambers Dictionary* the definition of 'switchel' is treacle-beer.

The Worldhams

Near Alton lies the village of East Worldham, situated dramatically on the top of an escarpment. The old road from Selborne to Binsted, now visible as two lanes, crosses the Kingsley to Alton road at East Worldham. Philippa Chaucer, wife of the poet Geoffrey Chaucer, is said to be buried in the pretty church at East Worldham, and the coffin lid from her tomb, found in the chancel, is in a niche in the church. Chaucer's son was lord of the manor at Worldham and Keeper of Woolmer Forest. A wooded mound, visible from the main road and called King John's Hill, is the site of a royal hunting lodge.

Away from the main road and about a mile and a half through peaceful countryside is West Worldham. Here the little church, medieval in origin, adjoins a 16th-century manor farmhouse. There is more history at Hartley Mauditt, still within the parish, where a few mounds in the soil mark a vanished village. St Leonard's church remains with its Norman architecture, delightfully situated beside a lake.

The Worldhams still cherish a strong sense of identity. Highlight of the year is the Fete and Flower Show. A Parish Walk takes place on Rogation Sunday.

The Worthys

The Worthy villages of Abbots Worthy, Headbourne Worthy, Kings Worthy and Martyr Worthy, lie just to the north of Winchester and along the valley of the river Itchen. These settlements and their fertile lands were, at various times, the possessions of royalty, the church, and great families. They are recorded in Saxon charters, the Domesday survey, and legal, public and personal documents over more than a thousand years. The archaeological interest of the area is considerable, including Iron Age sites, the remains of a Roman villa and a pagan cemetery from Saxon times. For many centuries the main business of the Worthy villages was agriculture. The censuses which were taken every ten years recorded most males as 'ag lab' – agricultural labourer. They worked for the owners of Bull Farm, Woodhams Farm, Hookpit Farm and Pudding Farm. They lived in substantial cottages, and gradually more specialised craftsmen and artisans found work as farriers, metalworkers, carpenters, joiners, to name but a few.

Other features that put the villages on the map were the churches and their location on the main route from Winchester to London. Headbourne Worthy church still contains the site of an important stone carving of the Rood, dating from the 10th century. And the Cart and Horses pub continues to serve refreshments to visitors, as it has since the 18th century.

The Victorian age saw great expansion and change in the villages, thanks in part to the arrival of the railway in Winchester. Successful entrepreneurs settled here and built substantial houses, for example Hinton House, Morton House, Kings Worthy Grove, Northleigh and The Cottage on London Road. The population of the Worthys has grown from less than a thousand before 1900 to around 7,000 and still counting in 2018. This is largely the result of the growth of Springvale in the mid-20th century and the continuing development all over the area up to the present. Headbourne Worthy is notable for being the home of three famous residents in the 1940s. Laurence Olivier and Vivien Leigh lived on School Lane while Olivier was a pilot at Worthy Down. Olivier had the reputation of being brave, full of mischief and a rule-breaker. He left Headbourne Worthy in order to star in, produce and direct *Henry V*. The third famous resident was *Lovely Cottage*, the winner of the 1946 Grand National.

Not famous, but well recorded in the history of Kings Worthy, was the woman who lived in a hole. She was Mrs Yoland Span, a well-educated woman who spoke several languages and had worked as an interpreter in the First World War. She was a widow and arrived in 1923, having bought a plot on Lovedon Lane where she lived in a wooden hut with her son Louis. They set up a smallholding with goats, chickens and some geese. Things changed when Louis decided to emigrate to Australia, and Yoland's life deteriorated until she was living in a hole about 3ft deep with a corrugated iron and wooden structure making a sloping roof over it. Newspapers were piled up to make a floor, with sacks on one side for a bed. There was a tin box oven on which she cooked, and tins and jars piled up high. After the war she acquired a Red Cross ambulance and a fish and chip van, but instead of living in one of them she used one to house her animals and the other as a food store. She took goats' milk, cheese and eggs to customers in Winchester in an old pram. Her unusual lifestyle must have suited her, for she lived into her eighties, dying in 1957 after a short illness.

In the last 40 years or so Abbots Worthy and Martyr Worthy have altered very little, but Kings Worthy and Headbourne Worthy are physically joined together and the population has doubled. The area has become quite suburban, with many residents commuting to London and Southampton. There are now two community halls as well as St Mary's chapel and the church rooms, which are both used for various classes and meetings. The sports and social club is another place to gather, with premises on the recreation ground. Kings Worthy is fortunate enough to have two post offices, a pharmacy, two general stores and a farmshop cum café, as well as a coffee shop and one which caters for fishermen and other outdoor pursuits. All in all this is a very pleasant place in which to live.

Thorney Hill & Bransgore

In the mid 1800s the areas of Thorney Hill and Bransgore were mainly farming communities and included the hamlets of Neacroft, Godwinscroft, Bockhampton and Waterditch. There were also a few large family estate houses, including Avon Tyrrell House, belonging to the Manners family and today Grade I listed. Bransgore was originally called Bransgrove and legend has it that the 'brans' part meant brains and the 'gore' blood. This seems to date back to the battles of King Alfred but is probably not true!

Somewhat surprisingly there were three churches and three public houses in Bransgore plus a village school, all of which still stand today. Henry William Wilberforce, son of the anti-slavery campaigner, was once vicar of St Mary's church and he also founded Bransgore school in 1841. There were several corner shops scattered about but sadly none of those exist any longer. The church of All Saints in Thorney Hill was built in 1906 by the Manners family for their own use and for the local residents. Paintings by Phoebe Anna Traquair adorn the interior of the church with faces of the Manners children depicted in amongst them. There was also a school in Thorney Hill but with the advent of extensions to Bransgore school in the 1970s the school was sold and is now a private house.

Another large family property was Bransgore House and at least one local resident whose family now own MacPennys, the garden centre, remembers working on a farm as a Land Girl during the Second World War and going with the milk churns full of milk to be poured into jugs provided by the maids of the house. Bransgore House still stands and is now divided into private flats.

Brickmaking was one of the early sources of work in Bransgore as there were two areas of clay pits essential for the production of bricks. Many of the bricks used in construction work in Bournemouth were from the Bransgore Brick Works.

Smuggling was a big part of the history of the New Forest and Bransgore would have been en route from the sea at Christchurch to Burley and beyond. A lady known as Lovey Warne used to stand on high ground at Burley wearing a red cloak to warn the smugglers of excise men in the area.

During the Second World War there was a lot of activity in and around the forest, some of it at Thorney Hill hidden well in among the trees. There is an impressive Airfields Memorial just off Forest Road where a service is held each year to commemorate all those who served locally. Additionally in the nearby village of Sopley there was an army and air force camp housing many servicemen and women well into the 1970s. During the war there was an extensive underground radar station as part of the camp which was eventually sealed off during the 1980s.

Bransgore today is a thriving and lively community with many new housing estates, two doctors' surgeries, a school with an excellent Ofsted report, a village hall with both indoor and outdoor activities and a comprehensive parade of shops meeting everyone's needs including an excellent coffee house jointly run by the churches and manned by volunteers.

The areas of Thorney Hill and Bransgore, with the arrival of several housing estates, are part of a thriving and lively community offering facilities and activities for all ages. The New Forest and the beaches are a short distance away and the larger towns of Bournemouth and Southampton are within easy reach, with train and coach services to London and beyond nearby. It is a brilliant place to live whether you are nine or 90.

🍁 Thruxton

Lying just to the north of the busy A303, Thruxton is a name familiar to those interested in gliding or car and motor-cycle racing. These events are held at the former Second World War airfield situated just to the west of the village and where there is also a busy little industrial estate.

Unlike the racing circuit, the village proper can hardly be seen from the main road. The centre of the village was declared a conservation area in 1985. There are many listed buildings, including cob boundary walls traditionally capped with thatch or tile. The village green, the seasonal stream and the surrounding houses, epitomise the idea of the English village.

Standing boldly in the centre of the village is the chapel of this former Wesleyan stronghold. It was built in 1875 and opinions differ as to its architectural merits. After the First World War it became the village Memorial Hall. It still hosts the full gamut of community activities.

The church of St Peter and St Paul dates back to the 13th century but much of what we see today is a result of 19th-century rebuilding and recent restoration.

Inside are a few treasures. Of particular note is a magnificent brass portrait of Sir John de Lisle, lord of the manor, who died in 1407.

Beyond the village there is evidence of Bronze and Iron Age occupation and traces of two Roman buildings have been discovered, the more important at Mullenspond. This was possibly a temple dedicated to Bacchus who is depicted on the mosaic pavement found under the rubble in 1823. In 1899 the owner of the site presented the mosaic and the terracotta candelabrum found at the same time, to the British Museum, where they can still be viewed.

Today it is wildlife found at Mullenspond which is of particular interest and fiercely protected. The present pond was created during the Second World War when gravel was excavated to lay the runways at the airfield. It naturalised quickly to become an outstanding feature of the locality and many villagers monitor the impressive variety of birds who use it as a home, or as a temporary stop.

🍁 Titchfield

The village of Titchfield has a long and chequered history. To celebrate it, one local woman conceived and co-ordinated a plan to record it in intricate and splendid detail.

Tessa Short found a local artist, John Harper, to design historical scenes of the past 2,000 years. She approached the Solent Stitchers and other local people, who used their varied skills to recreate the characters and events of the village past and present. The result can be seen, displayed in six panels of beautiful needlework, in the Parish Rooms.

Tessa Short, a former Mayor of Fareham, planned the tapestries as a community millennium project. Work started in 1998, on Tessa's dining table. The Stitchers prepared the background, on to which were added the buildings, banners, horses, coaches and characters, made by other volunteers. They worked using embroidery, stump work, collage, bead work, tapestry and metal work. The materials were gathered from local people, who posted through Tessa's letter-box old jewellery, buttons, ribbon, feathers, fabrics and beads. After hours of painstaking work creating authentic scenes in minute detail, the panels were completed in 2000.

Many women feature on these panels, some as important visitors, and others as notable residents of more recent years.

Titchfield has been frequently honoured by visits by Queens of England. Anne of Bohemia, wife of Richard II, came in 1393. She introduced the high horned hat to ladies of the court, and set the fashion for riding side-saddle. When Margaret of Anjou came to the Abbey in 1445, at the age of 15, to marry Henry VI, the wooden bridge at the foot of Fishers Hill was strengthened with stone, and is known as the Anjou Bridge. When the king suffered psychotic episodes later in life, she ruled the kingdom in his place but following the civil war and the death of her husband and only son, she was exiled and died in poverty in France.

In 1569, Elizabeth I visited the 2nd Earl of Southampton at Place House. His wife, Mary Browne, is one of many suggested as being Shakespeare's mysterious 'Dark Lady'. Another was her son, the 3rd Earl, who was Shakespeare's patron. The 4th Earl was a friend of Charles I, who brought his new wife, Henrietta Maria, to visit. She proved to be a strong and committed wife; during the ensuing Civil War, she led an army to Oxford, where she was styled 'Her She-Majesty, Generalissima'. The Queen's House at Greenwich was re-styled for her.

The pub sign at the Queen's Head, in the centre of the village, bears testimony to the visit of Catherine of Braganza in 1675. Wife of Charles II, she introduced the fashion of tea drinking to society. She had no surviving children, but had to suffer her husband's philandering, and his fathering at least twelve children out of wedlock. A devout Catholic, she returned to her native Portugal when William and Mary came to the throne.

The owner of Place House in 1741, Peter Delme MP, developed an extravagant life-style, incurring heavy debts. His wife, Lady Elizabeth Howard, known as Lady Betty, was made of sterner stuff. After her husband died, by astute management she was able to rebuild Cams Hall in Fareham using material from the dilapidated Place House. In 1777, she sat for a sumptuous portrait by Joshua Reynolds.

Achievements of local women were rarely well-recorded, but Dame Hart is one of the earliest, and is remembered for establishing the first village school in 1751. She taught local children reading and the useful arts of knitting and spinning.

The fortunes of Titchfield fluctuated over the years, and social benefactors feature in the tapestry. One was Charlotte Hornby, member of a renowned local family, shown distributing provisions to the poor.

Dr Margaret Dunton has worked as a doctor in the Titchfield area since 1961. As a committee member of the Titchfield Village Trust, she led the 1970s 'Traffic Organisation'. Their aim was to stop heavy lorries driving through the village. She organised lawful public action along South Street causing traffic to come to a halt and thereby attracting local media. Margaret and her team worked with planners to develop the new eastern bypass, diverting heavy traffic away from the village. Margaret is still a member of TVT and felt honoured to be in the tapestry.

Rita Prior has always played an active part of village life. From its inception in 1972, she was a controller organising the Friday WI Market whose aim was to sell locally grown produce and provide refreshments. It quickly became a place to meet friends and purchase local goods. In the 1970s, Doreen Evans (1923-2009) became the village pharmacist. She was on the PCC of St Peter's church, helping in many practical ways, and was recognised for her work in the village by receiving the Queen's Maundy Money. In 1999 she was Citizen of the Year in Fareham Borough Council.

Apart from instigating the Titchfield Tapestries, Tessa Short was a borough councillor for the Titchfield Ward and Mayor of Fareham in 1994. She has been involved in many important Titchfield village schemes, including helping to set up the Titchfield Christmas Trees, arranging to have the local sarsen stones moved for safe keeping to the village, instigating and winning the Best Kept Village competition for two years, and buying the village clock with the prize money.

All these splendid women can be seen on the tapestries when the parish rooms are open for Country Markets on a Friday morning. Titchfield WI would also be willing to arrange a viewing on request.

Twyford

Twyford, four miles south of Winchester, gets its name from the two fords across the river Itchen, world famous for its trout fishing. Today the village is bisected by the busy B3335 and the villagers would welcome two crossing places. However, the installation of traffic lights in the centre of the village has eased the crossing problem.

The present church of St Mary was rebuilt in 1878, but it incorporates the 12th-century nave arcades and the font. A window in the north wall dates back to 1520. Under the tower are twelve stones in a circle. These, combined with a well and an ancient yew tree, are said to provide the circle, wood and water needed for Druidic worship. The yew tree was mentioned in the Domesday Book.

The whole village is full of history. A Roman villa was unearthed, at the top of Roman Road, in 1891. The Dolphin Inn is reputedly an 18th-century coaching inn on the London to Southampton route. Twyford House also dates back to the early 18th century. It belonged to the Shipley family. Bishop Jonathan Shipley, Bishop of St Asaph, invited his friend Benjamin Franklin, the American statesman, to stay in 1771 and it was there that he wrote part of his memoirs.

Brambridge House stands on the edge of the village. The original house burned down in 1872, but the avenue of limes leading to the house was planted in the reign of Charles II. Brambridge House was the family home of Maria Smythe who, as the widowed Mrs Fitzherbert, contracted a morganatic marriage with the Prince Regent in December 1785.

The village has memories of various wars. The barn at Manor Farm was used to quarter troops during the Civil War. Army Row was built to house veterans of Waterloo. In the First World War troops were encamped on Hazeley Down, and in the Second World War Canadian soldiers were billeted in the village.

The only surviving custom is the Bell Ringers' Feast. Legend has it that William Davis was returning home on horseback over the downs when the mist came down. The bells of Twyford church warned him that he was on the edge of a deep chalk pit.

In his will he left a guinea to the bell ringers so long as they rang a peal morning and evening on 7th October. The bells are rung accordingly and the bell ringers enjoy supper together afterwards.

The footpaths by the Itchen Navigation Canal and others leading up over the chalk downs reveal a wealth of plants, birds and insects and contribute to the pleasure of living in Twyford.

Upper Clatford

Upper Clatford lies one and a quarter miles south of Andover. It is a most delightful village with a beautiful church and the river Anton flowing through the valley.

It was probably during the reign of Henry I (1100-1135) that the church of All Saints was first built. Its massive columns and round arches are typical of the first half of the 12th century. The church was partly rebuilt in the 16th century and the building transformed into an 'auditory church' in the 17th century.

The fine house known as Red Rice stands in the parish of Upper Clatford, having been built by General Webb in about 1740. General Webb was one of the Duke of Marlborough's subordinates, and it is said that the trees in the park surrounding the house represent the troop line-up at the battle of Malplaquet in 1709.

Bury Hill hillfort has no known history, unlike its famous neighbour Danebury Ring four miles away. Some exploration was carried out in the 1930s but did not bring forth much information.

A famous feature of Anna Valley (also part of the parish) was the well-known firm of Taskers which for more than 160 years provided employment for many local people. Founded in 1873 by three brothers, the foundry manufactured cottage pumps, agricultural machinery, steam engines, iron bridges (one is still in use today in the village by Fishing Cottage) and, during the Second World War, aeroplane trailers large enough to carry complete aeroplanes for the RAF.

The Tasker brothers provided housing, a school, church and a workman's rest for the people of Anna Valley. The school house can still be seen, called the Lodge. It has become one of the many listed properties in the parish, many being beautiful thatched cottages several hundred years old, including the post office and the village pub, the Crook and Shears.

Upton Grey

The village was formed from two Anglo-Saxon manors, called Aoltone and Odingetone in the 1086 Domesday Book. By the late Middle Ages they had become Upton and Hoddington respectively. John de Grey, one of King William's knights, owned the manor in the late 13th century and when he died in 1272 he left his surname affixed to Upton. Long before the Anglo-

Saxons were here, the Romans left their mark by building a road from Calleva Atrebatum (Silchester) to Noviomagvs (Chichester), passing close to both manor houses on the way.

In August 1601 Queen Elizabeth was on one of her progresses, which she used to undertake in order to get out of a stinking London in the summer. She travelled from Basing House to South Warnborough, via her hunting lodge, now Bidden Farm, a mile from Upton Grey. Her progress consisted of up to 400 carriages and carts as well as people on foot. Elizabeth had a lockable door on her carriage, several carts carrying items that she might want on her journey, plus a privy in a carriage in case the queen or one of her ladies in waiting was caught short. The appearance of this cavalcade on the edge of the manor must have been a mind-bending vision, which took over two hours to pass.

When the English Civil War broke out in the mid-17th century, the village found itself sandwiched between the Royalist Basing House to the north-west and Parliamentarian Farnham, with Colonel Waller in the castle, to the east. Basing House was under almost continuous siege from 1642 to 1645 and Parliamentary troops were billeted in several of the houses in the village, cannon balls were left behind, and are still here.

Some of the more notable residents of the village include Lady Dorothy Eyre, maid of honour to Queen Anne, the wife of King James I; Malachy Dudeny, nonconformist Lord of the Manor of Upton and senior revenue official throughout the Civil War; Admiral Sir William Fanshawe Martin Bart, entered the Navy aged 12 in 1813 and served with distinction until 1870; Lord Basing, a prominent member of Disraeli's cabinet in the 1870s and enobled in 1887; politician John Profumo; and actress Valerie Hobson. Henry Fielding, at one time London's leading playwright, political journalist, novelist (*Tom Jones*) and magistrate, who founded the Bow Street Runners, was banished by his father to Upton Grey, to remove him from the temptations offered by the fair sex. Amongst other things he wrote a poem entitled *A Description of U...n G... (alias New Hog's Norton) in Hants*, dedicated to a young lady called Rosalinda.

The famous Elizabethan poet George Puttenham (1529-1590) lived with his wife at Herriard House. He beat his wife and had affairs with all their maidservants, impregnating most of them. He also had a farm at Upton Grey. It was there that he kept his 17-year-old sex slave whom he had kidnapped in London. Eventually she was released when Puttenham's long-suffering wife discovered her existence. When two Royal officials came to arrest him, he had his servants tie them up in Herriard churchyard, where he beat them about the head.

St Mary's Church, Upton Grey

A church was in the manor of Upton at the time of Domesday, but the earliest parts of the present building date from the early 1100s. It is listed Grade I and has on one of its walls writing, in English, that has been dated to before 1340, and most likely reads 'For God's love beware by me'. Hoddington House probably dates from the late 17th century and is listed Grade II*. Parts of the Upton Grey manor house date from the early 15th century and it was extensively altered by Ernest Newton when owned by Charles Holme, the editor of the Arts and Crafts magazine *The Studio*, in the early 20th century. The garden was originally laid out by Gertrude Jekyll in 1908-9 and restored by the present owners.

In the 19th century the inhabitants of the village were almost all engaged in rural occupations, 'agricultural worker' being the most common occupation given on the census. If they weren't employed on the land they worked as baker, butcher, tailor, hurdle-maker, thatcher, shoemaker, maltster, etc. to provide what the community wanted. In the 21st century a farm which could have employed a dozen men in the 19th century now employs just a couple of men. Major changes in occupations were accelerated by the two world wars and timber-framed cottages, that once housed two or three families with up to a dozen children in one bedroom, were bought by educated professionals and 'restored' back to their 16th-century roots, helping to give the village its picturesque appearance.

One story that has withstood the test of time is that a ghost, in the form of a monk in full habit with the cowl raised over his head, was sometimes seen in Willow Cottage standing at the foot of the bed of the daughter of the house. It was believed that he came from Hoddington House, which in the Middle Ages had been a monastery. When the thatch on the roof was replaced with tiles the ghost was no longer seen.

There is a flourishing pub (the Hoddington Arms), a well-stocked shop and a post office, and numerous events are organised throughout the year including a spring flower show, a summer fete and an autumn festival with fantastic fireworks. A history society has been formed to preserve the information that has survived to this day.

Vernham Dean

Vernham Dean – 'the village in the valley of the ferns', with thatched cottages, a pub, a church, a gospel hall, village hall, playing fields and a primary school which attracts pupils from a wide area, as well as a popular pre-school. Perfect? No – in olden times the toughest policeman in Hampshire lived in the village to quell its rowdy inhabitants who made 'rough music', poached and stole. The 'Swing Riots' were here, a farm was targeted and villagers dispatched to Australia. Today? A collection of commuters, retirees, independent workers from home, and estate workers.

Vernham traces its history back many years; hand axes from the Bronze Age were found on a farm and now live in the Andover Museum. There are relics from all ages, up to a skiing medal dropped by an Italian prisoner of war in the 1940s. The village has developed from isolated farmsteads in Saxon times to the consolidated settlement it is today. Falling to 300 people, new housing in the 1960s saved the village from decline and today it contains 500 people. There is the tale of the priest in times of plague who housed sufferers and promised to provide food. He failed, and his punishment was to climb, again and again, up the road to Conholt for all eternity. One house was used as a hospital during the Civil War, and has a very cold presence in one of the rooms.

Surrounded by several estates, game shooting attracts many people during the season and provides casual work for beaters. The chalklands are good for sheep, the fields are well cultivated and there is a healthy horse population to serve keen riders and carriage drivers. The woods are managed and supply a superb array of bluebells in this hilly chalk area in the spring. Orchids can be found, rare butterflies appear and walkers are drawn to the area. The Test Valley Tour sets the cyclists off from the playing fields which are well used for football, a tennis/netball court serves the Vixens Netball team, and the village hall has its exercise classes.

People of note? The Duchess of Cambridge's grandparents lived here for many years. Marty Feldman, the actor and screenwriter, lived in the village for a short while. There is plenty of life in this hidden corner of Hampshire – carols round the pond at Christmas, Auld Lang Syne at New Year outside the pub, celebrations for royal occasions with decorated tables all down the street.

Vernham's history was written by a team of villagers some ten years ago, and they often entertain groups who want to see the highlights such as the Grade II listed church which, although a hotchpotch of styles, attracts many visitors whose ancestors have lived here. An Elizabethan manor house is sited nearby and stories are told of an underground passage to the church, through which the monks travelled in early days. Walking through the village, people can trace the history, see the structure of the ancient houses, thatched roofs, labourers' cottages enlarged to form 'desirable residences', new buildings on the site of post Second World War pre-fabs, the 'pond' which is no longer but serves as a sink for onslaughts of rain from the surrounding roads. The old village shop still sports the balcony to which the grain sacks were hoisted from the carts. Once there were two bakeries in the village, a blacksmith, visiting fish and meat vans. Today a fish van still calls, but as is now the way of the world, Vernham shops in Andover supermarkets.

Seeing the secondary school children congregate for the bus each morning, no one would say that Vernham is a backwater. The village is alive and kicking, who would want to live anywhere else?

WALLINGTON

Wallington is an old settlement within the Borough of Fareham. It lies on the lower slopes of Portsdown Hill, at the head of Portsmouth Harbour with the river Wallington running through it. Roman and Saxon artefacts have been found and the river has enabled a tannery and brewery to thrive and a pottery, which produced the bricks for the Royal Albert Hall, known as Fareham Reds.

The pottery also made chimney pots, decorated with a white band around the top, which proved popular in this country and abroad. Here in the village there is one of the largest collections of the chimney pots to be found. Sadly, these once-thriving industries have disappeared, but they could not have functioned without the river.

It is the Wallington river that gives us so much pleasure and grief in equal measure. Most of the time the tidal river has kingfishers, moorhens, coots, herons and cormorants and many ducks and swans nesting on the bank, which are of great interest, and are regularly fed by residents. However, a period of continuous heavy rain coupled with a high tide has produced flooding over the years, entering houses, garages and gardens. It was on 20th December 2012 that the river became famous, if only for a few hours! It had had the only severe flood warning issued across the UK, unknown to the village, but not to the press. From nowhere TV crews from the BBC, ITV and Sky News, with their helicopter hovering overhead, made it national news. Luckily the river's peak coincided with low tide so, with a few inches to spare, it passed under the bridge. During that evening many villagers had phone calls from anxious friends and relatives, checking that they had survived. It must be noted that Fareham Borough Council has funded current work being undertaken and the vast majority of Flood Mitigation work is funded by the Environment Agency.

There have been many incidents in the village, when it has been threatened by developers and others, so a call to arms goes out. The water meadows had been used by the villagers over many years, as a public footpath ran across them. Children played and fished in the river. Then the M27 was laid, slicing across the meadows, leaving a part of them in the village. A large area was designated as an industrial park, including 'our meadow'. The village formed a fighting committee. After much correspondence and getting a villager elected onto the council to fight on behalf of us to save the meadow, it was eventually decided that building work would not take place, and permission was given to use the meadow for village events. Little boys still fish in the river and people, with or without dogs, enjoy the green space. The village maintains the meadow and pays to have the grass cut for the wonderful village fete and musical evening. It is hoped that we will be able to enjoy the meadow far into the future.

There was an old drovers' lane which ascended to the heights of Portsdown Hill, where many farmers grazed their cattle. At the top of the lane there is Fort Wallington, one of Palmerston's Follies, built in the 1860s because of the fear of a French invasion that did not occur. However, Fort Wallington was the best preserved. In 1961 it was sold to a man who wanted to use it as a storage depot and plant hire unit. Unfortunately he was not a man who cared for preservation, and in 1962 proceeded to dynamite it! Red bricks rained down on the area without warning, except for the 'explosion', and one did fall through the roof of the bungalow. However, residents found a barrister and he was stopped, even though the Fort was sporting a banner stating it was an independent state! An Englishman and his fort! Later another enterprising businessman turned the fort into a nightclub, called the Dungeon Club, maybe frequented by some of our ladies in their youth!

The road through the village is mostly used by residents so traffic is not a problem, though parking can be. It is only a ten minute walk to the busy town of Fareham, but it is the river that keeps our identity and long may it continue!

There can be few villages such as this where most homes receive an excellently produced colour magazine three times a year called *Wallington Once-in-a-While*. For a small sum each year these are delivered to the door by street reps. It informs residents of the numerous clubs and societies using our well-maintained and excellent village hall. We are lucky to live in such a vibrant, friendly and well-maintained village.

Waltham Chase

A chase (or chace) was a piece of land reserved by the Crown for a local lord for hunting. After the Bishop's Palace had been built at Waltham in the 12th century, Waltham Chase was used as a hunting ground by successive bishops. The chase began at Waltham Park and ran to the south and east, stretching as far as the Bere Forest at Soberton, covering a much larger area than the present village.

The deer with which the Chase had been stocked were a nuisance to the labouring tenants whose crops they ate, but it was not until the 18th century that the Waltham Blacks appeared. They were young men who blacked their faces, disguised themselves and stole the bishop's deer. Further, they went on to rob stagecoaches and were much feared by travellers.

In 1722 Parliament, having been urged to do so by Bishop Trimmell, passed a Black Act which listed hundreds of offences, many punishable by death. A gibbet was erected by the roadside hedge of what is now the Triangle Recreation Ground.

Although scholars believe the Black Act was not called into use, the gibbet was used more than once. However in 1742 when Bishop Hoadley was asked to restock the Chase with deer, he refused, saying it had done enough harm already.

Waltham Chase village was enclosed in 1855, and, following enclosures, common wasteland was sold for seven shillings an acre. Market gardening became important and there were many smallholders. Strawberry growing was an important industry by the turn of the century, until the Second World War. Many growers took their fruit by horse and van to Botley station where they queued up for their turn to unload. The growers' carriage charges helped the railway and the service provided by the railway helped the growers. Much of the fruit was sent to London hotels.

Warsash

Warsash is situated on the eastern bank of the river Hamble, near the entrance of the river into Southampton Water, and opposite the village of Hamble. The parish is known as Hook-with-Warsash because of the links with the nearby village of Hook.

By the crossroads in the centre of the village is the clock tower, which was built as a water tower to supply Warsash House and estate with water. King Edward VII used to visit Warsash House when he was Prince of Wales. The house was pulled down and modern houses built just before the Second World War, but the water tower and model farmhouse remain. The clock on the tower struck ship's bell time until an electric clock was installed in 1945.

Shipbuilding and fishing were very important occupations – crabs, lobsters and shellfish provided the living for several families. Crab teas were provided near the shore and became famous locally. The Rising Sun (where teas were once served) is still a very popular public house.

The land in this area is very stony and is ideal for growing strawberries. Twenty years ago, on a fine summer's day the smell of strawberries was all pervading. The trade has been important to the area for many years, and you will still find strawberries being sold at the side of the road in season.

The College of Maritime Studies, situated where the old coastguard station used to be, has trained countless Merchant Navy seamen from all over the world.

It is possible to steer one of the world's largest oil tankers and bring it into port and never leave the college buildings, thanks to modern technology!

Very near here, a century or more ago, salt was collected from the salterns after the sea water had evaporated. Wooden posts can still be seen at low tide marking this area.

A ferry runs regularly across the river Hamble to Hamble village. Some people travel to work that way, and it is very popular with holidaymakers.

Wellow

The name of Wellow dates back to AD 885 when King Alfred left 'the toune of Welewe' in his will to his eldest daughter, Ethelfreda. It is also mentioned in the Domesday Book. Today Wellow is a desirable place to live and work. Why? Firstly its location – a couple of miles from the motorway network making access to the whole country possible. The fabulous south coast beaches, cathedral cities of Winchester and Salisbury, the busy port of Southampton, the pretty town of Romsey are just a short drive away and the New Forest is on our doorstep. With the coming of broadband people can choose to work from home. There are a growing number of retirees whose children have flown the nest adding to the thriving population who organise and run the fetes, cricket and football teams, tennis, badminton, golf, indoor bowls and youth groups. The village hall hosts many activities and of course, the WI that has been running since 1919.

We are fortunate enough to have a primary school that was built in 1875 by the Nightingale family from Embley Park. It has been a hub in the village since then and is thriving to this day. There are two pubs, the Red Rover, an old coaching inn, and the Rockingham Arms. Shops include two butchers, hardware, newsagent, chemist, hairdresser, beauty salon, a mini supermarket and a post office.

The church of St Margaret of Antioch was consecrated in 1215 but was built on the site of a much earlier building. The walls are covered by beautiful paintings rediscovered at the end of the 19th century. In the graveyard is the resting place of Florence Nightingale, our famous nurse who died on 13th August 1910. The Methodist church in Maurys Lane was built in 1867 and has a fine organ built by one of the best organ makers of the time, Thomas Elliot. There are also the Canada Road Gospel Hall, Canada Common Methodist church and the Wellow Christian Centre that all have a faithful attendance of parishioners.

Agriculture was the main occupation in East and West Wellow right up until the late 1970s and there are a couple of small farms still operating. The largest agricultural concern now is the growing of strawberries and raspberries under polytunnels that cover hundreds of acres. In the past other trades like butchers, blacksmiths, bakers etc were here to support the residents of East and West Wellow. The village was very self sufficient but in the late 1960s and early 1970s it was struggling, due to the lack of young blood to fill the school, scouts, guides, cricket and football teams. The development of housing estates like Brookfields, Barnes Close, Whinwhistle, Wheatears, to name but a few, and a beautiful new village hall built on farmland in 1980, breathed new life into the village and it prospered once again. Now, further development is on the horizon and who knows what changes, if any, Wellow will face again?

Nearly all the present day residents in Wellow know of Carlo's Ice Cream Parlour. This came about when Carlo Donnarumma was evacuated out from Southampton in the Second World War. He and his wife Thora lived in a little wooden house with a corrugated iron roof (as many people in Wellow did during and after the war). They started making ice cream in an outhouse at the weekends, selling this locally and also taking it to local towns and villages in their red and white van. If there was any left unsold, Carlo would telephone and say 'do you want any ice cream?' (never came the answer 'no, thank you'!). Whereupon he would drive round and give away the lovely creamy ice cream as in those days it was unsuitable to freeze. The queues on a sunny weekend would be all along the road and Carlo would be directing the traffic wearing his white apron and hat and a huge toothless grin. He and his wife Thora were a lovely couple. Carlo also used to drive the school bus to Bartley secondary school and there are many people who remember him making the bus sway from side to side and saying 'Shall we stop at the Birds Eye shop?' meaning, if you were lucky enough to have any money, he would stop at a little sweet shop in Winsor Road. Sadly, things like that would never be allowed to happen today.

Other connections to sweet things – Chatmohr House on the A36, now associated with small businesses, was the house built in 1900 by William Mackintosh of the confectionery family who manufactured Quality Street chocolates and toffees. Not forgetting the Cadbury chocolate family – Sir Egbert and Lady Mary Cadbury owned the Manor Farm near St Margaret's church where a dairy herd of pretty Jersey cows produced lovely creamy milk. We have no evidence it was used in the making of their chocolate. Their son Peter Cadbury also owned the farm that was managed by a Miss Apperley.

Our most famous resident was, of course, Florence Nightingale, as mentioned above. Her family bought Embley Park in 1825. Florence is known to have nursed her first patient here, a dog, owned by a local shepherd. She walked the paths and lanes in Wellow, visiting the sick and gave blankets to the poor. She is also known to have helped at the school her father had built.

Two other, slightly less famous people who are buried in St Margaret's graveyard include the artist Derek Hill. His parents lived at Spursholt House on the A27 and are also buried there. He tutored Prince Charles on watercolour techniques. Several of his paintings are exhibited in Mottisfont Abbey. The other is John Joseph Crosfield who lived at Embley Park in 1925. He was the High Sheriff of Hampshire. He paid for the building of the Crosfield Hall in Romsey and the installation of the organ in St Margaret's church, to name but a couple of his philanthropic endeavours. He died on 9th May 1940.

Wellow, sandwiched between the busy roads of the A27 and the A36, could be overlooked by many people as they rush along in their cars, going about their daily business. But if one were to stop a while and walk the ancient sunken lanes around St Margaret's, ponder there, then stroll over the beautiful Wellow Common on the edge of the New Forest, you may be able to imagine past inhabitants, rich and poor, famous and the not so famous, going about their daily lives too. Let us hope the present villagers can leave behind more history and stories that can be woven into the tapestry of the ancient village of 'Welewe'.

West End

The village has been here for many hundreds of years although the name West End did not appear until 1607. There was a time when many of the large houses were owned by gentry, now replaced by flats and houses. To name a few: Harefield House was owned by Edwin Jones, of the Southampton department store founded in 1860 that later became part of the Debenhams Group; The Firs by Richard St Barbe-Baker (1889-1982), environmentalist and founder of the Men of the Trees organisation; Holmecroft by Sir Arthur Rostron (1869-1940), the captain of RMS *Carpathia* who saved 706 souls from drowning when the *Titanic* sank in 1912; and C.B. Fry (1872-1956), the cricketer and footballer. Nurse Kate Oram (1879-1918), who nursed Florence Nightingale when she became elderly, also lived locally.

Hatch Grange (the house was destroyed by fire) is now officially a public open space where special events are held. Townhill Park House was used by the Red Cross from 1939 to 1969 as a convalescent home and still stands today with beautiful landscaped gardens, home to The Gregg School. Our local fire station was converted into a museum in 1996 and is run by West End History Society. South Stoneham Union workhouse for the poor was developed by the NHS in 1948 into Moorgreen Hospital, but today is a large housing estate.

The original parish church of St James was built in 1936 but the spire was struck by lightning in 1875 and had to be demolished. This heralded the beginning of the new and bigger church that we have today. West End has always had a school, the first built in 1871 funded by benefactress Harriet Haselfoot and known as West End Dame School for Infants. Later West End National School was built on the main road, now the Hildene Centre. Due to growth in numbers, St James Church of England junior school was erected in 1985 and today is being extended.

Most of the villagers were either mill workers of farm workers. Very different from today when the locals travel to many varying jobs, some as far as London on a daily basis. It is said there were originally 14 public houses and drinking houses in the area, but now only four exist.

West End is the home to Hampshire County Cricket Club – the ground now known as Ageas Bowl – where a large hotel, tennis and sports club and golf course are situated on the same site. We have a thriving parish centre with café, sports hall, library, hall and committee rooms. The staff and councillors organise an annual carnival, Christmas Party for senior citizens and a pantomime for children – all free! There are many clubs for all ages going on in West End and it still retains very much a village atmosphere, with everyone friendly and involved. Despite all the frequent building works, there are green open spaces and pleasant walks.

West Meon

This lively village, within the South Downs National Park, with a population of getting on for 1,000 people, has a church, primary school, pub, a doctors' surgery, and a number of picturesque thatched dwellings. There is also a village community shop, managed by paid staff and numerous volunteers, a separately run café, and a butcher's shop nearby. The village has been voted one of the most desirable places in which to live in England. With Winchester, Alton and Petersfield stations within 20 minutes by car, it is accessible by rail; and by road, being just off the junction of the A272 (east-west) and the

A32 (north-south). It is well known for the disused railway line from Alton to Fareham (now a footpath), which used to take watercress from Warnford, a mile south, also on the river Meon, to London, daily.

Its history encompasses Ancient Britons up on the neighbouring Old Winchester Hill, Romans, and Saxons. Finds from these periods are still being unearthed. St Wilfrid founded Warnford church in AD 682 and preached at the cross in West Meon. During the Civil War, troops from both sides passed through; the Battle of Cheriton took place in 1644. In 1648, King Charles I came nearby trying to escape, but eventually was caught, imprisoned in Carisbrooke Castle and then beheaded in London. King Charles II, escaping after the Battle of Worcester (1651), stopped for a beer in Warnford, on his way to catch a boat at Shoreham to his temporary exile in France.

More recently, two men were well known. Firstly, Thomas Lord, the founder of Lord's Cricket Ground in London. He lived in West Meon and died here in 1832 aged 76, and is buried in the churchyard; members of the MCC still come to pay their respects at his tomb, and to enjoy refreshment at the local pub which is named after him. Secondly, Guy Burgess, the diplomat and spy for the Soviet Union, who defected with Donald Maclean to Russia in 1951 and died there in 1963; as his parents lived in West Meon, his ashes were interred in the family plot in the churchyard.

West Meon is proud of its excellent primary school and of the active sports club. The latter runs teams for cricket, football, and hockey, and there is a flourishing drama group, the West Meon Players. The village hall is used by many groups and societies, including a thriving 52-year-old WI. A community bus runs regularly to several town shopping venues, and there is a 'care group' for those in need of transport for medical reasons. As you will have gathered, West Meon is a lovely place in which to live. It is an active and caring village; do come and visit.

West Tytherley

The village of West Tytherley is a rural community of just over 600 people and is situated in Hampshire but only a mile from the Wiltshire border. It is roughly equidistant from Romsey, Stockbridge and Salisbury. It is surrounded by woodlands, the most well known being Bentley Wood, a large area held in Trust for Conservation and the use of villagers. This was previously owned by the Forestry Commission but was purchased by Lady Colman, of Colman's Mustard fame, who gave the wood to the Trust. In order to preserve and increase species, the Trust has opened up clearings and replaced softwood with hardwood.

West Tytherley is mentioned the Domesday survey as Tederleg, meaning young wood, and was in the ownership of Waleran, William I's huntsman, together with much more land in this area.

During the late 11th century St Peter's church at West Tytherley was a chapel of Mottisfont Abbey. The site of the old church is indicated by a slight platform in the old burial ground opposite the present church. The old church was in use until 1833 when the nave of the new church opened and several items were incorporated into the new building including a black marble Norman font.

The three bells were removed from the church in 2010 in order to restore the frame and allow the bells to be rung again. During this process it was found that one bell dated from 1725, another from the 14th century, but the oldest is dated 1260. This seems to pre-date any other bell in the world set up for full circle ringing.

In the 1750s Robert Thistlethwaite had the present Norman Court mansion house built on the hillside above the site of the old manor house. Early in the 19th century Norman Court was bought by Charles Wall, who was succeeded by his son Charles Baring Wall in 1816. In 1853 the estate was inherited by Thomas Baring, the nephew of C.B. Wall's mother. Thomas Baring, the Member of Parliament for Huntingdon, was head of the Baring Brothers bank.

In 1906, Washington Singer, one of the many sons of Isaac Singer of sewing machine fame, bought the Norman Court estate. Large country estates were still very self-contained in the first half of the 20th century and the workers lived in estate cottages in what was a very close community. From Norman Court, the Singers owned the whole of the villages of West Tytherley and West Dean together with the outlying farms and cottages. The estate had its own sawmills, workshops and brickworks. As far as possible equipment was made or mended on site. During the Singer era, the school and King Edward's hall were built along with many estate workers' houses.

After Washington Singer died in 1934, the bulk of his estate went to his widow, Mary Ellen Singer, with the exception of Norman Court which was inherited by his adopted son, Grant, once he became of age in 1936. Unfortunately, Grant Singer, the new owner of Norman Court and Bentley Wood, was killed in the Battle of El Alamein in 1942 and left no children.

In order to pay the second lot of death duty tax, the whole of the Norman Court estate was auctioned off over two years in 1945 and 1946. All the estate houses and cottages were sold separately, many to the existing tenants but as some of the workers had lost their livelihood those unable to purchase their properties were evicted. The school, recreation ground and King Edward's Hall were given to the villagers.

Today the village has a thriving school, a community shop, the Black Horse public house, St Peter's church and the village-owned recreation ground and King Edward's Hall. The hall hosts the Forest Forge theatre company for their Christmas play, usually on Christmas Eve, a tradition that has been carrying on for many years.

WHERWELL

Wherwell is in northern Hampshire and is situated on the river Test, a chalk stream rising at Overton and flowing into Southampton Water at Redbridge. It is renowned for its fly fishing for trout, and occasionally salmon come this far up river to spawn.

When Winchester was the capital of England, Wherwell was a royal hunting

St Peter & Holy Cross Church, Wherwell

lodge. In the 10th century Elfrida married King Edgar, who owned the manor, but after his death she murdered his son at Corfe Castle. In expiation of this crime she founded the abbey of Wherwell and ended her life in penance. Nothing remains today, but 'The Priory' was built on the same site. The present church of St Peter and Holy Cross was built on the site of one destroyed in 1858. A painting of the original church hangs there today.

An interesting charity recorded in the church shows that in 1691 Philadelphia Whitehead, out of the yearly rent of the White Lion, made available twelve shillings a year for ever, to be paid to twelve of the oldest parishioners. Today the brewers who now own the White Lion give a lump sum of money to be invested.

In the centre of the lawn at The Priory is a tree stump. The tree was blown down some years ago, and under the roots was found the body of a man covered by a hurdle. Legend says a great treasure is buried there, but anyone trying to recover it would pay the penalty of sudden death.

A weather vane depicting a cockatrice used to be fixed on the church spire but is now in Andover Museum. The story goes that many years ago, in a dungeon beneath the priory, a duck laid an egg, which was hatched by a toad and produced a cockatrice, a fearsome monster. A reward of four acres of land was offered to anyone who could slay the monster and various people lost their lives trying. A servant at the priory called Green obtained a large steel mirror, which was lowered into the dungeon. The cockatrice, seeing another of its kind, exhausted himself trying to kill the newcomer, whereupon the valiant Green descended into the dungeon and slew it with a spear. In Harewood Forest today there is a piece of land, exactly four acres, known as Green's Acres.

Whitchurch

From *Evacuation Blues*, written by Bank of England employees evacuated to Whitchurch during the Second World War:

> In the wilds of Hampshire
> Among the cows and pigs,
> Montagu's young ladies
> Are living out in digs ...

Whitchurch doesn't now host the young ladies of the Governor of the Bank of England (Montagu Norman, Governor from 1920 to 1944), although quite a few stayed on after the war enjoying what the town had to offer. So, what makes Whitchurch distinctive? Here are some clues: silk, rabbits, trout, kingfishers, the Salvation Army, gin, paper money and the Law!

Nestled in the valley of the river Test, Whitchurch has the oldest working silk mill still in its Georgian building. The mill uses original 19th-century machinery that has woven silks for many purposes, such as gowns for the Law Courts. Today silk is designed and woven for heritage projects like National Trust houses and period television dramas, as well as special celebrations. Visitors can enjoy its beautiful setting, view the skilful production and see exhibitions around silk. Famed for its trout, the river Test flows under the mill wheel and on through the centre of the town. Generations of children have watched the trout, ducks and swans fight for food thrown from the bridges. Ron and Rosemary Eastman, who lived in Town Mill, filmed their ground-breaking, 1960s *The Private Life of the Kingfisher* nearby; whilst egrets and herons can also be glimpsed by the river banks and around the town's mills.

Within a few miles is the rabbit terrain of *Watership Down*, whose author, Richard Adams, lived in the town. Along the valley is Laverstoke Mill, where the company Portals once produced Bank of England note paper. The Huguenot refugee Henri de Portal originated paper production in the early 1700s at nearby Bere Mill, like the other mills now a private house. Today with payment cards and bitcoin, paper money seems quite innocuous, but in 1822 William Cobbett believed it was the 'curse of England'. He was therefore not complimentary about Whitchurch: 'there runs that stream which turns the mill of "Squire Portal" ... yet this river ... has produced a greater [negative] effect on the condition of men ...' (17 November 1822). Laverstoke Mill is now transformed into the distillery for Bombay Sapphire gin and is open for tours and tastings. Cobbett would probably not have approved of that either!

For a small town, Whitchurch has two claims to making significant changes to English Law. Following a demonstration in the town square in 1889, Salvation Army members were marched to Winchester for trial. The resulting ruling by the London Law Courts stated that English people had the right to gather peacefully in public places; a 'famous Victory for Liberty in England' (William Booth). Secondly, Lord Denning, Master of the Rolls from 1962 to 1982, was born, bred and lived in Whitchurch. He never lost his Hampshire burr even when he became possibly one of the most influential judges of the 20th century. A new bell, 'Old Tom', was hung in All Hallows church, to celebrate his 100th birthday.

Given its position in a river valley with routes to all points of the compass, it is unsurprising that Whitchurch's history stretches back to the Iron Age.

Roman tracks pass nearby, but it was in Saxon and medieval times that the town became a centre of trade. A church was established around AD 800 and the present one has Saxon, Norman and Tudor features. Whitchurch's position near to the Downs meant wool was an important commodity. A fulling mill lies beside the river and there were fairs for trading sheep and cloth. In Fair Close sits an original Fair House. The town's first charter was issued in the 13th century and there are many old buildings scattered around the town's conservation area, often hidden behind more modern facades. Both the famous and infamous would have travelled through this market town and visited one of the many inns. Perhaps the most famous guest was Charles I who stayed at King's Lodge before the Second Battle of Newbury in 1644. The Georgian town hall, where the town council meets, sits opposite the 15th-century White Hart Inn where Charles Kingsley stayed whilst fishing in the Test and writing *The Water Babies*.

In 1854 the railway (east-west) came to Whitchurch, and today London is about one hour away, so it is commutable; even so Whitchurch still has the atmosphere of a small country town where people linger. The town's many groups contribute to a vibrant and friendly place to live and work.

Whitchurch is a Walkers are Welcome town with lots of footpaths to explore in the environs, and has an active Walking for Health group. If you visit you will be warmly welcomed into the individual shops and varied eating places grouped around the Market Square. Like all old communities, there are rumours of ghosts inhabiting buildings where tragedies have occurred; such as at The Gables, originally the workhouse, and in shops off the Square where a little girl in blue is said to linger.

Whitchurch hasn't got the most distinctive of names; there are many other 'White Churches'. In fact, there are 14 known 'Whitchurches' in the United Kingdom, and one in Canada. In 2015 Hampshire's Whitchurch celebrated the first biennial Worldwide Whitchurch Weekend. But in many ways, as you have read, our Whitchurch is distinctive; a small town with a big heart. Charles Kingsley said of Whitchurch, 'I like this place', and so do we!

WICKHAM

The lovely village of Wickham has a large square, said to be the second largest in the country. Shops surround the square, along with Georgian houses, and there are 16th-century houses just around the corner.

Wickham was the birthplace of William of Wykeham, Bishop of Winchester and founder of Winchester College, in the 14th century.

The mound on which the church is built was used by Celts and Saxons for burial or religious rites. St Nicholas' was built by the Normans in 1120, but has been thoroughly altered since. Inside there is a large memorial to the Uvedale family, once lords of the manor.

In 1268 King Henry III granted a charter to the lord of the manor, Roger de Scures, to hold an annual fair. One has been held every year since – even during wartime.

The old Victory Hall, now converted into flats, beside the river Meon, was once a busy tannery where men from the village worked. Later it became a brewery, with heavy horses coming and going, pulling great drays loaded with barrels. After part of the building caught fire, it was rebuilt and there is still a plaque on the rear of the building saying 'Wickham Brewery rebuilt ANO DMI 1887 being the Jubilee Year of the Reign of H.M. Queen Victoria'. The brewery closed in 1910 and later the Victory Club was formed to commemorate victory in the First World War. It was used in the Second World War as home and refuge for many evacuees from Portsmouth and Southampton. There was an army headquarters in the King's Head public house, Canadian soldiers at Rookesbury School, and army engineers took over part of a garage along the Fareham road. A great many of the engineers married local girls and settled here after the war.

WIELD

Wield comprises the two villages of Upper Wield and Lower Wield, the first being a 'green' village with the houses formally arranged round a green, and the latter a 'street' village with the houses mainly along a single lane.

Upper Wield's most notable building is its 12th-century church of St James. It still retains most of its Norman architecture and there are many vestiges of wall paintings which date from medieval times to Queen Anne's reign. Her royal coat of arms can be seen above the chancel arch. The church also contains a large memorial to Henry Wallop and his wife. This is not only a beautiful piece of alabaster carving but the inscription is a remarkable piece of snobbery which eulogises Henry's brother and appears to mention the deceased almost as an afterthought.

Looking from the green there is a charming scene of a group of thatched cottages with the church behind them. This is best seen in the early morning when the sun glints on the golden weathercock on the wooden church spire. Only one cottage is still thatched in the 'longstraw' or 'Hampshire' thatch, the others favouring the 'wheat reed' style which is more hard-wearing.

There is a tiny Primitive Methodist chapel, which speaks of dissension in the village 100 years ago. Religion caused great disruption in 1851 when William Budge, a Mormon, came from America looking for converts. They were baptised in Wield Wood pond and some emigrated to Utah. Between 1851 and 1861 the population of the village dropped by over a quarter. Some of these probably emigrated, while others went to work in factory towns hoping for better wages. The census of 1881 shows that 90 per cent of the population were engaged in agricultural or allied jobs. Today the percentage has dropped to less than 0.5 per cent.

The Yew Tree pub in Lower Wield is a popular place to eat. It is directly opposite one of the prettiest cricket fields in the county. This is a pleasant place to have a picnic on a summer Sunday. Straying from the match and walking through the village will reward you with the sight of some very attractive houses.

Woodlands

Woodlands village is in Netley Marsh parish, a few miles west of Southampton. It is within the New Forest National Park and the centre of the village is now a conservation area.

There has been some habitation in this area from prehistoric times. There was an Iron Age hillfort at Tatchbury Mount, which is an area of raised ground commanding extensive views over the surrounding countryside and the river Test. The hill is entrenched and covers an area of five acres. Running north-west from this site there is a track dating from prehistoric times, leading to ancient Stagbury Hill. Tatchbury was used as a hillfort in Roman times and just north of here was a Roman road, probably connecting Winchester to Dorchester. Celtic objects have been found in this area, and we know from the *Anglo-Saxon Chronicle* that two Saxon chieftains came here in the 6th century and killed a local king called Natanleod and many of his men. They took over the land and called it 'Natan Leah' (later known as Netley). Tatchbury was mentioned in the Domesday survey in the 11th century.

Just south of here is the site of the deserted medieval village of Taceberie. The 10th-century manor house of that village had once been a hunting lodge for King John, and later became Tatchbury manor house. Tatchbury Mount is now occupied by a hospital and other medical units run by the NHS. Another historic house in this area is Little Testwood House. The original house was built in the 15th century, and was extended in the 18th. It is reputed to be haunted by a man in a top hat and caped overcoat, who is thought to have murdered the cook and dumped her body in a nearby lane, now known as 'Cook's Lane'.

Woodlands was originally known as just 'the woodland', a wooded area between Cadnam and Bartley to the north-west, Ashurst to the south-west and Totton and Eling to the east. Woodlands Road was just a track leading into the New Forest. Gradually the woodland was cleared and basic cob cottages were built along the track on the edge of the common. It was part of the ancient parish of Eling, in the Redbridge Hundred, and much of the land was owned by the Bishop of Winchester. Farms and smallholdings were established and later industries such as a timber business and a brickworks flourished. A beer house, a public house, and later, two hotels were built.

As the population grew, more houses appeared, and in 1873 a school was built. There was also a reformatory school, accommodating 50 boys. The boys were taken to the parish church every Sunday, but people complained that the boys' clothes had an unpleasant odour, particularly when damp, and they were not welcome there. In 1887 there was a scandal that was reported in the national newspapers. The vicar's warden had attempted to prevent the boys from entering the church. The staff complained, accusing the warden of assault and the case went to court. The issue was less about assault and more about the fact that the warden should not have prevented the boys from entering, and that only the rector should make such a decision. The warden was reprimanded and the boys were awarded nominal damages of one shilling.

In 1855 a new church was built at Netley Marsh, and Netley Marsh parish was officially created in 1894. In the 1900s the Bartley church reading rooms were created in a corrugated iron hall, which became known as the 'tin church', and is now used as a village hall. Another hall was built next to the parish church in the 1920s. More houses were built in the 19th and 20th centuries. In the 1970s a community centre was built.

Woodlands has a stable population, with some people descended from families that have lived in the area for generations. However, new people are welcomed into the community. People can be involved with the schools, the pubs, the church and the various clubs and groups which meet at the church hall, the 'tin church' and the community centre.

The Netley Marsh Carnival is held in June of each year. Children from the pre-school, primary school, Rainbows, Brownies and Guides, the Beavers,

Cubs and Scouts, all dress up to a theme and parade from the Gamekeeper pub to the church field at Netley Marsh, where there is a village fete with music, stalls, activities and refreshments. The Netley Marsh Steam Fair is held every year in July. Hundreds of steam engines of all sizes are gathered there, with demonstrations of threshing, wood-turning, etc and parades of engines, tractors and classic cars.

Woodlands is a great place for walking and cycling, and many families and groups come here for these activities. They often start or finish at the Gamekeeper pub. There are many rights of way, bridleways and footpaths and the New Forest is within easy walking or cycling distance. There are no shops in the village now, but there are many shops two or three miles away, also a doctors' surgery, a dentist, chemist and even an arts centre at West Totton, only two miles away. No wonder that people want to come here and stay!